*Aerial Photography
in Anthropological
Field Research*

Aerial Photography in Anthropological Field Research

Edited by Evon Z. Vogt

Harvard University Press
Cambridge, Massachusetts
1974

Preface

While anthropologists and, especially, archaeologists have been utilizing aerial photographs in field research for several decades, the potentialities of aerial photography for both ethnography and archaeology were greatly increased in the 1960s with the introduction of new types of cameras, improved high resolution film, and new techniques of photogrammetry. A number of anthropological field projects in various parts of the world began to turn more seriously to aerial photography for increasing the efficiency of mapping operations having to do with settlement patterns or land ownership and use, for compiling census data, and for placing archaeological sites and living communities in their ecological contexts. The advantages of aerial photography are especially apparent in areas of rugged or isolated terrain, where ground surveys would require weeks or even months of field work to accomplish a mapping task that can now be accomplished in far less time with the use of aerial photographs. Furthermore, an overview of large areas of terrain frequently displays patterns and regularities in the relation of culture to ecology that would escape notice on the ground.

In the application of the improved technology of aerial photography to anthropological field research, new methods and new concepts are being developed and tested, both in ethnography and in archaeology. These include new techniques for collecting data, as well as new ways of conceptualizing the relationship between culture and ecology and how this relationship changes with time.

The idea for this volume emerged during the course of an aerial photography project in the highlands of Chiapas in southeastern Mexico, which lasted from 1963 to 1969 and in which five of the authors participated. As we proceeded with the project, we kept in close touch with other anthropologists who were also developing new methods and techniques for the utilization of aerial photographs in field research. I assembled and chaired a working conference at Harvard University on May 10–12, 1969, to exchange information on concepts and methods in the uses of aerial photography in anthropology. The group included Michael D. Coe (Yale) and Elmer Harp, Jr. (Dartmouth), who were working with new uses of aerial photography in archaeological research; Robert A. Hackenberg (University of Colorado) and Thomas S. Schorr (University of Pittsburgh), who were specializing in novel uses of aerial photographs in the study of cultural ecology; Richard M. Kroeck (Mark Systems, Inc.), a professional air photo interpreter; Dennis Wood (Clark University), a geographer who had worked with aerial photos in Latin America; Priscilla Reining (Smithsonian Institution) and Conrad Reining (Catholic University), who had used aerial photos in their research on land use and tenure in Tanzania; and Frank Cancian (Stanford), George A. Collier (Stanford), Gary H. Gossen (University of California at Santa Cruz), and Richard Price (Yale; currently Chairman, Dept. of Anthropology, Johns Hopkins University), former members of the Harvard Chiapas Project who had worked with the aerial photos. The student participants included William W. Fitzhugh, Edward B. Sisson, and Carolyn Pope Edwards, the latter serving as rapporteur. Harold C. Conklin (Yale), a pioneer in utilizing the new techniques of aerial photogrammetry in Luzon, unfortunately could not attend because he was in the Philippines.

Out of the conference at Harvard came a plan for a symposium on the uses of aerial photography in anthropological field research, held at the Sixty-Eighth Annual Meetings of the American Anthropological Association in New Orleans in November 1969, where some of these papers were presented. Out of it also came the idea for this volume, which we hope will be helpful to others with an interest in using aerial photography in field research.

The National Science Foundation funded the aerial photography project in Chiapas, as well as certain travel expenses for members of the working conference at Harvard, and I am deeply grateful for the sustained interest of the foundation in our research. At Harvard, the project was sponsored by the Center for the Behavioral Sciences and the Peabody Museum, and I appreciate the continuing assistance of their staffs. Professors A. Kimball Romney and Norman A. McQuown, my fellow investigators during the first two phases of the project, gave generously of their time and expert advice. We also benefited from the advice of Professor Robert M. Adams of the University of Chicago. Despite a previous lack of familiarity with anthropological problems and with the geographical and cultural situation in the highlands of Chiapas, Richard M. Kroeck, project engineer for the Itek Corporation which carried out the photography and some of the interpretation, served with insight, intelligence, and tact and was crucial to the success of the project. I am deeply indebted to members of the Harvard Chiapas Project who performed so brilliantly in the field or in the laboratory during the course of the aerial photography project, especially Frank Cancian, George and Jane Collier, Carolyn Pope Edwards, Gary H. Gossen, Robert M. Laughlin, Richard and Sally Price, and Linnéa Holmer Wren. In Mexico, our work was sponsored by the Instituto Nacional Indigenista, where we obtained unflagging and loyal cooperation from the late Dr. Alfonso Caso and Dr. Gonzalo Aguirre Beltrán. Many Zinacantecos and Chamulas made important contributions to our research and learned to become photo interpreters in their own right; we are especially indebted to José Hernández Pérez and Domingo de la Torre Pérez in Zinacantan and to Mariano López Méndez in Chamula. Much of the manuscript was expertly edited and typed for publication by Catherine C. Vogt, Dolores Vidal, and Sharon Latterman.

Evon Z. Vogt

Contents

Illustrations

Tables

Part One

Changing Ecological Relationships: Prehistoric and Contemporary

Michael D. Coe

Photogrammetry and the Ecology of Olmec Civilization

The Olmec civilization of Mexico's Gulf Coast is now known to be the earliest high culture in Mesoamerica. Each year brings not only new Olmec discoveries within the so-called heartland—the wet lowlands of southern Veracruz and Tabasco—but also increasingly strong evidence for Olmec domination of much of central and southern Mexico, extending as far southeast as the Pacific Coast of Central America.

In an effort to answer questions posed by the existence of so early a civilization, such as its origin, nature, and demise, a three-year archaeological program was begun in 1966 at the great Olmec site complex known as San Lorenzo Tenochtitlán, in the Coatzacoalcos River drainage of Veracruz. The results of this project were altogether surprising, for it was found that the Olmec flourished at the most important site, San Lorenzo, during the 1200–900 B.C. time span, considerably earlier than at La Venta, which had previously been placed at 800–400 B.C. The great portrait heads, altars, and other basalt sculptures for which San Lorenzo is known thus stand at the very beginning of the Olmec developmental curve.

While the archaeological work concentrated mainly on the what of Olmec civilization—in particular its chronology, which was poorly understood—light was also thrown on the how and why of this strange civilization, which had no clear-cut antecedents elsewhere in the New World. Recently, increasing attention has been paid by archaeologists to the ecological contexts of native Mesoamerican cultures, that is, to placing each culture within a larger framework as part of an ecosystem, in which groups of people are mutually interacting with the natural environment and with each other. These relationships are viewed as dynamic, having changed over time to produce the major advances that appear in the archaeological record of the last eleven thousand years.

Mesoamerica is divided into a number of major biomes, such as desert, highland steppe, temperate forest, and tropical forest. As a result, most theorizing about ancient ecosystems has been limited to the supposedly permissive or limiting effects of these broadscale habitats on native cultural development. For instance, Betty Meggers (1954) proposed a controversial theory of the inhibiting nature of the tropical lowland forest biome, which altogether precludes the independent rise of a civilization within it and within a short time snuffs out such high cultures as that of the Classic Maya, which was supposed to have been transplanted to the tropical forest. Another school of thought that complements Meggers' view is an offshoot of Karl Wittfogel's theory of the despotic state as arising from the controls needed to administer large-scale irrigation systems (Wittfogel 1955). If one accepts the notion that this is the only way in which a state—and therefore civilization itself—could have arisen in Meso-america, it follows that such a development could have happened only in the semiarid-to-arid biome of the central highlands, within which irrigation would have been a requirement for productive agriculture. It also follows that lowland development would necessarily have been derived from the highland civilizations.

Unfortunately for proponents of the irrigation theory, such as Pedro Armillas, Eric R. Wolf, Angel Palerm, and William T. Sanders, the new dates of the Olmec civilization completely refute this idea. Recently William Sanders and Barbara Price (1968) tried to get around this problem by denying that Olmec was a civilization, but since there is strong evidence for the existence of an Olmec state, their argument is weakened (Coe 1968).

Over the years I have become more and more disillusioned with theories focusing on entire biomes. There is an enormous amount of variation within these biomes, which is usually overlooked. Anyone who has traveled through the tropical forest, for instance, knows how varied in vegetation, soil, fauna, and even climate this supposedly monolithic environment can be. The biome theorists have simply taken the wrong scale for what they are studying: human groups are adapted not so much to biomes as to smaller units within them, which Kent V. Flannery and I call microenvironments and which ecologists would call biotopes (Coe and Flannery 1964). The study of these microenvironments, however, requires far more detailed, fine-scale information than is usually provided by those interested only in the biome.

It was my intention to make such a detailed study of the San Lorenzo Tenochtitlán area as an adjunct to archaeological research, in hopes of discovering the environmental conditions that stimulated the precocious rise of Mesoamerican civilization in this purportedly restrictive tropical biome. An assumption was made, which later turned out to be correct, that the environment three thousand years ago was not much different, if at all, from that prevailing today. The analysis of wood charcoal and of animal bones found in Olmec refuse confirmed this hypothesis, since all were of species still prevalent in the area.

My aim in designing such an ecological project was twofold: to investigate the use of the environment by the present-day population, and to determine the ultimate human carrying capacity of the land, given the native systems of agriculture. For the latter, I was strongly influenced by the methodology of the British geographers working in Africa as outlined by William Allan (1965). There, administrators of native territories were sometimes called upon to move populations from one area to the next, and it was vital to provide figures on capacities that were not the usual "guesstimates," such as those in vogue among Maya archaeologists. For this, it was necessary to measure variations with great accuracy, including the areas covered by particular vegetation-soil types, the average years in cultivation and in fallow for each such type, and the production of each kind of crop within each type. Thus, the per capita area required within each vegetation-soil type could be calculated, as could the total carrying capacity of the entire area, including uncultivable lands. To carry out such an ambitious program in the shortest possible time, I clearly had to resort to photogrammetric methods. Other valuable data came from the agricultural and consumption studies carried out at La Venta island in Tabasco (Drucker and Heizer 1960) and in the area between the lower Coatzacoalcos and Tonalá rivers (Drucker 1961).

Photogrammetry

With the aid of the National Science Foundation, I was able to contract with the Cia. Mexicana Aerofoto to provide basic photogrammetric coverage of San Lorenzo Tenochtitlán. A sample area of 75 sq. km. was selected, based on an incomplete flight made by the company in the 1940s. It centered on the site of San Lorenzo itself and included representative portions of all the major microenvironments that could be tentatively identified on the older photo series (Fig. 1). In February 1966 the first flight was made at an altitude of about 4,400 feet with a Wild RC-8 camera, resulting in a complete set of extremely fine-resolution photographs in a 9 × 9-inch format, at an approximate scale of 1:8,000. These formed the basis for all subsequent photo inter-

Michael D. Coe

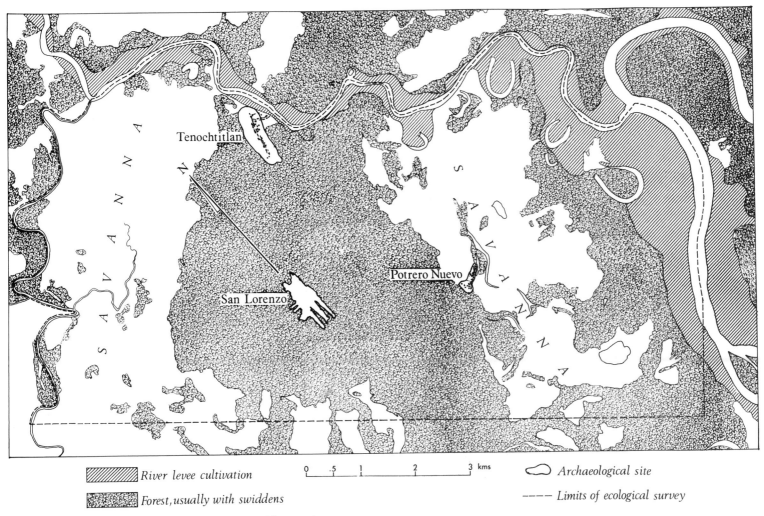

Fig. 1. Map of the San Lorenzo Tenochtitlán sample area, based on an uncontrolled index mosaic prepared by the Cia. Mexicana Aerofoto, which gives an indication of the main ecological divisions in the environment.

pretation and mapping of vegetation, land use, and soils. However, since the scale was too large for the economical production of topographic maps, subsequent flights were made in 1967 at a higher altitude, and this time the photographs were at a scale of 1:15,000, which made them very poor in cultural and ecological detail.

From these photographs, the Cia. Mexicana de Aero-foto produced a series of topographic base maps on Cronaflex film. The entire coverage is on thirteen sheets at a 1:5,000 scale, with a contour interval of two meters. A very thorough survey with transit and stadia rod was carried out by the company to provide the necessary ground control. Since the altitude of the area varies between only 20 and 80 meters above sea level, distortion caused by topography was not a problem. On these base maps appear not only topography but also drainage, houses, trails, fences, and other cultural details.

The second part of the contract with the Cia. Mexicana de Aerofoto focused on botany, that is, on vegetation patterns and land use. Here there were obvious problems, for while it was necessary to conduct field traverses to interpret the patterns seen on the photos, one of the basic kinds of land use being dealt with was one of shifting cultivation rather than fixed fields. Accordingly, by the time the team of botanists from the National University of Mexico got to the field, the patterns had shifted from what they were in February 1966. Nevertheless, mistakes of photo interpretation could be corrected. It was also a stroke of luck that the field botanists had been affiliated with a larger project on the flora of Veracruz. While in the field gathering information for the establishment of vegetation types, they made a fair-sized herbarium including over 187 wild species. One of the team was a practiced ethnobotanist, and he managed to collect 239 species and varieties of plants that were either cultivated or exploited by the inhabitants of the sample area. The final result was a series of overlays on the same scale as the topographic base maps showing field patterns, boundaries of second-growth areas of varying maturity, and areas covered by the determined vegetation types.

Lastly, the contract included an intensive survey of the sample area by soil specialists from the National School of Agriculture at Chapingo. Using the 1966 photo series as a base, seventy-five pits, each two meters deep, were dug at strategic spots over the entire zone, profiles were recorded, and soil samples were taken. The analysis of the soil samples included texture, pH, saturation percentage, field capacity, cation interchange capacity, soluble salts, and organic material. Four soil series were established on the basis of this information, and their boundaries plotted on another set of overlays. Once more, other information revealed that mistakes had been made on these maps, but it was possible to adjust what in some cases seemed to be armchair analysis with the ethnographic and ecological facts. Totally at odds with the realities of the situation was a final piece of work provided by the soil experts, namely, the ranking of soil classes according to their supposed potential. It turned out that this potential was purely an academic construct, based on what students in agricultural schools are told about modern agricultural practices and having little to do with the realities of wresting a living as faced by the farmers of the zone.

Land Use Patterns and the Human Ecosystem

Actually, photogrammetry was only the starting point for the ecological project. The principal aim was to get from this detailed mapping something usable. Thus, it was necessary to subject the maps and overlays to a thorough reanalysis, including a good deal of correction and redrawing, based on our having lived among the people of the area off and on for three years and having acquired an enormous amount of data to apply to the maps and photographs. We were anthropologists interested in people, while the photogrammetry specialists and soil scientists were interested in things, so that our aims did not always jibe. Nevertheless, out of all this came three separate maps at a scale of 1:16,000 (the largest scale that can be used to get a single-sheet map of 75 sq. km. onto a printing press). One sheet is topographic and "cultural"; the second shows vegetation and land use; the third represents topography-cum-soils.

Michael D. Coe

As we found out, archaeologists can do a great deal of ethnography if they have good informants and are equipped with tape recorders. We were not only prepared in this respect to gather a vast amount of information on human ecology in the area, but were joined by two zoologists, Dr. Elizabeth S. Wing, who studied fishing, hunting, and turtle-collecting practices, and Dr. Robert R. Miller, who investigated fish species. We were able to accompany farmers to their milpas and to join them on their fishing and hunting trips, so that we could flesh out the photogrammetry with some solid ethnography.

San Lorenzo Tenochtitlán is located in an area dominated by the Coatzacoalcos River and its tributary streams. Since the topography is low-lying, with only gentle hills rising here and there, most of the area is alluvium, and many oxbow ponds have been left by the meandering of the streams and rivers. The climate is unusually wet, even for the humid tropics, the average annual rainfall being over 2,000 mm. (80 in.). Since the annual evaporation averages around 1,100 mm., soil humidity is high. Because of the cool, rainy northers that sweep across the Isthmus of Tehuantepec at intervals from January through mid-March, the so-called dry season is not very dry; in fact, only March, April, and early May have low rainfall. The wettest months are from June through October, with a peak in September, when the rainfall may reach over 500 mm. in a single month.

Another basic factor of human ecology is what happens to the rivers and landscape during this precipitation cycle. The Coatzacoalcos, which is the second largest river in Mexico, borders the sample area on the southeast; on the northeast, the sample area is bounded by the Río Chiquito, a branch of the Coatzacoalcos, and on the northwest, by the much smaller Tatagapa. The rivers begin rising rapidly in June and reach crest height in July and September, flooding all land lying below the 24-meter contour and occasionally some land above this line. During the summer rains, it is a world afloat, with the people abandoning horse and foot travel for dugout canoes.

Soils are closely correlated with this flooding pattern.

The local farmers have their own classification of soils, which fortunately corresponds closely to that established by our soil scientists. Along the rivers are broad, naturally raised levees, which are called locally *tierra de primera* or "first-class land" (Fig. 2). Most levee soils are underwater from June through November, but once the rivers go down, they are planted, producing the greatest harvest of the area. Away from the levees are flat grasslands, which also become inundated every summer (Fig. 3). Their soils (*tierra de potrero*, "pasture soils") are highly acid, poorly drained, and useless even if plowed. Nonetheless, the savannahs play a key role as pastures for horses and cattle during the dry season, as loci of the oxbow ponds that are so important for native fishing, and when covered with water, as places to catch tropical gar and tarpon.

There are two kinds of upland soil above the 24-meter contour on the *lomas*, which are hilly regions presumably uplifted by underlying salt domes. The most important is *tierra barreal* (clayey soils) (Fig. 4), a rich, slightly acid soil. The other is *tierra de grava* (gravel soils), localized at and around the San Lorenzo site, and characterized by a sandy texture full of gravel. The archaeological work shows that it consists mainly of artificial fill brought in to construct the Olmec ceremonial center.

The area covered by our study comprised 7,574.8 hectares, with the following breakdown according to soil class: tierra barreal—1,697.8 hectares; tierra de grava—670.5 hectares; the lomas land total—2,368.3 hectares, or 31.2 percent of the study area. Tierra de primera covered 1,588.3 hectares or 21.0 percent of the study area, which with the lomas land adds up to 3,956.6 hectares or 52.2 percent as the total amount of cultivable land. The remaining 3,618.2 hectares were classified as tierra de potrero, accounting for 47.8 percent of the area studied.

The land use patterns that can be seen today are considerably more complex than is apparent at first glance and are closely correlated with patterns of climate, soils, vegetation cover, and especially with the annual regime of the river system. There are two principal corn crops on the upland soils. The *temporal* is the wet season crop. It

Fig. 2. Contact print of *tierra de primera* along the Coatza-coalcos River, at the point where it branches off into the Río Chiquito. Maize, cucurbits, and citrus crops are among the cultigens that can be identified.

Michael D. Coe

Fig. 3. Ground photograph of savannah (*tierra de potrero*) interspersed with forested "islands" during a February norther. This landscape is exploited only for hunting, fishing, and grazing.

Fig. 4. Contact print of *tierra barreal* between the town of Tenochtitlán and the site of San Lorenzo, February 1966. The lighter patches in the upper right quadrant are *tapachol* fields, some with manioc interplanted with maize. Abandoned fields regenerating to bush and low forest can also be identified.

Michael D. Coe

fits the usual slash-and-burn description: a patch of forest or bush is cut down, allowed to dry for twenty days, and then burned just before the rains. It is planted in late May or early June with a digging stick. In August the resulting corn is doubled, to keep the water out, and it is harvested in September. The *tapachol* is the winter crop, usually planted in December fields that have been cleared in low second-growth, or even in part of the previous temporal field. Because of the northers, the brush cannot be burned properly but is left on the ground and then piled up around the young plants; thus, the tapachol is a mulched crop, harvested in late February or March. Such mulching of the winter crop is practiced widely in southern Veracruz and Tabasco, for instance, at La Venta island (Drucker and Heizer 1960:39).

On the tierra de primera along the rivers, only a dry season crop or tapachol is possible; anybody who tried to plant temporal there would be taking a tremendous risk. Once the natural vegetation cover has been removed, the typical fallow cover is *camalote* grass (*Paspalum fasciculatum*). It has sometimes been claimed that Meso-american farmers do not plant in grass, but this is not so. Typically, the grass is felled with machetes, and the maize is planted down through the grass roots in holes made by a dibble stick; the maize grows so fast in such soil that it outstrips the regenerating grass. A high fertility—for tierra de primera is recently deposited alluvium—and capillary water ensure enormous yields.

This pattern is still relatively simple. To complicate matters, two extra crops can be planted. One such crop is the *chamil*, planted in March in low, humid, sandy soil, preferably with fairly high forest on top; both flat lomas and uncleared land along the river can be used. The chamil is harvested after three months. The *tonamil* or *aventurero* (adventurer) is a mulch crop, planted in late August or early September in the lomas on well-drained tierra barreal and harvested in November. The name aventurero is applied to it because the tonamil is considered a risky business, especially subject to insect pests.

A further complication is that many varieties of corn are in use, each with different growing and production characteristics. There are nine kinds of *maiz corriente* or native races, and two recently introduced hybrid corns. Although hybrids produce significantly greater yields than the native races, they are not planted in the temporal because they are subject to rot. Conversely, maiz corriente is not favored for the tapachol because it can be blown down by the strong, hot south winds that blow across the Isthmus of Tehuantepec from March through May, whereas the hybrids are wind-resistant.

Other crops are cultivated as well. Two varieties of sweet manioc (*Manihot esculenta*) are grown, usually interplanted with maize in the lomas soils. The black bean is also very common and is a major item in local diets, the best harvests being obtained from plots along the river. A wide variety of cucurbit cultivation is found along the rivers in the very sandy soils on the margins of the tierra de primera. Small pits called *zurcos* are dug into the soil and filled with beach sand; three to four seeds are planted in each. This technique is now used extensively throughout the middle Coatzacoalcos drainage area in the production of watermelons for sale downriver. It can easily be spotted and the zurcos counted on aerial photographs; in fact, since the average production of a single zurco is known, it is possible to estimate the entire crop. Other food and condiment plants include sweet potatoes, jícama (*Pachyrrhizus erosus*), chili peppers, cherry tomatoes, malanga (*Xanthosoma violaceum*), yams, and annatto (*Bixa orellana*). A wide variety of fruit trees are cultivated, including citruses of many varieties, mangoes, bananas and plantains, sapodilla, avocado, and breadfruit. Coffee and cacao are occasionally grown on nonflooding land close to the rivers.

Citruses, bananas, and watermelons are all cash crops. In recent years there has been a great upswing in wet season production of swamp rice, which is sown in lowlying tierra barreal. All of these are shipped in river boats, the only form of transport out of the area, to be sold to middlemen in the market city of Minatitlán.

Wild plant products also play a role in the local ecology. A number of fruit-producing species are not cultivated or otherwise encouraged by man. Most important is the palma real (*Scheelea liebmanni*), which provides thatching material, palm nuts for oil and meat, and a nutritious palm heart. The local pharmacopeia is extraordinarily rich and heavily dependent on wild plants for active ingredients. At least two species, one of them a Sapindaceae, produce barbasco or fish poison, while several trees and one bromeliad are sources of cordage. Sources of wood include ceiba, Mexican cedar (*Cedrela mexicana*), nacaste (*Enterolobium cyclocarpum*), and many others.

In an effort to understand what appears on the photographs, one must also take into account fishing, hunting, and turtle collecting, which go on year-round. The species captured and the techniques used change with the annual round of rainfall and the rise and fall of rivers. In spite of the fact that cattle, pigs, and chickens have been in this drainage area since the sixteenth century, the first two are generally kept for sale outside the area and only enter into the diet during feasts. By far the most important source of animal protein is fish, including snook (*Centropomus*), gar (*Lepisosteus tropicus*), mojarra (*Cichlasoma*), and catfish. Favorite fishing places are the oxbow ponds, located out on the savannahs, which are literally harvested rather than fished, for as they shrink with the advancing dry season, the fish are concentrated and surrounded by seine nets. When the waters once again flood the landscape, they are naturally restocked. Second to this as a source of protein is game, primarily Virginia deer and brocket deer, collared peccary, and the lowly armadillo. During November and December, quantities of migratory geese and ducks are taken on the ponds.

Production, Consumption, and Land Ownership

From a number of informants in the village of Tenochtitlán, it was possible to obtain meaningful figures on production, mainly for maize, within the sample area. For the year 1966 in tapachol, informants supplied the following figures on maize cultivation and production according to soil classification: tierra barreal—41.2 hectares were seeded; tierra de grava—12.2 hectares; for a lomas land total of 53.4 hectares, producing 121.1

metric tons of shelled maize. The tierra de primera area planted was 196.8 hectares, producing 619.9 metric tons of shelled maize. A 24.8-hectare plot of tierra de potrero soil was planted by a local landowner after plowing with a tractor, but the entire crop was lost. All informants clearly distinguished between the alluvial levee lands—tierra de primera—and the upland soils. One hectare on the levee lands will produce an average crop, using native races, of 3.15 metric tons of shelled corn, but there is only one crop. In the two upland soil series, the average per hectare production for each crop is considerably lower, only 2.25 metric tons, but there are at least two such crops possible.

A number of consumption figures were compiled which are probably somewhat inaccurate but show the kind of thinking involved in the economic decisions that local farmers must make. It is believed that a family of five persons needs ten *cargas* of maize per year, about equal to 1.00 to 1.20 metric tons of shelled corn; this comes out to 200–240 kilos per person. The addition of pigs and chickens raises this figure considerably, since one pig is said to eat no less than 270 kilos a month. Turkeys are also great eaters of corn and thus a luxury kept only for ceremonial occasions. Therefore, a person who grows only one hectare on the lomas land can in a single season obtain more than enough to feed his family. He uses what is left over to sell for cash, so that the other things in life which he has come to need—transistor radios, wrist watches, canned goods—can be bought.

The question of buying power raises the question of economic and political power. This is based directly on land ownership. Most of the upland soils belong to the ejido of Tenochtitlán and thus are commonly held among eighty or so ejidatarios; any outsider wishing to farm these lands must pay a small fee to the ejido. These soils are farmed in a shifting fashion, and although individuals have vague rights over where they shall place their milpa at any one season, these are customary and are not frozen into any rigid property system. The opposite is true of the levee lands, the tierra de primera. With the exception of a few community *parcelas*, which are set aside for the use of the primary school in each settlement, much of this land is in private hands, occasionally absentee. In the village of Tenochtitlán, for instance, the most powerful family has arisen through a gradual acquisition of such lands. This group of brothers began by working hard in the lomas soils of the ejido, where anyone who wants to put in extra labor will get out a tremendous per capita income. Eventually the brothers accumulated enough capital to pay laborers to work with them on the lomas, thereby increasing their purchasing power even more. With this, these caciques began to buy up the riverbank lands and thus almost doubled their income within a few years. Then they became storekeepers, loaning out money at huge rates of interest against future crops, whose ultimate price disposition they controlled through their deals with the owners of the river boats and with the buyers and middlemen in Minatitlán. By 1966, the brothers occupied all important political posts in Tenochtitlán and were among the richest men in that part of the Isthmus of Tehuantepec.

Carrying Capacity of the Land

The 1966 population of the sample area was approximately 1,400 persons, a density of only 18.7 persons per square kilometer. Simple calculations based on the minimum consumption figures for maize show that given the current production of the tapachol crop alone, as many as 3,700 persons (counting five to a household) could subsist in the area. Adding to this a possible temporal production, for which there are no figures, equal to the tapachol crop in the lomas, one arrives at a total probable production of 862 metric tons. This amount of maize would support about 4,310 persons, with a population density three times as high as actually observed. The conflict between observed and expected is owing to the exportation of the bulk of the crop outside the sample area, an important factor in the accretion of economic, social, and political power.

These observations are all drawn from the actual exploitation of the land. However, only a fraction of the usable land is in fact used. This low efficiency is in large part dependent on the factors of fallowing and of the "cost" to the farmer of increased exploitation in terms of labor and distance traveled. These factors are fairly well known for the sample area. One might think, therefore, that it would now be possible to come up with accurate figures for the carrying capacity of these 75 sq. km.—that is, the maximum population which the area could support under conditions of native agriculture. Yet there are very great problems. One is that the Cia. Mexicana de Aerofoto made serious errors in interpretation of field patterns and crops. They were working with prints at a scale of 1:8,000, whereas it is impossible to identify growing maize accurately and to distinguish it from recent *acahual* (second growth) at this scale, even with stereo pairs, because morning glories (*Ipomoea*) and other vines wrap themselves around old cornstalks in such a way that the patterns produced on the photos look like rows of growing corn. Accordingly, I obtained enlarged prints at a scale of 1:5,000, which easily enabled me to identify actual tapachol crops from second growth and to correct the maps, using stereo pairs and a Fairchild F–71 viewer. However, even though I knew that beans and manioc were growing at that time and had hoped to spot such plots on the photos, only old manioc plants in abandoned plots stood out. There is little question that if aerial Ektachrome or Ektachrome Infrared photographs were available, such crops could be distinguished from maize.

There are also mathematical difficulties in dealing with several soil series, a number of vegetation types, different seasons and methods of cropping, and a multiplicity of crops or varieties of the same crop with varying characteristics of production. All these factors complicate the picture. Nor is the fallowing cycle easy to determine. Esther Boserup (1965) proposed a classification of land use based on frequency of cropping as follows:

Forest-fallow cultivation—20–25 years fallow after
    1–2 years in cultivation
Bush-fallow cultivation—6–10 years fallow after 2–8
    years in cultivation

Short-fallow cultivation—1–2 years fallow, during which time only wild grasses can invade the fallow land

Annual cropping—land left fallow between harvesting of one crop and planting of next

Multicropping—same plot bearing several crops a year, with little or no fallowing

Fallowing is extremely important for the farmer planting in the two kinds of upland soil, since grass competition (not loss of fertility) is an almost insuperable problem. Usually, after three crops have been planted successively in the same place, a grass called *zacate de elote* (young corn grass) (*Panicum fasciculatum*) will begin crowding out the young corn shoots, and the field will be abandoned because it cannot be successfully weeded. Also, when planting tapachol in second growth, the lower the bush, the worse the grass problem. Accordingly, after three crops have been planted—that is, after 1 1/2 years—the field will be abandoned to bush so that the trees and shrubs can shade out the grass, with the fallow period usually lasting 3–6 years. Thus, the upland cultivation falls somewhere between Boserup's bush-fallow and short-fallow types, but great variation is possible on the pattern. Along the river levees, one finds a mosaic of annual cropping and short-fallow cultivation. Obviously, upland and levee areas will have to be separately calculated for carrying capacity. One might agree, therefore, with the correctness of Harold Brookfield's observation (1968:419) that "an approach based on precise description of what is found in any agricultural system would better enable us to understand agriculture as the manipulation of ecosystems than would continued use of the shifting cultivation-permanent cultivation dichotomy."

The complexities involved in such calculations are enormous. These complexities would have been invisible if it had not been for the information provided by photogrammetry and field work. They must also exist elsewhere in the tropics, in spite of claims for the simplicity of some areas, such as the Maya lowlands. For instance, Ursula Cowgill (1961:53) proposed a maximum carrying capacity for the central Maya area of 100–200 persons per square mile, on the basis of agricultural studies made near Lake Peten Itzá. She obviously meant that on cultivable soils of the type or types found there (not specified), this might be the carrying capacity, but surely the figure does not apply to the whole area, which has never been studied from that point of view.

There is little doubt, however, that the carrying capacity of our 75 sq. km. sample is many times the present population figure. This state of affairs is found in other parts of the world where tropical swidden agriculture is the rule, as in Black Africa, where the present population density is only one-tenth that of the carrying capacity (Henshall 1968:449). Unfortunately, it may be almost impossible ever to know what the carrying capacity in San Lorenzo Tenochtitlán might have been three thousand years ago, since Nal-Tel, a much more primitive and less productive race of corn, was probably dominant in those days. It may also be that attempts to arrive at maximum possible densities are in themselves meaningless and that we should be asking other questions of the data.

Models of Land Use and Demography

When I conceived the ecological project outlined here, I, like many other archaeologists and anthropologists, was a fairly straightforward Malthusian. That is, the premises of the model are: under given systems of food getting, the amount of food available is strictly limited; populations are the dependent variable; and after new forms of production have come into use, their levels tend to rise to the new limits set by them.

A new school of geographers and economists has turned this notion upside down. Esther Boserup (1965), for instance, marshaled impressive evidence from around the world to show that agricultural systems are elastic and highly responsive to changes in population. In other words, demography would be the independent variable, and agricultural systems the *dependent* one. The "new demography" can demonstrate that population growth in a given area is a response to a number of factors which may be social, cultural, ceremonial, religious, and perhaps not even subsistence or consumption-oriented (Wrigley 1967).

In line with this view, William Clarke (1966) in New

Michael D. Coe

Guinea and Clifford Geertz (1963) in Java have shown that the response to such population pressures might be the stepping up of labor input and only secondarily the adoption of new techniques of production. The eventual result is that as total production rises, per capita income may actually be falling because of rising population, and the amount of free time away from agricultural pursuits becomes negligible. This "agricultural involution," as Geertz called it, leads to a very definite lessening of the qualities that make a farmer's life worth living.

The relationship between production, population, and the rise of civilization is therefore by no means clear. While I am convinced that the Nile-like situation along the Coatzacoalcos River, in which the road to power lies in the possession of the river-levee lands, had something to do with the crystallization of Olmec culture and all its paraphernalia, new models are needed to explain why and how this happened.

It is my view that such models are going to depend on microgeographical studies of the sort that photogrammetry can provide, and I also am convinced that they are going to stem less from anthropological investigations and more from the "new geography" (see, e.g., Chorley and Haggett 1968; Haggett 1965; Chisholm 1962; Brookfield 1968). Locational studies, including central-place theory, nearest-neighbor analysis, and von Thünen's "isolated state" theory for the location of agricultural activity are the kinds of models I have in mind. These would necessarily be based on very accurate, large-scale mapping of settlements, fields, communications, and other data for which photogrammetry is a sine qua non. Computer analysis of such maps can now be done, through devices which can digitize information by co-ordinates and put it on tape for storage and retrieval. It would be theoretically possible, for instance, to have the computer produce a map showing all areas suitable for a chamil crop.

Another model is game theory, defined as the optimizing of decisions in the face of imperfect knowledge (Henshall 1968:448). It has been said that "the best general rule to the behavior of primitive farmers is that they work to get the maximum return for the minimum effort" (Nye and Greenland, in Clarke 1966:357). To get such a return, every adult male in San Lorenzo Tenochtitlán is faced with making decisions throughout the annual cycle. Some of the variables of which he has quite detailed knowledge are soil quality, pests, winds, amount of sunshine in a particular season, slope, vegetation cover, grass competition, land ownership, prices, maize varieties and qualities, transportation costs, and how much time he wants to leave for other activities, like hunting and fishing. The average farmer here probably does little gambling, and does not need to since crop failure, unless caused by pests or poor weeding, is unknown. An aspirant to local leadership, however, might have to follow a rather complex strategy to acquire economic power, extended over a number of years and with a considerable amount of risk taking. These and other problems could certainly be posed and worked out with game theory in mind.

In conclusion, photogrammetry, like the computer, cannot substitute for concepts. It may destroy them, or it may even help the investigator explore for new ones, but productive use of photogrammetric techniques in the study of human ecology requires the formulation of models, that is, of realistic and productive concepts, which focus on specific parts of biomes instead of on the entire biome. To reverse an old saw, we have not been looking at the trees because we have been concentrating on the forest; it is now time to look at both.

This project was carried out with the authorization of the Instituto Nacional de Antropología e Historia. Financial support was provided by Grant GS–1593, National Science Foundation. Collaborating in the ecological and ethnological studies were Richard A. Diehl (University of Missouri), Elizabeth S. Wing and Stephen Carr (Florida State Museum), Robert R. Miller and Mr. and Mrs. James Lackey (University of Michigan), and Mr. and Mrs. G. R. Krotser (Jalapa, Veracruz). Botanical studies were undertaken by Javier Chavelas Polito and Miguel A. Martínez Alfaro (Instituto Nacional de Investigaciones Forestales) and by Arturo de la Cruz Trejo (Cia. Mexicana de Aerofoto). I am especially grateful for the cooperation and advice of Arturo Gómez Pompa (Universidad Nacional Autónoma de México).

Elmer Harp, Jr.

Threshold Indicators of Culture in Air Photo Archaeology: A Case Study in the Arctic

Air photos are not an immediate panacea for all the problems that beset a field archaeologist, but if taken at optimum scales and in the most efficient emulsions (Harp 1968), they are potential sources of much valuable cultural data. Generally, these data may either contribute to the discovery of new sites in hitherto unexplored country, or they may aid the elucidation of cultural phenomena previously recognized. Unfortunately, however, the information potential of air photos is not automatically available to the untrained or random viewer, for it can only be developed through systematic and persevering analysis and interpretation. This observation suggests that a photoanalyst must operate within some specific conceptual framework, and it follows that his ultimate problems of interpretation can only be solved if they, too, have been logically and clearly formulated.

In order to secure the maximum retrieval of useful archaeological information from air photos, it is necessary to focus on the detection and interpretation of threshold indicators of culture, that is, all relatively minimal traces of man and culture on the surficial landscape. Often it happens that archaeological ruins are instantly visible in air photos, as in the case of Stonehenge, an Iron Age hilltop fortress, or prehistoric irrigation systems. Also, one does not require extensive ethnographic training in order to identify these remains as unnatural phenomena, or to go one step further and deduce that they are remnants of human culture. However, archaeologists are involved more often than not with cultural traces that are less complex, smaller in size, and frequently incomplete or vestigial. This kind of fragmentary evidence may indeed stand on the verge of one's ability to perceive it; it may be at the very threshold of recognition. Presumably, then, in order to detect and grasp the significance of such penumbral detail, it may help if we first examine the parameters of the man-environment relationship, and also it may be necessary to clarify the intellectual problems inherent in the act of translating and interpreting information obtained from two-dimensional photography.

It is a reasonable assumption in all anthropological studies that man is fundamentally a part of nature and, therefore, a member of one or more ecological systems or communities. The general patterns of his existence are always conditioned to some extent by the surrounding physical environment. Furthermore, if man's activities have any degree of social magnitude, or sufficient routineness to be described as cultural, he will inevitably alter that environment, either unconsciously or with purpose, in response to cultural imperatives.

Recently it has become fashionable to condemn ourselves as despoilers of the natural environment, although ecologists and natural historians have long been aware that men are important modifiers of nature. However, we err in thinking of this as a phenomenon only of the past several decades, or even of the Industrial Age, for man has been a major factor in the evolution of the earth's surface for perhaps the last two million years, or at least since he acquired control of fire in the middle of the Pleistocene period. As Robert F. Heizer (1955) observed, "at any point in time or space where man has occupied a region he has materially affected the soil, the fauna, the flora, and even the climate, through the intermediacy of that one distinctive human possession which we call culture." Pursuant to his proliferation of culture and his deployment of it as a shield and a set of techniques to mediate between himself and nature, he effected profound changes in preexisting natural ecological processes. This new adaptive system, culture, enabled man to become a wide-ranging predatory species and to conquer the entire habitable world, excluding only Antarctica, by approximately 2000 B.C.

In this geographic spread, man exerted a drastic influence on the natural environment almost everywhere he ranged. He has hunted certain species of animal life to extinction and still threatens many others, while artificially conserving some as pets and as domesticated sources of food and energy. He has interacted similarly with the floral kingdom, destroying some species, cultivating others, and selectively breeding new ones. His use of fire has turned forests into prairies, by design or accident, and has denuded land across countless thousands of square miles. His untold numbers of camp and settlement sites scattered throughout all the continents are enclaves of refuse and deposits that have completely upset natural chemical balances, vegetative cover, and soil profiles. He has caused both devastating erosion and monumental construction. In short, man has been one of the most significant agents of change in the latter-day history of the earth's surface.

Given these observations, we might theoretically expect to find residual evidence of man's occupations, whether past or present, in any air photo imagery that covers a sufficiently large area. However, such human evidence may not be immediately apparent, for man has been only one factor within a large complex of natural agencies of change. As Edward Pyddoke (1961) expressed the matter, "archaeological strata are nothing more than comparatively recent examples of the effects of geological processes and are manifestations of the same fundamental causes." In the vertical case of soil stratification, we must know something of the dynamic agencies of sun and air, wind, rain and hydrology, frost, and flora and fauna, before we can fully comprehend the origin and development of cultural deposits. Correspondingly, in the horizontal, or surficial, case, as reflected in an air photo image, I believe the very same agencies must be factored out of the total context before the human element can be fully exposed to examination.

Thus, for general purposes we can begin by saying that air photos record two primary sets of information, one consisting of the natural landscape, and the other, the cultural landscape. From an anthropological point of view, we may conceptualize these as separate but interacting subsystems. Hence, wherever man is present, or has been at some time in the past, the images of these two subsystems, or landscapes, can be fully understood only with reference to each other.

The Analytical Procedure

The interpretive analysis of aerial photography is largely an intellectual procedure, involving both deductive and inductive reasoning. As in all varieties of scientific investigation, a successful outcome hinges on the presence of repetitive phenomena, whether these be individual basic elements or patterned complexes of such elements. Also, the analysis must operate from a series of assumptions, among which the following are paramount: landscapes are derived by natural processes through the alteration of residual and transported materials; these surface and subsurface materials combine to form discernible patterns; through variations of color, tone, and texture in the photo image, such patterns can be analyzed for component elements; these component elements are conceptualized as indicators of the complexes themselves; like associations of indicator elements produce like pattern complexes; and like pattern complexes, in turn, denote similar dynamic processes and developmental trajectories.

The analytical and interpretive process must include a continuous criticism of the nature of the evidence observed in the air photos, as well as of the modes of perception and identification. Cultural biases can lead to notoriously mistaken conclusions in photo interpretation, as they do elsewhere in the realm of human behavior, for we tend to be object-oriented in culturally determined ways, and an apparent familiarity of shapes and patterns will often short-circuit the reasoning process. Therefore, the actual data observed and the criteria used to classify them must be rigorously questioned and evaluated at all times.

The fundamental approach of environmental analysis advocated here derives from the work of Robert E. Frost and Jack N. Rinker (1968). For maximum results, they recommend deployment of a team of specialists, including perhaps a geologist, physiographer, biologist, hydrologist, anthropologist, and engineer. However, as a team of such experts may not always be available, a single person can often progress surprisingly far in air photo analysis within the limits of his own training and experience. It is the background knowledge of the analyst that rises to the stimulus cues obtained in photo reading, and as noted before, there is no automatic transference of information from photograph to viewer.

The analytical procedure begins with a scanning of the regional environment. This is best accomplished with a mosaic of small-scale panchromatic photography, for massive patterns and regularities of the landscape can be seen more readily in their entirety, and gross relationships of form and process can be determined. We can learn something of the general geography of the region from its physical and cultural aspects and their spatial relationships; next, physiographic attributes can be described, and the bedrock geology deduced. In this phase, knowledge is gained about the origins of the crustal materials, whether transported or residual, as well as about the processes that have contributed to the formation of the regional topography. Also, we can characterize the climate of the region through a study of erosion patterns and vegetation, as well as of the patterns of man's economic exploitation, if these are clearly portrayed in the air photos.

The second stage involves more intensive study of local aspects, or minor features, in the region. This is best pursued through stereoscopic examination of larger-scale panchromatic photography, on the order of 1:20,000 or 1:15,000 (cf. Figs. 5, 6). At this level of procedure we can obtain more detailed and accurate comprehension of land forms, drainage patterns, and erosional characteristics. We can analyze the occurrence of vegetation in fine detail, achieving at times clear understanding of its structural character and relationship to land forms, even perhaps its specific identification. At this scale we can also analyze the arrangements, contrasts, and design of photo tones: a panchromatic emulsion records all colors in the visual band of the electromagnetic spectrum as varying shades of gray, numbering on the order of two hundred, and it is necessary to examine these variants carefully in order to determine their significance as pattern elements.

At this stage, we should also attempt more refined analysis of the cultural landscape, differentiating broadly between urban and rural patterns, and describing man's general alterations of the landscape and the intensity of these activities. Here, of course, the analyst is concerned not only with overt cultural patterns but also with any special features that may seem anomalous in the otherwise natural context.

In the third and last stage of procedure, the data from regional and local analyses are correlated, and finally, interpretations and evaluations are made with respect to a specific set of problems. At this point we enter the picture primarily as anthropologists or archaeologists and focus our attention and effort on the man-environment interface, for that is the crucial plane of interaction. It is understood that we are concerned here chiefly with social and cultural systems, and less with individual man.

Given the earlier assumption that any human activity

Elmer Harp, Jr.

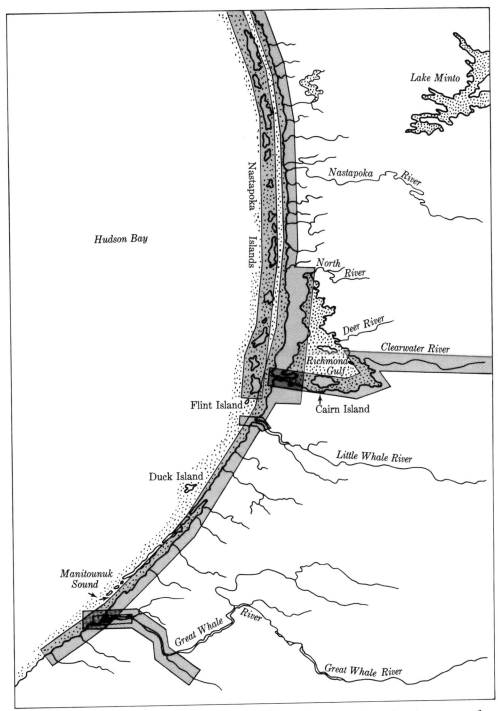

Fig. 5. Map of east coast of Hudson Bay north of Great Whale River, showing extent of experimental photography flown in summer of 1966.

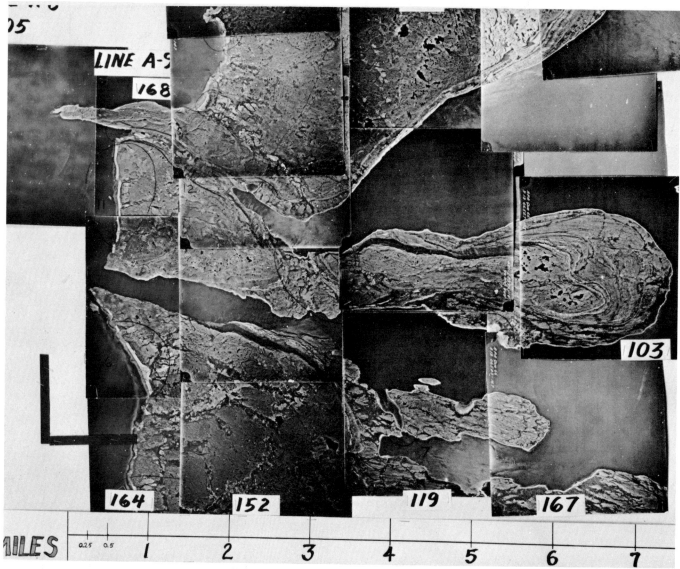

Fig. 6. Mosaic of panchromatic air photos, showing Gulf
Hazard inlet from Hudson Bay (left) to Richmond Gulf (right).
Panchromatic, 1:15,000.

Elmer Harp, Jr.

with social magnitude or cultural routineness will always leave a trace on the surface landscape, we realize that such traces may in time become obscured, perhaps even entirely obliterated, by erosion or cataclysm. However, short of such drastic elimination, any cultural deposition or alteration of the surficial environment will establish a chain of unnatural effects that will long endure, and the reflected images of these events may be recorded in suitably scaled air photos. Although the erasure of cultural signs, particularly as it relates to processes of physiographic changes in Pleistocene and more recent time, poses serious problems for both the field archaeologist and the archaeological photo analyst, that topic is beyond the scope of this paper.

Assuming that the analysis has showed the constituents and properties of a given environment, we can now inquire about the range of man's cultural responses to that environment. Or, from a slightly different point of view, we may ask about man's specific purposes in occupying that environment. At this juncture the chief matters of interest are his basic modes of subsistence, levels of tool development and technology, methods of transportation, sources of energy for work performance, and other systematic cultural techniques for resource exploitation. For example, the extremes of man's reactions to his environment may vary from that of an aboriginal hunting-fishing-gathering economy to the modern expression of advanced Western civilization. The first of these types involves subsisting on the land with a minimal technology that is closely adapted to the exploitation of local food resources and of such other materials as may be prerequisite to survival. The latter type of cultural response has sufficient technological ability to transport its own environment anywhere, now even to extraterrestrial spheres, and wherever the locale may be, is able to carry out large-scale programs of exploitation in response to its more elaborate needs.

Clearly, these different culture systems will exert significantly different influences on any natural landscape, and each will leave its own kind of distinctive traces. Likewise, there should be identifiable signature

traces for various other stages of culture and technology that are intermediate between the two extremes. These statements may seem to imply that anthropology includes a universally acceptable scheme for the hierarchical classification of culture systems, but that is not the case. However, there is nothing to prevent the use of any taxonomy that contributes to the solution of a given problem, and in this instance one can benefit most from a classification of culture stages that expresses the broad, vital relationships between subsistence economy, technology, and environment.

D. L. Clarke (1958:322) recently formulated a scheme of gross cultural groupings that appears to meet admirably the needs of air photo archaeological analysis. He postulated a basic cultural entity, which he named a "technocomplex" and defined as a large group of approximately similar culture systems that have in common "the same general equilibrium pattern based on similar economic strategy, in similar environments with a similar technology and a similar past trajectory." There may be a wide range of differences in the component culture systems of a technocomplex, as in language, ethnic affiliation, or any number of other cultural patterns. However, the important point for our present analysis is that the various components of a technocomplex show basic likenesses in their strategic responses to comparable environments. For this reason, all members of a common technocomplex should alter their environments in a similar set of ways, and their individual signatures in air photos should therefore be comparable. Regardless of space or time, then, if we can characterize a given environment with sufficient accuracy, we should be able to identify the range of technocomplex systems that can, or could have, successfully exploited it.

If technocomplexes are categorized in terms of subsistence economy, a classification familiar to anthropologists, three basic varieties emerge: hunter-fisher-gatherer, pastoral nomad, and agrarian. Of these, the first has been the fundamental and most widespread throughout all of human history, for it has existed in one form or another ever since the advent of the hominids. According to the developmental level of its component culture systems, tool kits, techniques, etc., and depending also on the nature of the natural resources to be exploited, the hunter-fisher-gatherer technocomplex can be effective in virtually any terrestrial environment, although it may be constantly at the mercy of ungovernable cyclical changes in any given environment. Clearly, however, it will achieve optimum efficiency wherever rich staple food resources can be exploited in a socially organized fashion, or wherever a sequence of such resources can be utilized in a formal rotation pattern through an annual round of seasons. Clarke (1958:276–283) referred to this as a "climax development," and it is this heightened level of sociocultural elaboration that is most likely to leave its signature traces on a natural landscape.

Whereas the hunter-fisher-gatherer can subsist in almost any environment, the pastoral nomad technocomplex, despite its possession of advanced cultural techniques, is strictly limited to environments that naturally supply sufficient food for its domesticated staple animals, such as tundra, steppes, grasslands, or suitable portions of desert and mountain areas. Also, the origins of this technocomplex lie within the last five thousand years of man's history, so that the category allows for the possibility of further analytical refinement, insofar as its geographic and time-horizon boundaries can be used to define signatures in the cultural landscape.

The agrarian technocomplex is likewise a relatively youthful cultural phenomenon, although it may well be twice the age of the pastoral nomad systems. Also, it is subject to sharp environmental boundary limitations, even though some of its component culture systems may represent the acme of man's technological abilities. The signature traces relating to this category are the most complex of all, because they can express numerous levels of subsistence economy ranging from primitive village horticulture, possibly combined seasonally with hunter-fisher-gatherer pursuits, to the highest elaborations of modern urban civilization.

It is not my purpose to examine or even specify the full spectrum of culture systems within each of the aforementioned technocomplexes, but only to clarify the potential usefulness of this classification for air photo analysis in cultural anthropology or archaeology. Archaeologists, who customarily "think Indian" (or "Eskimo," as in the case study that follows) as they explore for new sites, may regard this basic theoretical approach as commonplace. However, it furnishes the kind of exact conceptual framework that we need for an orderly, efficient approach to interpretation of the cultural landscape. Once the character of the physical environment is thoroughly understood, we can then predict its potential interrelationships with each of the several major technocomplexes, and if the archaeologist wishes to project his inferences still further, he can then define a limited range of sociocultural subsystems that might be linked with one or another of these technocomplexes. A final caveat is necessary: inasmuch as an archaeologist may sometimes experience difficulty in defining or classifying a culture even after he has excavated its vestigial remains, we should not suppose that he can be any more successful in identifying a specific culture from the information reflected in an air photo.

In summary, when the veneer of natural landscape patterns has been perceived, analyzed, and figuratively stripped away, any visible traces of human activity will stand highlighted and separate. Only through the conduct of such structured analysis, proceeding from macro- toward micro-levels, can one hope to understand the full scope of cultural information that may be recorded in air photo imagery.

A Case Study

The case study concerns a transitional Arctic and sub-Arctic environment on the east coast of Hudson Bay, an area that was originally selected for archaeological exploration for at least one compelling reason that is relevant to problems of air photo analysis and interpretation. Aside from the fact that valid and pressing archaeological questions can be posed, this part of the Quebec-Labrador peninsula confronts us with a strong challenge of limited and simplified archaeological potential. The

Elmer Harp, Jr.

territory has always been thinly populated, at least in the northern region of Ungava, and before the arrival of European fur traders and colonists its only known aboriginal inhabitants were semimigratory Indians and Eskimos. As subunits of the hunter-fisher-gatherer technocomplex, these small band societies were closely integrated with their surrounding environments and lived in tightly balanced ecosystems. They had a meagerly developed technology and material culture, which were seldom elaborated beyond the dictates of their subsistence economies. Therefore, we can expect that these primitive hunters exerted a relatively slight impact on the austere, Arctic landscape and left behind them a bare minimum of archaeological residues.

In the summer of 1966 I had selected lines of experimental photography flown in this general area, using various scales (1:15,000; 1:7,500; 1:2,500) and several different emulsions (panchromatic, infrared, true color, camouflage-detection). The extent of coverage was considerable (Fig. 5), and the examples illustrated (Figs. 6 and 8) consist of 1:15,000 panchromatic, at which scale the original 9-inch photo width is equivalent to 2.13 miles and one photo inch equals 1,250 feet. The area pictured includes the central section of the east coast of Hudson Bay, portions of Richmond Gulf, and part of Gulf Hazard, which is the entrance to Richmond Gulf.

Because it is not feasible to document this paper with original stereo photography, the following analysis cannot be construed as a complete presentation. Moreover, inasmuch as I spent the following summer of 1967 in a ground reconnaissance of this country and am now thoroughly familiar with conditions there, it should be emphasized that this summary contains only evidence that can be derived from a systematic examination of the air photos.

Geography. Hudson Bay composes the westerly section of the photo mosaic (Fig. 6), and a large body of almost landlocked water known as Richmond Gulf lies to the east. Richmond Gulf is connected with the outer bay through Gulf Hazard, which makes it a tidal body. A broad regional analysis of this and other mosaics elicits no immediate signs of economic exploitation, no discernible roads or trails, no apparent indications whatsoever of a cultural landscape. One sees essentially a natural landscape of wilderness.

Physiography. The face of the land is composed of barren rocky hills or mountains, and headlands, occasionally interspersed with patches of variable-toned grays, which indicate areas of vegetation. The topography is rugged. Its most outstanding features are two north-south lines of cuestas, one of which forms the offshore chain of the Nastapoka Islands, and the other the primary mainland shore, including the major peninsula that separates Richmond Gulf from Hudson Bay. These cuestas slant gradually upward out of the sea, attain heights in excess of one thousand feet, and then plunge abruptly to the sea again in a series of east-facing escarpments. Farther inland the country assumes a jumbled, unpatterned aspect, and there is no consistent alignment in the distribution of the rounded bedrock hills and mountains. The basic organization of the drainage is from east to west.

Geology. The two lines of cuestas are capped with basalt flows, beneath which is a complicated series of strata. These could no doubt be identified by a geologist after careful examination of the boundary characteristics and talus slopes along the scarps, but there are signs of metamorphic and sedimentary layers in the series. The country lying east of the cuestas shows features which are characteristic of granitic rocks, in that the barren hills and mountains are all dome-shaped with convex slopes, and the fracture lines are complex and unpatterned. This is typical Canadian Shield terrain, totally residual in origin except for the lowland fill.

The valleys and lowlands are floored with unconsolidated sands and gravels, which are of transported origin. Where these valleys are wide, the drainage systems are dendritic and show no signs of immediate bedrock control. In other places close to a coastline some of the filled valleys contain extensive series of concentric raised beachlines and wave-cut terraces. The soil mantle, as evidenced by vegetation patterns, is sporadic and thin, and confined strictly to the intermontane lowlands.

Drainage Patterns. No major river systems show in the mosaic illustrated here, although photography of the adjacent region reveals the several important rivers that drain from the interior Ungava plateau into Richmond Gulf and Hudson Bay. Wherever small streams do appear, the valley systems through which they flow are clearly under bedrock control, and their general trend is from east to west. Otherwise, there are no large-scale patterns or organization in the drainage.

Land Forms. This landscape shows strong traces of past major glaciation. The rocky upland surfaces have been stripped clean of soil mantle; they are pockmarked with myriad basins and ponds, and deep striations are clearly evident in many places. The granite hill country to the east is characterized by rounded knobs and open, U-shaped valleys.

The valleys and lowlands, however, are filled with glacio-fluvial deposits of gravel and sand, as well as marine sediments. In the systems of raised beach lines we see the post-Pleistocene history of the landscape plainly recorded: as the glaciation retreated, the depressed land mass experienced marine submergence to heights between 500 and 600 feet; subsequent crustal upwarping caused a relative lowering of the sea level and the cutting of a long sequence of receding beach lines.

Erosion Patterns. Several agencies have contributed to the reduction of this landscape, most notably continental glaciation. Seasonal frost action is still operative, as indicated by the block-fractured materials in the talus slopes. The deposition of shoals and sand bars in coastal waters shows localized fluvial erosion, and occasional complexes of sand dunes and blowouts in valley areas supply evidence of strong wind action in the present and recent past.

Vegetation. Floral cover is scanty, owing in large part to the widespread denuded rock surfaces, and vegetation occurs only in the intermontane lowlands. Much of the country may be described as barren, although it is obviously close to or within the extreme limits of the northern tree line. In certain well-protected areas, such as the southeastern slopes of Castle Peninsula and some of the deep interior valleys, there are thin-to-moderate stands of conifers. Under optimum conditions these reach heights of thirty or forty feet. Some portions of this forest are identifiable as open lichen woodlands, for dense surface patches of *Cladonia rangiferina* (reindeer moss) can be distinguished from ordinary grassland by their lighter gray tone in the panchromatic prints. Elsewhere in moist valley bottoms are concentrations of thick, high brush, deduced as Arctic willow or alder; and higher, well-drained soils support heath vegetation, including clumps of low brush, deduced as dwarf birch.

Fauna. On the mosaic illustrated here there are no indisputable signs of local fauna, but the 1:15,000 coverage of adjacent areas affords clear evidence of both land and sea mammals. For example, the larger rivers draining into the east side of Richmond Gulf clearly act as barriers athwart the north-south migration paths of the interior caribou herds, and concentrations of caribou trails can easily be seen on panchromatic at habitual crossing places along these rivers. Also, in a coastwise line of camouflage-detection coverage, two frames show a small school of beluga cavorting at the surface just a few miles south of the entrance to Richmond Gulf. These are not visible to the naked eye at 1:15,000, at which scale the school appears to be a fleck of white water, but with a 5X viewing magnifier the individual whales can be counted and identified.

Photo Tones. The range of tones in this panchromatic photography is relatively limited, although the pattern differentiation tends to be rather clear and definite. The general monotony derives from the low reflectance of the dominant rock surfaces, and all of these have darker

057542

Elmer Harp, Jr.

values than most of the vegetated lowlands. The highest reflecting surfaces are associated with certain subsurface rock strata and the narrow sandy beaches that rim the land. Otherwise, there are no apparent tonal anomalies that might relate to a cultural landscape.

Climate. Many indicators suggest an Arctic or sub-Arctic climate. One might be tempted to use the flow ice in Hudson Bay, for example, but this is ephemeral and even unnecessary, for gullies below some of the higher bluffs contain perpetual banks of snow and ice. The evidence pointing to past glaciation and present frost fracture also suggests high latitude. Although there are ample supplies of water in the region, the floral cover is limited; low temperatures and short growing seasons are obviously important factors in this distribution. Even the species themselves suggest the transitional zone of a northern tree line. The presence of innumerable ponds on impermeable rock surfaces prove a high incidence of rain or snowfall, as well as cool summer temperatures and consequent low rates of evaporation.

Summary of the Natural Landscape. Even if we had not originally known the exact location of this case study, there would have been no difficulty in identifying it as a high-latitude region. It is clearly a coastal environment, which has been powerfully affected by major, continental glaciation, leaving exposed its residual bedrock strata. In the modern period it has been subject to the seasonal changes of a polar or sub-Arctic climate, and its limited boreal forest cover is additionally controlled by distinctive physiographic factors. The faunal resources can be identified from limited evidence and inference as high northern in content. It is a totally rugged and difficult environment for man, and any considered estimate of its potential resources can only be minimal. In fact, there seem to be no indications of a cultural landscape.

Cultural Interpretations. Although we may not have discovered any cultural evidence in the prior analysis, the quest for archaeological signs cannot be ended here. This inhospitable environment may still be subjected to further examination in the light of our culture classification. In particular, a test can be made of its degree of fit with our ecologically oriented concept of the technocomplexes.

Clearly, an agrarian technocomplex would find this region impossible for major agricultural production, but of course, a climax component of the same type could exploit it for other purposes. From an intensive study of the aerial photography a team of specialists could no doubt predict a number of potential resources, including the existence of valued minerals, stands of timber suitable for sawmill operations, the feasibility of and the best routes for roads or trails, the location of gravel deposits for road building, safe harbor areas for seagoing transportation, and even the most tempting fishing water for visiting sportsmen. There are many such possibilities for the future, but they are not relevant here; and there were no comparable cultural events in the past.

Any representative component of the pastoral nomad technocomplex would similarly have experienced insuperable difficulties in attempting to operate a subsistence economy here. The specific area of the case study does not support sufficient pasture to attract large numbers of the native caribou, although signs of these animals are plentiful in the deep interior. Moreover, the very notion of pastoral nomadism is untenable in this setting because of what is already known about the ethnography and culture history of northern regions in the New World.

This leaves the hunter-fisher-gatherer technocomplex as the only agency that could possibly be responsible for archaeological remains. Given the environmental attributes that have already been reconstructed, the basic subsistence pursuits in this country would involve hunting large land animals and sea food. Caribou are available in the interior, but not in the rocky, barren coastal area of the case study, although it is possible that an occasional animal might wander in at random. Also, it is probable in this kind of environment that no other land species exists in sufficient strength or concentration to serve as a staple food crop. Therefore, any archaeological remains

Fig. 7. Aerial oblique view of Gulf Hazard, looking eastward from Hudson Bay toward Richmond Gulf.

pertaining to the hunter-fisher-gatherer technocomplex must have a direct relationship with the sea.

The presence of white whales in these waters, as well as all the other facts observed, emphasizes the strong probability that these are cold, Arctic seas. If so, they will be inhabited by a bountiful crop of sea mammals, including seals and walrus. There is no direct evidence of this, but it is virtually the last lead available. Therefore, it must next be determined where the best and most convenient base location is for a settlement of hypothetical sea-mammal hunters.

Although there are numerous probable site locations in the area, photo analysis indicates one section that probably affords the greatest potential for subsistence activities, which is Gulf Hazard, the narrow slot connecting Richmond Gulf with the outer bay (Figs. 6, 7). This

gulf is subject to tidal flow, and the photography suggests that the channel currents and terminal areas of tide rips are occasionally fast and turbulent. In all likelihood, then, because of the continual interchange of water between the bay and the gulf, one could expect an exchange of many or all of the seaborne animal species. This natural funnel should therefore concentrate the staple game animals at predictable times, and it follows, too, that the best possible hunting sites should be situated in Gulf Hazard itself. Such a location would serve a hunter especially well by eliminating the otherwise frequent need to negotiate the difficult stretches of the channel before reaching the most fruitful hunting area.

Additional stereoscopic analysis of the shores of the channel (Fig. 8) focuses our attention on one small area on the north shore that seems to have all the attributes

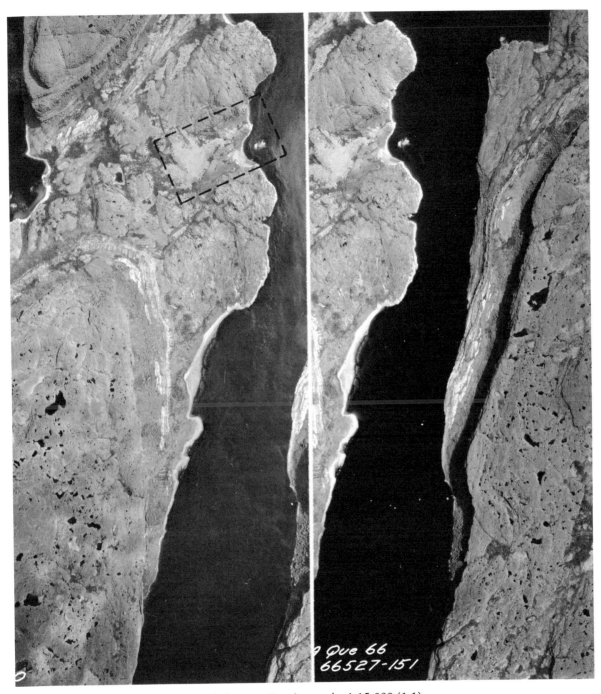

Fig. 8. Stereogram of the Gulf Hazard site area. Panchromatic, 1:15,000 (1:1).

of an excellent settlement site. It is adjacent to the narrowest throat of the channel and fronts on a small embayment, sheltered by two rocky points. A freshwater stream drains into the western corner of this cove. The land rises gently back through a series of raised sand and gravel beach lines, studded here and there with outcrops, and the small valley that these features compose is almost totally enclosed by granite cliffs and hills. The vegetation consists of dry heath, patches of low brush, and a few sporadic conifers beyond the height of land to the north. There is easy access over this rise to the bay on the north side of Castle Peninsula.

Intensive examination of this area now reveals several tiny anomalies that do not conform to the normal patterns of the natural landscape. They appear as depressions surrounded by earthen ridges, each measuring on the order of twelve-to-fifteen feet across. Given their location, individual conformation, size, and tendency to alignment on one of the raised beach lines, and in consideration of the rest of the information deduced, the most logical interpretation is that these are semisubterranean, winter house pits of a type normally associated with Eskimo culture. They do not appear to be contemporary, and therefore they may be prehistoric.

Because of degraded object resolution in the stereogram, it may not be possible to perceive all these minute details, but their relative location is shown as Complex 3 in the field sketch (Fig. 9). One can also vaguely make out several of the house pits in Complex 5, but these tend to be masked by vegetation. The surface rings in Complexes 1, 2, and 6 are not visible in the air photos because they are either buried in turf or set against noncontrastive beach shingle. Complex 4 has no external features at all.

At any rate, the emergence of Complex 3 in the photos led to a later discovery of the others during the field reconnaissance. Excavation of Complex 1 proved it to be a summer dwelling attributable to late-period Dorset Eskimo culture, and test cuts in one of the winter house pits of Complex 3 yielded additional slight evidence of Dorset culture.

Although there have been drastic shortcuts and gaps in this presentation, the thematic line of development should be clear. As we have proceeded from the photographic base line of general information toward more specific details, each stage has logically prepared the way for more refined levels of observation and inference. Through systematic and complete environmental analysis it has indeed been possible in these circumstances to detect and interpret certain threshold indicators of prehistoric culture. I think it is remotely possible that the same discoveries and similar interpretations might have been reached intuitively by an unusually well-trained and experienced archaeologist or ethnographer, but certainly only by one who had previous first-hand knowledge of northern environments. However, a comparable level of achievement could not be obtained by any investigator operating in a random fashion.

Therefore, I suggest that exploratory archaeological research still has much to gain from this kind of systematic air photo analysis and interpretation. Too often we are stimulated in our research efforts by vague subjective urges and covert assumptions, and thereby led into an attractive cul-de-sac. But here is a tool, a set of analytical techniques, that can help to retrieve sound empirical data and prepare the way for field investigations in a manner that has seldom been possible before. In terms of cost efficiency, it can save much time and money.

This research was supported by Grants GS–1216 and GS–2915, National Science Foundation. I am greatly indebted to Robert E. Frost and Jack N. Rinker for their help and advice.

Elmer Harp, Jr.

#7

#4 — _Dorset_ chipping station and lookout on N side of height of land.

#8

MAG

N

1
○

2
○

#3

3
○

#1-_Dorset_
○

2
○

3
○

#5

1
○

4
○

5
○

Granite Outcrop

#9
○

#6

Modern ○

Recent

2
○○

1
○

Contact Sites

○○

#2

RICHMOND GULF

← Narrows

Fig. 9. Field sketch of the Gulf Hazard sites.

Robert A. Hackenberg
Ecosystemic Channeling: Cultural Ecology from the Viewpoint of Aerial Photography

An area in continuous human use is like a theater in which a number of plays have been produced. But each subsequent performance takes place among props remaining from the previous set. The later performances may displace or partly demolish the earlier sets. Occasionally, the theater itself is partly remodeled, so as to obliterate a portion of the stage with its accumulated scenery and permit a new form of drama to be produced.

The essentials of cultural ecology as an anthropological pursuit may be inferred from this metaphor. A culture in its environment enacts dramatic events, deposits their remnants, and remodels the surroundings to suit the next group of players. Unlike plant or animal populations, postindustrial man is no mere occupant of an ecological niche. He either builds his own or remodels the one vacated by the former tenant.

A constructed or remodeled environment has a very different composition from one found in nature. Certain "given" elements have been consumed or removed, while others have been added. Because of the altered potentials for life support, the possibilities for growth have been limited, with some paths of development, or channels, becoming more probable than others. In this fashion, cultural ecology becomes a dimension of cultural change: the study of ecosystemic channels.

To the extent that such channels represent Markov processes controlling the probabilities which may elicit a certain course of development, a justification may be offered for seeing the present pattern of environmental utilization in time perspective. There is no better way to "see" this culture-environment configuration than with aerial photography, which captures present patterns of land use within the context established by the past.

Early anthropological research efforts were frequently devoted to constructing temporal inferences from distributional data. This effort was defeated by the removal of artifacts from their spatial (and functionally meaningful) context and by the general lack of a suitable inferential structure. Through the use of aerial photography, both the spatial coordinates necessary to place the data accurately, and the total context necessary to interpret them, may be captured. Since this visual matrix includes not only objects that are in contemporaneous usage but also evidence (remains) of objects formerly in use, it provides the basis for translating spatial data into temporal sequence. Aerial photography thus becomes a technique for performing retrospective studies of culture change.

The rich variety of meanings that may be extracted from the visual matrix includes both etic and emic dimensions. With suitable measures, external comparisons

Robert A. Hackenberg

of intrasocietal or intersocietal data collected through aerial photography can be made with great precision. But the aerial photograph possesses even greater advantages for working with informants. A map represents terrain selectively in terms of symbols dictated by the culture of the mapmaker. But an aerial photograph permits informant and interpreter to view the same terrain, each from his own cultural perspective. Nothing that is potentially meaningful to the informant has been removed by the abstractive mechanism of the mapmaker.

This attempt to visualize ecosystemic channels through the examination of aerial photographs differs on a basic issue from Eugene Odum's recently formulated strategy of ecosystemic development. Odum (1969:2) held that "ecological succession . . . results from modification of the physical environment by the community; that is, succession is community controlled even though the physical environment determines the pattern and the rate of change, and often sets limits to how far development can go."

Odum followed conventional anthropological usage in ascribing a determining role to the community and a passive role to the environment, which is generally held to be "acted upon." But if this view were a truly systemic one, it would postulate interdependence between the environment and the community. Each would be permitted to impose limits and constraints upon the other in a continuous dialectic of stimulus and response.

The ecosystemic channel concept allows not only for this interplay but also for its temporal consequences: the restriction of choices available to future inhabitants of the region as a result of options consumed or eliminated by those who have gone before. Such a limitation of possibilities exercises a channeling function, rendering behavior more predictable and some of its consequences more inevitable.

Ecosystem channeling can now be viewed in the context of an example, a microenvironment of four square miles located in the Gila River valley of central Arizona. This region has come under the successive influence of three radically different cultures: Hohokam,

Pima, and Anglo-American. By the examination and interpretation of the features contained in an aerial photograph (Fig. 10), a succession of occupations can be identified and placed in sequential relationships which form an ecosystemic channel. The area to be examined is adjacent to the present Pima Indian community of Bapchule, on the Gila River Indian Reservation, occupying the eastern halves of Sections 30 and 31, the western halves of Sections 28 and 33, and all of Sections 29 and 32, within Township 3 South, Range 5 East, Pinal County, Arizona.

Since the data contained within the visual matrix of an aerial photograph are theoretically without limit, rigorous selection of the variables to be employed for comparison and evaluation is necessary. Each of the three strata of cultural occupation is described in terms of four visible criteria that may be spatially related: residences, fields, ditches or canals, and other cultural orientation features. All visual evidence of these variables is keyed parenthetically to one of the 16 1/4 mile squares of which the picture is composed, such as Bapchule Mission (NW corner, B–2).

A description of the environmental setting is followed by discussion and interpretation of the variable-sets for each of the three cultural strata. A systemic development of interstrata patterns is then constructed, to form the ecosystemic channel.

The Casa Grande Valley

The central portion of the valley shaped by the Gila River, which runs from Silver City, New Mexico, westward to its intersection with the Colorado River, is known as the Casa Grande Valley—named after the Casa Grande National Monument, a cluster of Hohokam archaeological remains near Coolidge, Arizona. Today, this region appears as a heat-blasted wilderness of sandy plains, rocky pinnacles, and ridges, with a thin scattering of thorn-bearing shrubs and cacti. Twisting through it from east to west is a mile-wide scar of lighter colored sand (northern quarter of Row A), flanked by straggling rows of mesquite trees. This is the channel of the Gila River,

Fig. 10. Aerial photograph of four square miles in the Gila River valley of central Arizona.

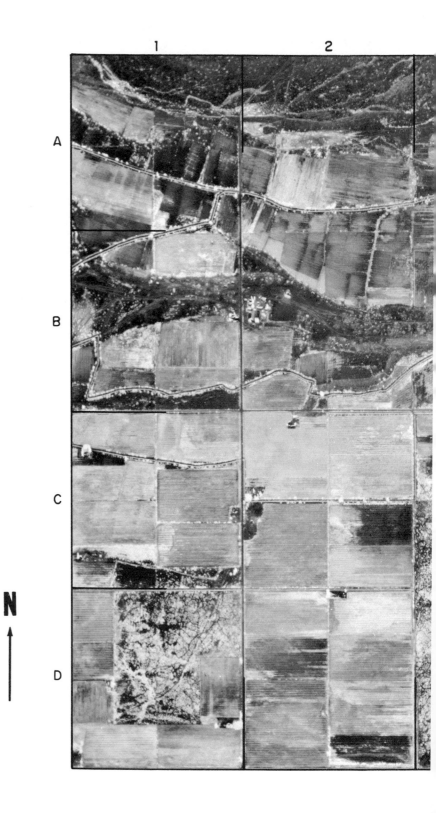

3　　　　　4

dry except for mid-winter and late summer floods, when a half-million acre-feet of water race between its crumbling banks (N 1/4, Row A), further eroding them and dissolving additional tons of topsoil.

This inhospitable portion of the Sonoran Desert, though always sparsely populated, is nearing the end of its second millennium of occupation by man (Haury 1967). The banks of the Gila River, below the town of Florence and above its junction with the Salt River sixty-five miles to the west, have furnished community sites successively to the Hohokam, Pima, and Maricopa Indians, and more recently to the Anglo-Americans. Within the four square miles covered by the aerial photograph, the occupants today include approximately three hundred Pima Indians, distributed among sixty households.

During the nineteenth century, this historic country evoked a very different description. An early geographer of southern Arizona, J. W. Hoover (1929:41), described the valley as it appeared in 1875: "Old settlers are united in describing the Gila as without braided shifting channels. Cottonwood, brush, tall grass, and weeds bordered the river which was confined to a narrow channel . . . There were no stretches of bare and sandy waste such as are found everywhere along the river now. Tall grass, sometimes several feet high, covered the whole countryside yearly . . . Lakes and ponds were once common over the river flat where there is no trace of them today." In the 1850s, estimates of the width of the Gila ranged from 40 feet (Eccleston 1950:207–215) to 120 feet (Parry 1857:20). The channel of the Gila confined within these narrow borders was entirely north of the area within the modern photograph.

In the mid-nineteenth century, above the rich silty bottomlands bearing cottonwoods and arrow-weeds were two distinct terraces. The lower terrace, which was nearly four miles wide in the Casa Blanca District opposite Gila Butte, contained level, fertile soil and was subject to occasional inundation. Beyond it, on both banks of the river, were relatively sterile areas of heavy salt impregnation, which comprised an upper terrace supporting little

vegetation except saltbush (Parry 1857:20; Hoover 1929:46–48). This terrace extended to the foothills of the surrounding mountain ranges. The lower terrace fell within the area between the base of Row D and the river channel. This was also approximately the 1,200-foot contour line of elevation. The lower terrace also dropped twenty-five feet to the river. The upper terrace extended southward from the base of Row D.

On the east, the upper and lower terraces were bounded by a formation frequently called an island. This island, roughly a mile in width, lay between the main channel of the Gila on the north and an extensive prehistoric canal on the south. This excavated channel, which carried water westward for twenty-nine miles, appears on many maps as the Little Gila River. The dimensions of the island, which was an extremely fertile strip of bottom land below the first terrace, were fixed by Richard Savage (1871), who also determined that the width of the main river channel was one hundred feet and that the Little Gila was fifty feet wide. Clay Southworth (1919:130–131) was the first writer to note the frequent confusion of the Little Gila Canal with the main channel by nineteenth century writers: "It is evident that some of the earlier adventurers into this region were of the opinion that the Little Gila was the main river channel . . . The banks of the Little Gila in many places are fifteen feet or more in height, while the banks of the main river are seldom more than six or seven feet high."

Quoting George Pablo, a Pima Indian born in 1849, Southworth (1919:29–40) reported that he thought the Little Gila was the important stream during his youth. Since it was cut deeper than the main channel, it carried the continuous flow of the river during the major part of the year. The main channel of the Gila received only flood water. This prehistoric canal continued to carry the major portion of irrigation water to the fields along the middle Gila until the disastrous floods of the nineteenth century had silted it partly shut and cut a pathway from the end of the original canal back to the bed of the main river. Until altered by the heavy floods of the present century, this canal terminated in the salt-impregnated upper terrace. The junction of the Little Gila with the main channel of the river is off the aerial photograph to the right. Salt impregnation of the upper terrace is visible, however (D-3, D-4, C-4), where the 1,200-foot contour bends sharply to the northeast from the base of Row D.

The Hohokam Ecosystem

Between the beginning of the Christian era and the end of the fifteenth century, the middle Gila River valley was occupied by the archaeological culture known as the Hohokam (Gladwin et al., 1937). The architectural remains of this occupation, consisting of a vast mound of melted adobe once utilized for earthern walls, appear at Casa Blanca Ruin, unexcavated, one-half mile to the west of the aerial photo, on the road that forms the base of Row D. The use of canal irrigation by the earliest Hohokam has been recently documented by Emil Haury (1967) through re-excavation of Snaketown, a site on the north bank of the Gila.

Along this section of the middle Gila, Hohokam residences were placed at the edge of the upper terrace. In this respect, Snaketown and Casa Blanca Ruin are identical. Building above the flood plain permitted a kind of structure whose use could be projected into the indefinite future, which encouraged permanent construction. The location of homes on the upper terrace likewise permitted the widespread use of adobe, which would have melted easily if placed either on the flood plain or within range of the marshy, irrigation-saturated fields.

The Hohokam preference for the upper terrace was not restricted to homesites, however, for they also placed their canals and at least a portion of their fields at this level of settlement. The capacity of their irrigation system, as well as the relative absence of animal remains in the excavations thus far conducted, indicate their nearly complete reliance on agriculture.

The Hohokam canals were in every case longer and wider than those later employed by the Pima Indians. Their dimensions are explained in terms of the destination of the water conveyed by these impressive examples of hydraulic engineering. The canals terminated in the salt-impregnated upper terraces, several miles away from the main channel of the river. To bring water to this elevation, twenty-five to fifty feet above the level of the stream, it was necessary to locate the headings at points far up the river. Also, since the upper terraces were removed from the flood plain of the Gila, their cultivation required complete reliance on moisture provided through irrigation. Richard Woodbury (1962) provided data indicating that the average bottom width of Hohokam canals on the Gila was ten to eleven feet, and they were six to seven feet deep. In reaching these figures, he did not consider the dimensions of the Little Gila Canal (fifty feet wide and fifteen feet deep), which have been greatly increased by the action of floods.

The Hohokam cultivated portions of the upper terraces to which their canals conveyed irrigation water, but because the canals ran very close to the edge on both the north and south sides of the Gila, it would have been possible to bring laterals down to the level of the lower terraces as well. In the aerial photograph, remains of a Hohokam canal originating in the Little Gila are visible as a dark line running from southeast to northwest below the base of D-3. This canal, after serving the long-abandoned alkaline fields located on the upper terrace, seen in D-3, D-4, and C-4, bends toward the river and drops to the lower terrace in D-2, preventing irrigation water from reaching the residence area.

Salt deposits today on the surface of the sterile upper terrace lands indicate the possible cause of the removal of the Hohokam from this area. It is the consensus of archaeologists that this situation resulted from intensive prehistoric cultivation (Halseth 1932:167–168; Hayden 1945:373–378; 1957:105–111). Through heavy irrigation, the ground water table rose, bringing dissolved salts in solution to the surface of the land. When soils dried, these salts crystallized as visible deposits. If such deposits formed on the lower terraces, they were washed away through continuous flooding with river water following the departure of the Hohokam cultivators. In the photograph, these deposits appear in the sections designated as fields above D-3, D-4, and C-4.

The location of Hohokam canals on the upper terrace may be explained in analogous terms. The placement of irrigation structures above the flood plain obviated the need for frequent replacement and for the massive investment in labor required. Canals of this capacity could utilize the entire flow of the Gila. The water thus diverted could be used in part on upper terrace fields and in part on the lower terraces.

The Hohokam culture appears to have called for labor-intensive rather than labor-extensive forms of investment in economic development. This feature of their ecosystemic pattern is seen also in their noncultural achievements. The construction of platform mounds and ball courts (neither of which is visible in the photograph) are further evidence of labor-intensive activities invested in permanent additions to the community. Like modern community planners, the Hohokam sought to reshape the habitat through residential, agricultural, and ceremonial-recreational improvements.

In their time, the main limitation on development was the total water supply available rather than the terrain. However, the water dispersed through their ditch systems had the capacity neither to flood out alkali from the fields nor to make fresh depositions of silt. It appears that the Hohokam conquered their environment for the time being, but were eventually conquered by it. Like most such interpretations, however, a considerable speculative component is involved. One is on safer ground when considering the impact of Hohokam community-habitat interplay as a limit upon the options open to the subsequent occupants, the Gila River Pima Indians.

The Pima Ecosystem

The center of Pima settlement, like that of the Hohokam before them, appears to have been in the Casa Blanca District. It was here that, in 1746, the cultivation of wheat and the use of canal irrigation was first observed by Jacobo Sedelmayr. By 1775, the Anza expedition reported five canals in use and a dam under construction that involved the employment of communal labor supplied by several villages.

The full details of later Pima-Maricopa land use are contained in the many mid-nineteenth century accounts that were contributed by the Kearny and Cooke expeditions of 1846 during the Mexican War, the gold seekers' journals of 1849, and the reports of the United States Boundary Commission, which in 1852 attempted to survey the line established by the treaty of Guadalupe Hidalgo. From these it is learned that the communities of the Pima Indians were contracted into a single contiguous settlement of huts and fields, ten miles in length, in which they had been joined by the entire Maricopa tribe, making a combined population of nearly five thousand. The center of this "Indian city" (Couts 1961) was in the Casa Blanca District, and all habitations were concentrated on the south side of the Gila, where they formed a defense perimeter against Apache raiders. However, some fields on the north bank were located on the lower terrace below Snaketown. This combined settlement represented the most intensive development of irrigation agriculture since Hohokam times.

Since the Pima were flood plain cultivators, they attempted to place their communities as close to their fields as possible. Mid-nineteenth century residences contained within the four square miles represented by the photograph were located at Old Mount Top Village (SW 1/4 of D-3), Stotonic (E 1/2 of C-4), and Bapchule (B-2). The former two communities were at the edge of the upper terrace, overlooking their former fields (N 1/2 of D-3, C-3, W 1/2 of C-4), and Bapchule was at its present site, on an elevated ridge running from east to west through Row B. The fields cultivated by the Bapchule village lay, then as now, between it and the river channel (S 1/2 of A-1, S 1/2 of A-2, N 1/2 of B-2).

The appearance of three large villages within four square miles indicates that the Pima settlement was dense, though not confined to a single group of structures. The three village sites in the photograph, approximating an equilateral triangle if connected by straight lines, are nearly equidistant from each other. The reason for this placement was the continual, shared defense requirement, to which John Bartlett (1854 2:232–233, 262–264) called attention:

The valley or bottomland occupied by the Pimas and Cocomari-

Robert A. Hackenberg

copas extends about 15 miles along the south side of the Gila and is from two to four miles in width, nearly the whole being occupied by their villages and cultivated fields . . . On the northern side of the river there is less bottomland, and the irrigation is more difficult. There are a few cultivated spots here, but it is too much exposed to the attacks of their enemies for either tribe to reside upon it. The villages consist of groups of from 20 to 50 habitations, surrounded by gardens and cultivated fields, intersected in every direction by acequias which lead the water from the Gila.

From both historic sources and contemporary testimony, it is known that during the early Anglo-American period, Old Mount Top Village was the home of the head chief of the Pima nation, Antonio Azul. The hillock visible in the photograph immediately to the north of the village site (center of D–2), known as Rattlesnake Home to the Indians but called Pima Lookout Mountain by the military observers, was the point at which sentinels were posted continuously to warn against approaching Apache war parties. If attacked, each of the three villages was equally well-placed to call for assistance from the others.

Despite the frequent search for a purely environmental reason for Pima homesite placement, it was based on a combination of water level and defensive considerations. Moreover, Pima home construction—ribs of ocotillo and sahuaro covered with brush and dirt—reflected the cultural requirement, observed throughout the nineteenth century, that a house must be burned upon the death of an occupant. The role of the habitat appears more clearly in the placement of Pima fields.

Pima Indians lived in villages and went out to their farms, which were uniformly located on bottom land. Since the upper terraces were sterile as a result of Hohokam cultivation, there was no choice in this matter. Because the lower terrace was subject to annual flooding, these farmlands were continually refertilized with silt deposition, so that their productivity is undisputed.

The size of each Pima field (see small rectangles with northeast-southwest orientation in Rows A and B, C–3, and N 1/2 of D–3) was determined by the food requirements of the family owning it, and its utility was determined by access to irrigation water. The historic Pima diverted water directly from the Gila River with brush dams. The intake ditch for old Bapchule Village is clearly visible in the northern portion of A–4, although the canal becomes part of a more recent system at the intersection of squares A–3 and A–4. Stotonic Village received its irrigation water from another ancient ditch originating farther upstream and crossing Row B from east to west. These systems, formerly separate, have been connected since 1930.

Old Mount Top Village was served by a branch of Stotonic Ditch, originating at the center of B–4 and proceeding southwest across C–4 and D–3 to a point immediately in front of Rattlesnake Home (hillock in center of D–3), which it skirts on the west side. The northeast-southwest orientation of all historic fields served by these canals was determined by the topographic requirement that all field ditches originating in a canal must be at right angles to the slope of the terrain in order for the irrigation water to serve the entire field. In A–1 and A–2, all locations of historic fields are oriented at right angles to Bapchule Ditch.

Since the flood plain was regularly inundated, continuous re-excavation of ditches and replacement of ditch headings and brush dams was a Pima way of life. However, soil fertility and crop production were unimpaired so long as the regime of the river itself was unimpaired. Thus, the Pima adaptive strategy for the four square miles contained within the photograph was the opposite of the Hohokam. The Pima were labor-extensive in their approach to the terrain, constantly replacing ditches, borders, and dams with others that were equally crude instead of refining and improving those which already existed. The explanation lies partly in the impaired fertility of the region that they inherited from the Hohokam, and partly in their defense requirements, which diverted much of the labor supply from agriculture to warfare. The sterile fields of the Hohokam (D–4), useless for agriculture, became a dance ground where the entire tribe assembled for war rituals to celebrate defeats of the Apache enemy.

The same square that contains a portion of the dance ground (D–4) also preserves the image of the spiderlike pattern of the intervillage road network of the historic period. These trails actually ran between compounds rather than communities, and were family wagon tracks whose life span was limited to that of the houses they served. Those still in use may be seen at the east approach to Bapchule Village (B-2). Very few of these have ever shown any signs of improvement because of their discontinuous use. They do not serve as orientation points for home location or as coordinates marking the center of each village.

Because of the Pimas' conservative use of the environment, their ecosystemic pattern remained substantially the same until the last quarter of the nineteenth century. At that time, a radical change in the character of the Gila River took place, which forced reorganization upon them. The behavior of the water supply became erratic and undependable. There was a disastrous flood in 1868, eliminating three entire villages and their fields. The decade of the 1870s was characterized by extreme drought, which in several years parched the mesquite trees and prevented the beans from maturing. The water supply was generally less than normal for the remainder of the century, although there were some good years. Two of the villages washed out by the flood of 1868 were Stotonic and Old Mt. Top. Families from both of these villages abandoned their fields and moved to less threatening locations beyond the four square miles of the photograph. Although the village of Bapchule received less damage, seven hundred acres of its fields were washed away.

The alteration in the course of the Gila was at first thought to result from the upstream diversion of river water by non-Indians, which had begun in the post-Civil War period. The simultaneous overgrazing of the watershed by herds of cattle and sheep was held to be a contributing factor. These forces were held responsible in the conventional interpretation offered by J.W. Hoover (1929:41–45):

The changed behavior of the Gila is generally attributed to overgrazing in the upper basin. Before 1870, there were few cattle, but they increased rapidly after the settlement of the Apache Indian troubles . . . During the eighties there was a series of wet years with abundance of natural forage. The ranges built up rapidly and overgrazing resulted. During the same time the mountains of the upper basin of southeast Arizona were being rapidly stripped of their timber for use in the mines . . . The end came with the disastrous flood of 1891. Before this, the floodwaters of the Gila merely spread out over the flats and irrigated them. Now, with the banks of the river unprotected by grass and brush, the channel suddenly widened and many good ranches along the river were cut out.

As a result of recent research, however, summarized by James Hastings and Raymond Turner (1965), two less visible independent variables have been acknowledged. During the latter quarter of the nineteenth century, the Southwest was seized by a more severe dry cycle than any since the thirteenth century. Simultaneously, slight but stable and significant temperature increases were taking place, which altered the regional vegetation pattern. The introduction of cattle only served to aggravate factors that were already inexorably at work.

The Anglo-American Ecosystem

During the twentieth century, the federal government has taken many steps to arrest and reverse the deteriorating tendencies that have been present along the Gila River since 1865. The steps have included land tenure, irrigation, and land subjugation. Between 1914 and 1921, the Bureau of Indian Affairs issued title to 98,000 acres of Gila River Reservation land in the form of ten-acre allotments. Between 1924 and 1930, various government agencies constructed the Coolidge Dam and San Carlos Reservoir and organized the San Carlos Indian Irrigation Project. The aim of this reclamation program was to store 900,000 acre-feet of irrigation water for the purpose of irrigating 100,000 acres of crops in the middle Gila River valley. The land within the irrigation district is equally divided between reservation Indians and non-Indian holdings west of Florence. Between 1930 and 1938, the Bureau of Indian Affairs conducted a massive subjugation program, clearing, leveling, and ditching over 45,000 acres of Pima-Maricopa lands within the San Carlos Irrigation District. Most of this land was also planted in barley or alfalfa, both soil-building pasture crops, instead of the soil-depleting wheat grown in the past by the Indians.

Because the entire four-square-mile area making up

the microenvironment under discussion is included within the San Carlos Irrigation Project, it has sustained the impact of all these changes. The effect on it has been determined in part by the previous interplay between the human communities and the natural habitat, and in part by the new cultural premises on which this final cultural stratum has been erected. Unlike the earlier situations, however, the results have not been uniform, and the variation is clearly disclosed by selected variables that are visible within the photograph.

The four square miles pictured are now divided between two communities: the old, conservative, but still surviving village of Bapchule, and the new, relatively more prosperous settlement of progressive Indians known as Casa Blanca Community. The dividing line between the two settlements runs east-west between Rows B and C. Both groups have received certain benefits from the San Carlos Project. Each group has been given the opportunity to exchange its smaller, older, one-to-five acre tracts of family-owned, northeast-southwest oriented farmland for ten-acre tracts of individually owned, east-west oriented farmland. The ten-acre tracts, divided into two rows of eight allotments each (sixteen to a quarter-section), are clearly visible in C-2 and C-3. In addition, each group has received the offer of county roads to be constructed along the quarter-section lines dividing each sixteen allotments, as may be seen between C-1, C-2, D-1, and D-2. Finally, each group has been offered the possibility of receiving irrigation water from a government-operated system originating in the San Carlos Reservoir and providing a water supply along fifty miles of mainline canal—an achievement surpassing that of the Hohokam. The linkages between the remaining sections of Bapchule Ditch and Stotonic Ditch may be located in B-4. As the joined canals are followed toward the western side of the photograph, their further division into five major ditches may be observed (all five are easily seen by glancing from south to north along Column 1).

Both groups, Bapchule and Casa Blanca, have accepted the government allotments, but each has utilized them differently. The Casa Blanca Indians have moved their homes to their allotments, breaking up the old pattern of concentrated residence within a village. The new pattern of farmsteads may be observed in C-1, C-2, and D-2. Bapchule Village, with its houses clustered on its traditional site, remains at B-2. The Casa Blanca Indians operate larger farms, each consisting of as many as four allotments (forty acres); hence, there are fewer homes per unit of land area in the region that they occupy.

The San Carlos Irrigation Project was intended to increase Indian farm efficiency by the use of modern techniques in traditional agriculture. The old fields were made level at the same time that they were reapportioned into larger farm units. These level subsections are easier to irrigate and to operate with farm machinery. The Bapchule Indians refused to give up their traditional land tenure pattern, however, and ignored the new allotments almost entirely. Within the northern half of the four-square-mile area, the cultivated farms show the older field orientation and the smaller unit size, even though the new irrigation system makes this orientation no longer functional.

The county road system has been welcomed by the Casa Blanca Pimas, who have located their homes at the roadside in order to gain maximum access to transportation for their families and their crops. The Bapchule have refused to allow more than one road to be constructed through their village territory, and that one is primarily for the service of the Franciscan Mission. Traditional Indian travel patterns east-west along the old ridge roads are maintained by the Bapchule residents without interruption. It is significant that the Bapchule Pima are Catholic, and thus the church is the center of their community. The Casa Blanca villagers are Presbyterian, and their homes are oriented toward the communications links with the sources of wage labor and trade: the road network.

The canal system that is part of the San Carlos Project has been equally acceptable to both communities, although the uses to which water is put are at variance. The Casa Blanca Pima rapidly became growers of barley and alfalfa, which are commercial crops that may be sold for cattle feed off the reservation. In Bapchule, wheat and other subsistence crops were grown for several decades after the initiation of the project, and are still grown by some.

The San Carlos Project has been able to counteract the worst effects of the environmental conditions attributed to the last quarter of the nineteenth century, but it has been unable to repeal the history of this human ecosystem. Of the area contained within the four square miles pictured, over seven-eighths, or everything except the northernmost quarter of Row A, has been allotted to individual Indians. Less than one-quarter of the area has been utilized in the manner anticipated by the development planners. At work here is an interplay between habitat and community factors. Not even the methods of modern agriculture can restore the fertility of the alkali flats destroyed by the Hohokam. Those sections located in C–3, C–4, D–3, and D–4 that have been allotted remain unproductive. The Indians who were issued portions of them received a useless resource.

The Bapchule Pima, in contrast, present a cultural obstacle to the efficient use of farmland for commercial crop production. It appears that nearly 50 percent of the land which they own, located in Rows A and B, is removed from production because of their failure to abandon traditional practices of land tenure, residence, and transportation. They retain their traditional cohesiveness. And of the 7,500 Pima still residing on the Gila River Indian Reservation, they alone preserve the definitive characteristic of the historic village; that is, they are a group of closely related families who receive their irrigation water from a common ditch. Although they are no longer responsible for the maintenance of the ditch, they continue to share in its benefits as a discrete unit.

The Ecosystemic Channel of a Microenvironment

In developing his concept of ecosystemic strategy, Odum (1969:262) asserted that the game theorists' alternatives, "minimaxing" and "maximizing," can be applied to human ecology. The former strategy, which he calls that of "maximum protection," refers to the acceptance of minimum gains in order to prevent maximum losses. The latter strategy aims for maximum gains regardless of possible detrimental effects, which Odum referred to as "maximum production" strategy.

In the ecosystemic channel described by the sequential cultural strata of Hohokam, Pima, and Anglo-American occupation, these strategies have alternated with each other. First the Hohokam "forced" the environment to yield the utmost good that their technology could extract. The price for this may have been eventual elimination of the habitat's capacity to provide for them at even a survival level. Their strategy was control, and they may have failed because they controlled too much for too long. The Pima then adapted to the environment as it had been altered by Hohokam occupancy. They sought a balance between the soil and moisture components of their environment. Their homeostatic treatment of the habitat, like that of the Hohokam, succeeded for a number of generations. But unlike the Hohokam, they were defeated by a change in the regime of the river and ultimately have failed because they controlled too little. The Anglo-American period of intervention is again characterized by an attempt to force the environment. Where irrigation water is insufficient, deep wells and power pumps are introduced. Where soil fertility seems inadequate, agricultural chemicals are made available. Where traditional crops prove unprofitable, cotton, safflower, milo maize, and many others are brought to the Pima farmers for experimentation. The innovations of the Anglo-American period, however, are superimposed on an environment now altered by both Hohokam and Pima occupation. Each successive cultural stratum, in paving the way for the next, has curtailed its options by the interplay of community and habitat.

The less-than-complete success of the San Carlos Indian Irrigation Project in this small corner of Casa Blanca District is not an isolated, atypical case but is reservation-wide. It illustrates that not even the power of postindustrial man can exceed the constraints imposed on him by the efforts at environmental remodeling attempted by earlier human communities. It remains to be more broadly

Robert A. Hackenberg

demonstrated elsewhere that the modernization process moves within an ecosystemic channel shaped in part by the past, and that, to the extent that there are "Bapchule Indians" everywhere, the past is still present. But it has been demonstrated here for these four square miles.

Portions of this paper were published earlier (Hackenberg 1964). The field work and aerial photography were supported in part by Grant RG–6709, National Institutes of Health. The aerial photography of the Gila River and Salt River Pima Indian Reservations, Arizona, was undertaken for a comprehensive study of sociocultural change in total Indian populations (Hackenberg 1967). The 221 aerial photos in the Pima series were taken in 1960 by Blanton and Cole, Tucson, Arizona. Plates may be obtained on mylar film from William Cooper, Aerial Survey, Tucson and Phoenix, Arizona. I am grateful to Terence E. Hays for providing the Odum paper.

Thomas S. Schorr

Aerial Ethnography in Regional Studies: A Reconnaissance of Adaptive Change in the Cauca Valley of Colombia

A photointerpretation manual in recent use by the U.S. Navy advises the reader that the "image interpreter must be able to recognize all natural and man made features on the surface of the earth from their film images and to fit them into a pattern from which he can deduce the nature and significance of man's activity (past, present, future) in the area" (Naval Reconnaissance and Technical Support Center 1967). If the photointerpreter could actually accomplish what this manual sets as his goal, he would surpass much of the present achievement of professional anthropology.

Objectives

Data acquired by the systematic use of aerial photographic methods have thus far largely conformed to the standards of photomapping for cartographic and geodetic purposes, established historically to answer the needs of effective military operations. The high cost and technical demands involved in producing air photo images that can satisfy these exacting requirements understandably prohibit wider application of the method, especially in anthropological field projects financed by modest budgets. Fortunately, aerial photographic coverage already exists over a great portion of the earth's surface (Stone 1959, 1961), and in some instances, regions have been photographed at regular intervals for fifty years or more. For those parts of the world where air photos may be nonexistent, the anthropologist could feasibly contract with a commercial firm for the necessary reconnaissance, as some have done (Vogt and Romney 1971; Conklin 1967; Hackenberg 1967).

Convinced that aerial photographic reconnaissance and interpretation could both be brought into wider, more systematic use by anthropologists as a supplement to ethnographic data gathered by conventional means and be employed to survey extensive zones for their human ecological patterns, I undertook to assess how the method might be simplified and adapted to the limited technical means and restricted financial circumstances facing most field workers. The techniques that were developed use existing, large-format aerial photographs where available and also take advantage of the high quality of photographs that today's small-format hand cameras are capable of producing at low flying altitudes. These two types of aerial photographs, used together, complement each other in the way they present information (St. Joseph 1966:17). The large-format

photographs can be overlapped with each other to form a continuous plan view in stereoscopic depth, from which precision maps and measurements may be made of pertinent features. While providing a mine of information, however, photographs of this sort may be deficient in a number of ways; the small scale, vertical view, infrequency, and hence age of the photography, seasonal variations, improper lighting, or circumstances of rapid change in the target region, all could limit their usefulness. Reconnaissance with the hand camera overcomes this photographic "obsolescence" because it offers a quick, economical way to obtain up-to-the-minute surveillance of conditions or features not represented in the large-format images. Close-in views, valuable for their detail, are also easy to take from light aircraft when flown at low altitudes. In regions where large-format photographs are not available, then, reconnaissance solely with the hand camera still produces a wealth of indispensable information unobtainable by any other means.

This project was one of the secondary objectives of a larger study of mine designed to investigate the pattern of adaptive changes that are presently taking place in the social structure of rural populations inhabiting Colombia's Cauca Valley. For at least two decades, the Colombian government has implemented a plan for the unified development of resources in the region of the Cauca Valley and adjacent zones. This program has had the effect of producing a rapid change in ecological relationships, involving among other things a reorganization of the valley's water supply through flood protection, irrigation, drainage, and the drilling of new wells. Accompanying these engineering modifications is a plan for agrarian reform, which introduces more elaborate patterns of subsistence, technology, and resources directly into the traditionally structured way of life by agents from the outside representing the Colombian government. Of particular interest is the adaptive restructuring that is taking place in rural agricultural society as the bases of life are shifted from a dependence on seasonal rainfall agriculture of the paleotechnic type to the neotechnic

ecotype associated with land reclamation, reparcelization, and irrigation agriculture.

Applications

Essentially, aerial ethnographic techniques were applied to this investigation for a number of purposes. First, they were used to make a regional survey of the ecological relations that contributed over time to the formation of the settlement patterns which are visible in the photographs. Second, they were employed to arrive at a classification of zonal settlement patterns. Third, the photographs allowed me to make a selection of communities representative of each type in the classification, for further study by a resident ethnographer of the effects produced by the government resources development program, concentrating on the process of cultural adaptation of these small populations to changing habitat conditions. Fourth, planimetric and topographic maps of the selected settlements and their immediate surroundings were constructed from the photographs to a scale of 1:1,500, for use by the ethnographer during residence at the locales. Fifth, the photographs served as the basis for preparation of a photointerpretation key while in field residence, to assist in interpretations both in the field and after. And sixth, they led to the eventual construction of transparent map overlays, each graphically representing the pattern of a specific class of data for direct visual readouts of variable correlations (Schorr 1965). The region of study was the first one to be chosen by the Colombian government for development. It consists of an area of approximately 25 km. by 5 km., situated on the west side of the valley floor between the Cauca River and the eastern slopes of the Cordillera Occidental, located between the towns of Roldanillo to the south and Toro to the north (Fig. 11).

Procedures

Ethnographic data acquisition by means of aerial photographs proceeded in three stages. First, copies were procured of the previously existing air photo coverage along a number of different flight lines. For a

Fig. 11. Photomosaic of the southern sector of the development region in Colombia, showing, as no map can, the complex interrelations between human populations and geophysical features that produce the two principal settlement zones: along the riverbanks and up against the mountains. Photographed through a medium-yellow filter on panchromatic film, Jan. 27 and 30, 1957. Courtesy of the Instituto Geográfico "Agustín Codazzi" (I.G.A.C.).

Thomas S. Schorr

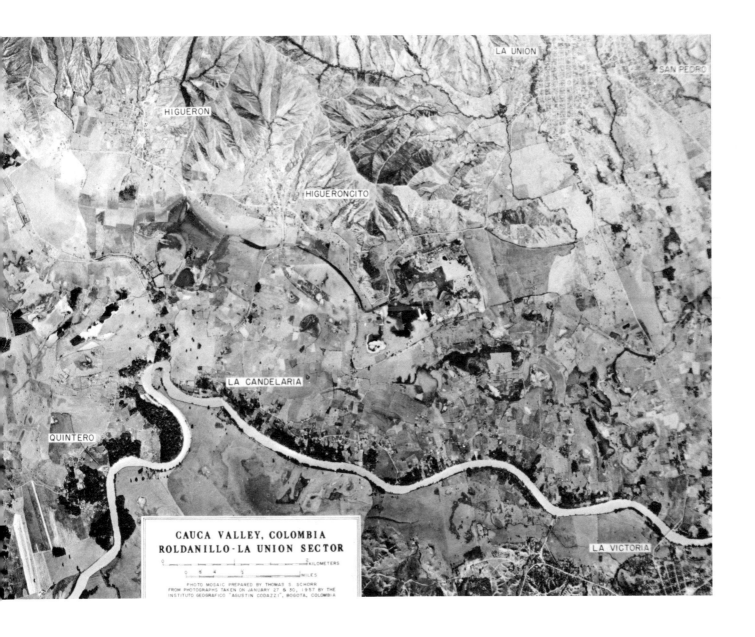

CAUCA VALLEY, COLOMBIA
ROLDANILLO - LA UNION SECTOR

PHOTO MOSAIC PREPARED BY THOMAS S. SCHORR
FROM PHOTOGRAPHS TAKEN ON JANUARY 27 & 30, 1957 BY THE
INSTITUTO GEOGRAFICO "AGUSTIN CODAZZI", BOGOTA, COLOMBIA

Cauca Valley of Colombia

43

nominal fee, the Colombian Geographic Institute (Instituto Geográfico "Agustin Codazzi") provided three sets of precision, vertical photographs: from 1947, at a scale of 1:60,000; from 1957, at 1:20,000; and from 1959, also at 1:20,000. These were studied to obtain a preliminary familiarization with the region in time-depth. The second step involved taking views, from the ground, of familiar objects, materials, and environmental conditions that were likely to appear in the aerial views. These photographs were printed, captioned, and bound for later reference during interpretation of the aerial views, so as to provide a standardized photointerpretation key—the so-called "ground truth"—for the positive identification of aerial images (Bigelow 1963; O'Neill 1953). The third step in data acquisition called for scheduling flights in a light, single-engine aircraft over a vast area between Cali and Cartago, for the purpose of photographing, with hand-held cameras, targets of interest, identified on the existing vertical coverage. The prints from this operation yielded recent information from which representative locales could be recognized and selected for study in greater detail on the ground. The combined coverage, consisting of the three earlier flight lines procured from the Geographic Institute, the interpretation key of terrestrial photographs, and the most recent photo flight results, supplied a compendium of information for use in interpretation and field work covering more than 3,000 square kilometers of the valley, in which about thirty population clusters were reconnoitered in detail, and the whole seen in a time depth spanning a period of twenty years.

Limitations

The entire project was undertaken with severe limitations placed on the use of the aerial photographic method, both financial and technical, which represent a very practical condition to be found in most anthropological field research situations. Budgetary considerations restricted operations in a number of ways: to commonly available hand cameras of the "advanced amateur" class familiar to most anthropologists; to locally procurable sensitized materials; to inexpensively rented light aircraft; to a minimal possibility for repeat flights because of aircraft rental fees; to a minimal opportunity for choosing optimum flying conditions, again because of cost considerations; and to processing and printing services that were available in the field. These factors were assumed to be the most likely ones to confront a field worker who was employing aerial photographic data-gathering techniques.

Purists in the classical applications of aerial photographic reconnaissance may find it difficult to agree with me on the nature and utility of the photographs obtained by means of such minimally controlled, shortcut efforts as were necessitated by these restrictions. Some would even deny any recognition of the effort as a "legitimate" form of aerial photography because precision aerial cameras and stabilized mounts were not used (Strandberg 1969:28). There is a presumptuously exclusive air about this stance, which is arbitrary and unwarranted, because of the erroneous impression it produces in the uninitiated of the inaccessibility of the method and techniques. Reliable, reproducible data derive from a wide range of technical and methodological adaptations, based on easier and infinitely more economical procedures than those standardized to the specifications of military and geodetic surveys. The degree to which image accuracy and control should be maintained is a decision that must be made by weighing together the factors of cost, convenience, and the final use of the results. Therefore, adequacy for the specific job at hand, and not unrealistic exactitude in fulfilling a set of ideal criteria established for other ends, should define the particular aerial phtographic methods and techniques to be employed. In fact, small-format, light-aircraft, aerial photography has been systematically employed for more than two decades by field workers in other disciplines, notably in archaeology, geography, geology, sociology, agronomy, and forestry (Solecki 1957; MacFadden 1949; Karan 1960; Fisher and Steever 1973; St. Joseph 1966; Willingham 1959).

The resulting images represent a compromise between what is ideal and what is possible, given the circumstances.

In aerial ethnography, the image requirements of the photointerpreter should be placed foremost. The requirements of the photogrammetrist differ in many important respects and, although not to be dismissed, are secondary. It should be emphasized that anthropologists make their own best photointerpreters, either performing the operation by themselves on the strength of their first-hand knowledge of the region, or performing it with the help of selected informants who have been trained in identifying image patterns and relationships in the photographs with their real counterparts on the ground. The primary characteristics needed in photo images destined for interpretation are: multiple coverage of the target region at various scales and specifications, including multiband photography; scant emphasis on distortion control; stereoscopy; image sharpness; tone and color contrast; and interpretability of all detail on each photograph (Coleman 1960:758).

Although most of these image specifications could be fulfilled with the restricted technological means at hand, those of photogrammetry could not. However, for regions similar to the Cauca Valley, where photographs flown to cartographic standards already exist, it was entirely feasible to use such photographs as a base on which to plot subsequent changes discovered by field observations and by the more recent, small-format reconnaissance flights. As a result, some of the minimum requirements for photointerpretation coverage could be eliminated, such as the production of stereo views, as this was available from the older sets of photographs. Instead, the project design favored the use of two cameras simultaneously for multiband sensing, although the cameras could have been used stereoscopically by tripping each shutter in turn at precalculated time intervals. When more than one band of energy is detected and recorded of the same view, the operation is known as multiband sensing, which most commonly involves the use of two or more cameras synchronized together in an appropriate mounting, to simultaneously expose films sensitive to different spectral ranges, for example, panchromatic film used in a camera with a yellow filter, mounted together with a suitably filtered camera loaded for infrared photography (Marlar and Rinker 1967). One camera records images by reflections of the visible spectrum, while the other registers its images from reflections of infrared radiation that lie just beyond visibility. The combination of images produces a broader range of spectral information, revealing by comparative interpretation much more about the photographed objects than either of the single views could produce alone (Colwell, 1961a). Acquired in this way, most views taken in flight from the open windows of the aircraft were obliques, and near verticals made with the aircraft in a tight bank at varying altitudes and directions to include the desired ground coverage.

Techniques

The aircraft used was a single-engine Cessna 180, piloted by a person experienced in photoflying as well as with the flight characteristics of the valley. In addition, I was usually accompanied by an assistant, who kept records of the order of shots, the locations being photographed, and the altitude and compass heading of the aircraft. The two cameras employed were 120 roll-film size, twin-lens reflex, with provision for open finder viewing. They were mounted to a binophoto bar and fired simultaneously by hand, using a double cable release. The entire apparatus was rigged from hardware available at most camera stores (Fig. 12). The total cost of the outfit was about $225 new.

During the flight, film advance was accomplished by manually cranking each camera individually, which was rapid enough for multiple exposures of the same target when the air speed of the aircraft was reduced to about 100 m.p.h. The highest shutter speed of 1/500 of a second was fast enough to overcome all but the most severe aircraft movements, which were usually caused by strong updrafts from the bare, heated slopes or newly plowed fields. Aperture settings corresponded to average readings made with a reflected light meter. The angle of view and altitude of the camera above the terrain varied according to the area of ground to be covered. The average coverage turned out by experimentation to

Fig. 12. Twin cameras mounted on a bracket originally intended for taking pictures through binoculars, to be used either for stereoscopic photography or, as here, for multiband sensing.

include about one kilometer in the low obliques and near verticals, measured horizontally across the line of sight, which was satisfactory for most interpretations of land use, soil drainage conditions, settlement patterns, crop identification, and population census estimates.

The experiments with simultaneously exposed, multiband, spectral recording employed combinations of panchromatic, infrared, color negative, color reversal, and infrared false-color film emulsions during three separate flights, each of approximately three hours in duration. For the initital flight, one camera was loaded with a medium-speed panchromatic film used with a deep yellow filter, and the other with an infrared film and filter, this last recording a spectral range of approximately 6,400A° to 8,400A°. Subsequent flights provided the opportunity to try combinations of simultaneously exposed color negative film with infrared and, by using cameras of the 35 mm. size, to try color reversal with false-color films (Kodachrome II used with Ektachrome Infrared Aero Type 8443 and a Wratten 15 filter).

The images produced by the 75 mm. lenses of the twin-lens reflex cameras measured 2-3/16 " square (5.6 cm.). When enlarged to the standard four-diameter practical limit set by emulsion grain and resolution, this format yields a print with an image which is 8-3/4 " (22.4 cm.) on a side, approximating the conventional 9" square format of the larger cartographic cameras. The twin-lens reflex camera also compares favorably to the 9 " format cartographic camera with a standard 12 " lens cone for the internal geometry and image/focal-length ratio; that is, both cameras will include the same area of ground in their photographs when used at the same altitude. In practice, the negatives were enlarged to slightly less than four diameters and printed without cropping on 8 × 10-inch paper, the only paper size available on the local market. The author processed the negatives but allowed a local commercial firm to enlarge the prints. Dimensions of the final image, excluding borders, were about 7-1/2 " square, which left approximately two inches of margin on the bottom of the prints for interpretation key captions, and enough of a

Thomas S. Schorr

margin on the sides so that they could be punched for three-ring binders and inserted facing each other in pairs corresponding to the simultaneous multiband images. This arrangement allowed for convenient, side-by-side viewing during interpretation.

From a technical standpoint, and judging by information content and ease of image interpretation, the best results were achieved by using color-negative simultaneously with infrared films. The infrared images extend the visible spectrum recorded on the color negatives to provide additional information for the photointerpreter. Many materials, the foremost being water and vegetation, reflect infrared radiation in proportionately different intensities from visible light. Hence, a wider range of materials can be distinguished with infrared images when interpreted alongside corresponding images made by visible light. An experienced interpreter working with an informant or a good key can identify types, ages, and estimated yield of crops during the growing season. Conditions of moisture, drainage patterns, and soil characteristics show more clearly in the infrared view. Construction materials take on a distinctiveness that lessens the chance for mistaken identity. Infrared radiation also penetrates the atmospheric haze to produce photographs of distant views with a clarity unequaled in the color or panchromatic images (Colwell 1961a; Estes 1966; Goodman 1959; Harp 1966, 1968; O'Neill 1953; Olson 1960, 1967; Tomlinson and Brown 1962; Wellar 1968). The only disadvantage of this combination is the greater expense of printing color, although cheaper black-and-white enlargements could be made from the negatives and color printing reserved for selected views. The use of panchromatic film with a deep yellow filter in combination with infrared material is a less expensive, acceptable alternative, though it entails some loss of image information. The 35 mm. format employing reversal color film, along with panchromatic, infrared, and false-color infrared materials in various combinations, was abandoned because it was difficult to maintain high resolution in the small images produced by any but the most expensive cameras. However, the present trend of improvements in 35 mm. cameras and film emulsions may eventually eliminate the problem. False-color infrared film is an interesting product with yet undiscovered potentials, but which unfortunately is not manufactured in the popular 120 roll size.

Any calculation of the cost of these operations is, at best, a rough estimate. The field worker who intends to apply the method will very likely encounter conditions that may vary widely from those described here. Of the total budget, a large portion must be allocated for flying time, using the figure of $40 per hour as a safe base for calculation. There are no set prices for aircraft and pilot rental from one region of the world to another, and sometimes the anthropologist can take advantage of opportunities to fly gratis. The number of hours will depend on the distance between the airstrip and the target area, the cruising speed of the aircraft, and the length of time spent in obtaining the photographic coverage. The cost of the raw film stock exposed during flight is the smallest part of the budget, while processing and printing expenses can total a substantial sum, even surpassing the cost of the flight itself if color negatives are exposed and enlarged in color. On an average flight of three hours' duration, I expended approximately ten rolls of film numbering twelve exposures per roll. Half of these were color negatives at $1.20 per roll, the other half were infrared at $0.60 per roll. Processing charges averaged $4.00 per color print made on 8 × 10-inch paper, and $1.50 per infrared print made to the same size. Printing costs were reduced by ordering proof-sheets made by contact printing each roll at the time of processing and then selecting for enlargement only those negatives of interest. Overall cost of printing would be further reduced by substituting panchromatic film in place of color in one of the cameras. The cost of processing and printing these materials would equal that of the infrared film. The maximum, gross cost, then, of producing a set of finished prints from an average flight, based on the figures quoted here and assuming that every negative is enlarged, would be $440 for the color/infrared combination and $270 for the panchromatic/infrared combination.

Prices of the large-format vertical prints will vary widely, as these are usually made to order by the agency in possession of the negatives. The Colombian Geographic Institute charged a special price of $0.40 per 9 × 9-inch print in 1967, or $40, for a total of one hundred prints needed to cover the region over twenty years of time depth. This low price was offered in exchange for a set of the small-format prints. By comparison, commercial rates commonly vary in cost from $1.50 to $5 per print, depending on the quantity of prints in the order.

Interpretation

Photointerpretation of the central Cauca River valley reveals that population nuclei are consistently concentrated in two zones. The larger settlements usually occur within the spurs of the ranges forming the walls of the valley, while smaller, ribbon settlements populate the natural levees along the present course of the river. This distribution is manifestly the result of a total ecological process involving geophysical, biotic, and sociocultural components operating over time (Schorr 1965, 1968). Briefly, the combined effects of the need to cultivate in the face of frequent flooding, poorly drained soils on the valley floor, and the requirements for protection from persistent violence on the part of hostile neighboring groups, contributed to the establishment and maintenance of larger, permanent settlements on the higher ground toward the foot of the mountain walls, where water supply and land form permitted (Fig. 13). On the valley floor, there are fewer numbers concentrated in settlements established on the slightly elevated, natural levees bordering the river (Fig. 14). Although the soil is richer on the valley floor than anywhere else, there is little soil to till away from the riverside because of anaerobic conditions. The periodic danger of flooding, generally warmer temperatures, lack of protection against recurring raids, and increased exposure to disease vectors thriving in the extensive, stagnant, backwater swamps that cover much of the valley floor, all lead to diminished population over this zone.

The systems of agriculture correspond to this dual zonal distribution of cultivable soils. The infield-outfield system is characteristic of the upland communities, where continually cultivated backyard gardens are supplemented by mountainside plots, while the riverside settlements practice permanent infield cultivation, made possible by the extraordinary fertility of the alluvium forming the soils of the levees and the convenience of bucket irrigation during the long dry summers. Until fairly recent times, the Cauca was the principal artery for bulk transport, and some of the riverside settlements also functioned as ports for the larger towns situated on the higher grounds nearby. In both zones, the cultivated plots have taken the shape of the small minifundio (Fig. 15). On the lower valley floor, the soil away from the river was formerly unsuited for cultivation but later was maintained in a natural pasture which provided the basis for livestocking and the accompanying larger latifundio tenure patterns. Prior to the Spanish introduction of cattle during the mid-sixteenth century, this zone of the valley floor was marginal and unoccupied, except for occasional fishing expeditions to the many lagoons.

The photographs also identify Spanish-founded or modified communities by their grid system of streets and their central plaza with civil and religious buildings nearby. In contrast, the pattern of pre-Colombian communities may be recognized by the organic, veinlike tracings of their trails and roadways, which follow the principal runoff channels or otherwise conform to features of topographical relief, as these gave access to resource centers. This pattern appears to have originated as a result of free-flowing pedestrian activity in limited areas where wheeled transport or beasts of burden are absent. Occurring in many places of the world, "its linear forms will tend to be slightly wavy but nongeometrical, hugging all external angles, with a variety of radials from fixed points and a general absence of parallel lines" (Esher 1966:156). The communities exhibiting this configuration in the photographs, especially in the uplands, have clearly been inhabited continuously since before the Conquest. Until recently, this part of the Andes has been unstudied archaeologically. The spotty work that has so

Thomas S. Schorr

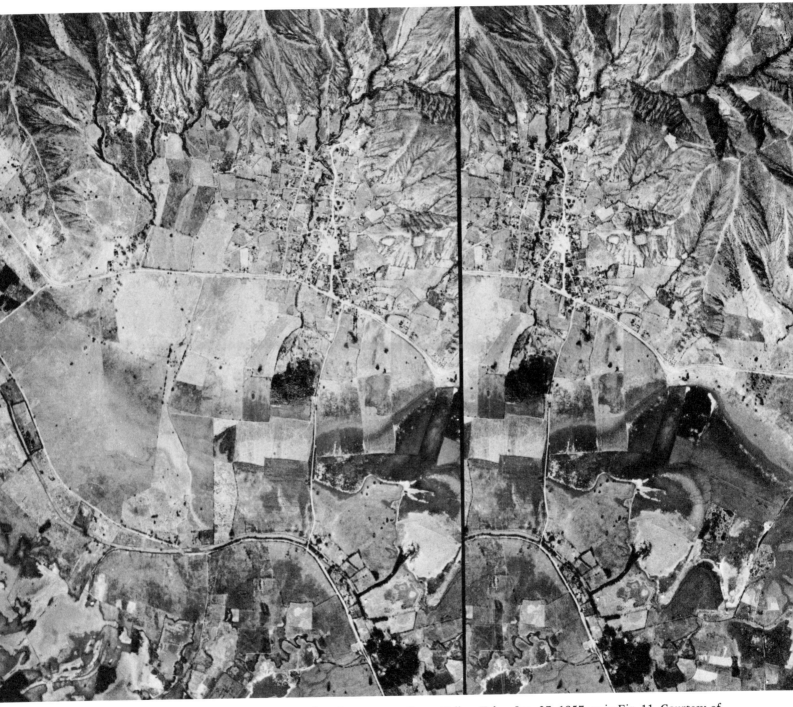

Fig. 13. Stereogram of the community of Higuerón, of pre-Colombian origins, which nestles protectively within the spurs of the Cordillera Occidental above the wet floor of the Cauca Valley. Taken Jan. 27, 1957, as in Fig. 11. Courtesy of the I.G.A.C.

Cauca Valley of Colombia

Fig. 14. Aerial photograph of the community of La Candelaria, typifying the smaller, ribbon settlements on the elevated banks of the Cauca River. Taken Jan. 30, 1957, as in Fig. 11. Courtesy of the I.G.A.C.

Thomas S. Schorr

Fig. 15. Low, oblique infrared photograph of Higuerón, presenting contrastive tones that aid in the identification of many ground features: the minifundio land tenure, a new school (circle), and a new runoff canal.

Cauca Valley of Colombia

51

far been carried out is insufficient to produce more than erroneous conclusions about the size and the way of life of populations inhabiting this valley in pre-Colombian times (Bennett 1944; Ford 1944; Schorr 1965:75–78). The recent excavations of Warwick Bray and M. Edward Moseley (1971) on the valley floor about 75 km. to the southwest have already substantiated many of my conclusions derived by means of aerial photos.

It is also possible to demonstrate that the riverside settlements were not static in their locations, as were those of the uplands, but that as time went on, they drifted over the valley floor following the river, as it migrated in a generally eastward trend. Major floods, occurring on the average of every nine years, periodically swept away established settlement structures, and when the settlements were rebuilt, their position shifted to conform to the changing course of the river. Boundaries of former house compounds can be identified on the photographs along the old courses of the river. Where the physical remains of the river's former channels have become obliterated through erosion and human activity, some viable field boundaries still persist, attesting to its former influence.

Present-day house counts from the photographs provide an estimate of overall population numbers, and more significantly, they form the basis for calculating the number of inhabitants in each of the nucleated settlements photographed. This information is not available in the national census figures, which by convention show only the number of residents in the *cabecera* (county seat), which is usually the principal town of the *municipio* (county), and the total of those residing outside of the cabecera, combining all of the inhabitants of the hamlets scattered throughout the remainder of the municipio into a single figure. This segment of the population can commonly amount to 75 percent of the entire municipio. The use of the original tracts of the national census, on which spot checks have shown inexact results, is tedious and perhaps even less reliable than estimates made from the photographs.

A comparison of the sequence of photo images taken over the last twenty years reveals information about the rate and quality of socioeconomic change (or lack of it) in the populations of the region. Visible differences in the proportions of land in agricultural and other productive uses can be used to reconstruct the past trends of change in labor specialization, technology and productive output. Changes in the frequency and proportion in which construction materials appear in the views can be related to origin and cost. For example, the frequency of change from palm thatch to tile, to galvanized iron, or to asbestos roofing materials over twenty years tells much about economic conditions and class preferences. Surfaced roads cost more than unsurfaced, so that when and where these make their appearance, coupled with other modifications occurring in the vicinity, offer substantial evidence from which to infer the nature and trends of change. The rate of appearance of new objects and configurations, such as power lines, mechanization, wells and reservoirs, schools, service structures, recreational facilities, barriers, shrines, and other specialized constructs, are further concrete indicators of the collective trends of change resulting from decision making and choice, of reallocation of time and resources, of shifts in interests, preferences, activities, and expectations of the population (Figs. 14 & 15).

In essence, then, the physical modifications and material reconstructions that a population introduces in the landscape are tangible representations of those aggregate, human behavioral procedures that make up the epiphenomenon of organized social systems. An analysis of the characteristics of this physical signature in the context of the total ecology, as conveniently presented in the reduced scale and compressed time of the photographs, yields interrelated patterns of information about many of the processes that contribute to the generation or restriction of change in the group. To be complete, this "external" analysis of the system's characteristics over time must be combined with "internal" investigations, such as those suggested by Fredrik Barth (1967), into the way in which time and resource allocations are changed by the members of the society

Thomas S. Schorr

and become institutionalized. Neither external nor internal views alone can provide the totality of information needed for an understanding of the processes of social change.

The use of photographic records should continue as a part of the long-term plan to pursue an ecological analysis, in time depth, of the central Cauca Valley region, and of the interconnections that link this area to other specialized regions of the northern Andes, the Pacific, and the Caribbean coasts. In summary, my use of the Colombian government's aerial photos with the more recent small-format photos made it possible to record, survey, and classify over thirty communities within a larger development region of over 3,000 square kilometers, and to assess numerous changes that occurred during a time span of twenty years. Representative sites were selected from the photographs for further study by a resident ethnographer. In addition to maps and to other kinds of information routinely produced by photogrammetry, the images were indispensable for making comparative evaluations of culture-adaptive (ecological) interrelationships in the valley's population as it adjusted over time to the changing requirements of life in the region. The photographs were also valuable in the way that they stimulated interpreters to generate testable hypotheses about the observed structural relationships in force for thousands of years.

Anthropologists interested in the comparative study of sociocultural change, especially on the regional level, must be prepared to gather and to relate classes and quantities of data that traditional field methods and techniques were never designed to handle. They must also operate with more than a casual knowledge of areas that have long been the separate domains of other professions, particularly within the behavioral, economic, earth, and medical sciences. Moreover, this need is intensified by the growing emphasis and support being given to multidisciplinary projects in which anthropologists can participate: rural and urban relationships, economic development and sociocultural change, community health and welfare, and many more all depend upon the successful coordination and direction of a variety of specialists, all contributing toward a single, unifying, research objective. With aerial photographic interpretation now long in routine use in many areas of investigation, cooperating scientists find that they can unite their separate disciplines around this common source of information, from which the trained eyes of diverse professions can identify and compare quantities, structures, and patterns of data relevant to the problem at hand.

John Rowe (1953:909) has commented that, in view of the possibilities which the method offers, it seems incredible that until recently only the French had consistently acknowledged and employed systematic aerial reconnaissance and photographic interpretation as a legitimate data-gathering technique serving ethnographic purposes (Chombart de Lauwe 1948, 1951; Griaule 1937, 1946; Poidebard 1934, 1939; Rey 1921). Of the subdisciplines that comprise American anthropology, archaeology alone has a legitimate history of systematic development and training in the use of aerial photographic tools (Rowe 1953:907; Anson 1963; Brock 1966; Coleman 1960; Heath 1957; Merchant 1963). Yet, aerial ethnography is capable of producing, quickly and economically, a large amount of unique, ethnographically relevant information over extensive zones of human habitation, which has hitherto been an impossible task for the ethnographer working alone with traditional field methods and techniques. Through wider training and practice, anthropologists of all specialties will discover in the method of aerial ethnography new avenues for research and interdisciplinary collaboration in the comparative study of contemporary sociocultural change.

Portions of this project were supported by grants from the Foreign Area Fellowship Program; the International Center for Medical Research and Training (award TW–00143), administered by Tulane University and the Universidad del Valle; and the Department of Anthropology, University of Pittsburgh. I wish to thank Edgar Caldas, Forrest E. LaViolette, Walter Escorcia, Miles Richardson, Robert MacLennan, Hernán Caicedo, and Peter Frazer for their invaluable assistance.

Part Two
Ethnographic Research and Analysis

Evon Z. Vogt
Aerial Photography in Highland Chiapas Ethnography

The highlands of Chiapas in southeastern Mexico are inhabited by over 200,000 Tzotzil and Tzeltal-speaking Maya Indians living in thirty municipios within a fifty-mile radius of San Cristóbal las Casas, the non-Indian, Ladino town that serves as the principal marketplace for the highlands (Vogt 1969a; Fig. 16). The limestone and volcanic mountains are high (rising to over 9,000 feet), rugged, and covered with tropical cloud forests, making travel slow and difficult, especially during the rainy season, when as much as sixty inches of rain fall between May and October. With few exceptions, the Indians maintain the ancient Maya settlement pattern. Each municipio has a political-religious center inhabited by only a few hundred Indians, while the bulk of the population lives in outlying hamlets in the mountains. Most of the hamlets are connected to the political-religious centers and to the outside world only by trails, so that anthropological field work involves hours or days on foot or horseback in order to reach the remote hamlets where most of the Indians live (Fig. 17).

I first visited the highlands of Chiapas in the summer of 1955, where I began to plan the Harvard Chiapas Project, on which field research was initiated in 1956. By 1960 I reached the conclusion that highland Chiapas would make an excellent site for exploration of the uses of aerial photography in ethnography. I had used some aerial photos taken by the Compañía Mexicana Aerofoto in 1954 for a preliminary mapping of the hamlet of Paste', but it was Duane Metzger, then of Stanford University, who in 1962 called attention to the astonishing new advances in aerial photo technology that were being used by the Itek Corporation of Palo Alto to count grape-drying trays (2 × 3 feet) from photos taken at 17,000 to 20,000 feet in altitude to estimate the size of the raisin crops in California. It was evident that this new technology could be highly useful in solving many of the ethnographic problems in the highlands of Chiapas. However, I knew it would have been inefficient for the members of the Harvard Chiapas Project to attempt to carry out the proposed aerial survey, that is, to hire a plane, take the photos, interpret them, and prepare the necessary maps. In the summer of 1962, field workers from Harvard and Stanford had hired a small plane, taken aerial photos of Aguacatenango and of two hamlets of Zinacantan, and used the photos to prepare rough maps for the purpose of speeding up census-taking operations. Although the results were interesting and promising, they had limitations. It was impossible, for example, with photos taken out of the window of a small plane, to obtain the kind of controlled cartographic coverage needed for the production of maps of large areas, or to obtain the kind of controlled overlap of photos necessary for stereoscopic examination in a study of the topography.

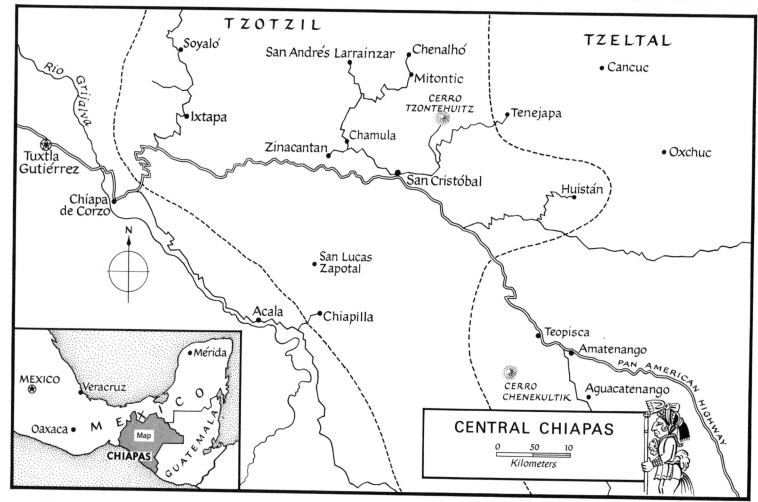

Fig. 16. Central Chiapas.

In consultation with Norman A. McQuown, University of Chicago, and A. Kimball Romney, Stanford University, both of whom were then also directing field projects in Chiapas, I decided to employ experts to carry out an aerial survey of the highlands of Chiapas, to interpret the photos, to train some of our graduate students in the techniques of photogrammetry, and to produce the necessary photomosaics and maps. Our investigation into this matter convinced us that the Itek Corporation was best equipped to carry out such an operation. Itek expressed strong interest in the project and agreed to work closely with us at each stage of the operation. In the

aerial photography and ensuing ethnographic research, I served as the principal investigator while McQuown and Romney served as co-investigators during the first two phases (1963–1967). I carried on alone as principal investigator during the last phase (1967–1969).

During the first phase of the project, the operational flying and photographing were completed, as well as the production of photomosaics and planimetric maps. Richard Kroeck, who served as project engineer from Itek for this research, came to Chiapas for a week in August 1963 to survey the area we wished to cover, to take ground photographs, and to familiarize himself with

Evon Z. Vogt

Fig. 17. Aerial oblique of the hamlet of ʔApas.

the Indian communities. He also began negotiations with the Mexican government to obtain permission for the operational flights, which would take off from Tuxtla Gutiérrez, Chiapas. After some months of negotiating, permission was arranged for Itek to subcontract the flying and photography to the Compañía Mexicana Aerofoto, using their plane, pilot, and Wild Heerburg RC–9 camera for the 9 × 9-inch photo coverage, and using Itek's 70 mm. High Acuity (HyAc) camera for the panoramic photography.

During the months of February and March 1964, while the dry season was in progress but before the swidden farmers had set fire to their fields, the entire Tzotzil-Tzeltal habitat of 6,400 square miles was covered with the 9 × 9-inch photography, as well as 985 square miles of selected area with the HyAc photography (Fig. 18) and other selected targets with oblique photography.

By the fall of 1964 we had in hand 1,226 exposures in the 9 × 9-inch format covering the Tzotzil-Tzeltal habitat. These were taken with the Wild Heerburg RC–9 super wide-angle mapping camera, with a focal length of 3 1/2 inches and an angular field of 120. Nominal flying height for the RC–9 photography was chosen at 11,600 feet above mean terrain. However, because of a large difference between the highlands and the Grijalva Valley in the average terrain elevation, the RC–9 coverage was divided into two zones. The lower terrain was flown at an indicated altitude above mean sea level of 13,100 feet. The more mountainous terrain was flown at an indicated altitude of 18,100 feet. Each exposure covered an area of approximately 30,000 square feet, providing an approximate scale of 1:40,000 (one inch = 3,333 feet). Flight lines were programed to provide 80 percent overlap between successive photos and 50 percent sidelap between adjacent lines to give the potential for stereoscopic viewing.

The flights also produced 1,732 exposures of selected municipios taken with Itek's HyAc panoramic camera. The HyAc is a direct scanning camera with a maximum scan of 120. It has a curved film plane and a high-quality narrow-angle lens, which scans across the flight path of the aircraft. As it sweeps back and forth, it photographs a wide swath of ground. The advantage of the HyAc camera is that, by using only the center lens field over the total angle scanned, it photographs the entire swath of coverage in high resolution. However, the scanning action of the center lens also produces a good deal of distortion not inherent in frame photography. This distortion, occurring at both ends of the sweep, involves the displacement of images of ground points from their expected perspective. Consequently, much overlap is desirable, and flight lines were programed to provide 40 percent forward overlap and 40 percent sidelap. The least distorted image of an area is the one most directly beneath the flight line. The HyAc photography covered the three areas centered around the municipios of Zinacantan, Chamula, Tenejapa, and Aguacatenango, where ethnographers from the three universities had done the maximum amount of enthnographic field work. Flying altitudes for the HyAc photography were chosen to provide an average terrain clearance of 10,000 feet along the flight path. At this altitude, the scale of photography was approximately 1:10,000 (one inch = 834 feet). Each HyAc exposure covered approximately 1,875 feet in the flight direction and a swath of 4 1/2 miles.

Finally, we obtained 59 low-level oblique photos of selected targets in the research area, especially of ceremonial centers, hamlets, and sacred mountains. They were taken with a hand-held Fairchild K–3 camera having a 10-inch focal length and a 7 × 9-inch format.

We also had Itek make a number of excellent photomosaics of the municipio centers and of the hamlets of Zinacantan, Tenejapa, and Aguacatenango, as well as a number of planimetric maps. We soon discovered that the maps were not as useful as the photomosaics, because the Itek photo interpreters, being unfamiliar with Chiapas, were unable to select geographically and culturally relevant details to place on the maps. We found during the summer of 1964 that our field anthropologists and, more especially, our Indian informants were better photo interpreters for our purposes.

Active research was begun on the photos, to explore a

Evon Z. Vogt

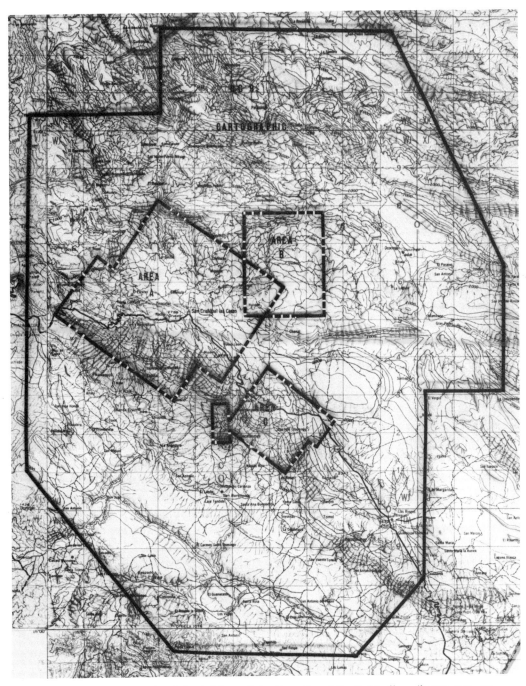

Fig. 18. Aerial photomosaic of the habitat of the Tzotzil and Tzeltal Indians (larger area outlined), photographed with an RC-9 cartographic camera except for the areas labeled *A*, *B*, and *C*, which were photographed with a HyAc panoramic camera.

number of ethnographic problems of settlement pattern, land tenure, and sacred geography. A preliminary report on the results was presented at the Seventh International Congress of Anthropological and Ethnological Sciences in Moscow in August 1964 (Vogt and Romney, 1971).

The second phase of the project (1965–1967) focused on the establishment of a system of information retrieval and interpretation. It was supervised from a Harvard Chiapas Project aerial photography laboratory in William James Hall at Harvard. We again turned to the Itek Corporation to provide a system that included a set of graphics consisting of photo plot indexes for the RC–9 and HyAc flight lines, which made it possible to locate easily any area covered by the photos.

The necessary viewing equipment for the retrieval system included an Itek Modified 18 × 24 reader-printer and a Bausch and Lomb Zoom 70 stereoscope (Model II) with a scanning stage. It was also necessary to have indexed duplicate rolls of the 70 mm. HyAc negatives and to have some of the RC–9 negatives reduced to 70 mm. size, in order to fit them into the reader-printer and the Zoom 70 stereoscope.

The reader-printer provided the capability for screen viewing of all the Chiapas aerial photography reproduced as roll film positive transparencies. The reader-printer projects the 70 mm. films onto an eighteen by twenty-four inch viewing screen at an eight times enlargement ratio. Screen viewing makes it possible for the user rapidly to scan a large volume of photography for orientation and general observation, or for detailed analysis of a selected area. Moreover, from the roll film negative transparencies, the reader-printer can produce in only thirty seconds sharp, high-contrast photocopies of the identical images on the screen. These prints, because of the speed, simplicity, and economy of their production, are invaluable as working materials, both in the laboratory and in the field.

The Bausch and Lomb Zoom stereoscope can be used in the analysis of all 70 mm. roll film transparencies. Equipped with 10x-wide field eyepieces, it provides a continuously variable magnification range from 7x to 30x. The stereoscope can be used for single-image viewing

of the HyAc photography, or, with overlapping frames of the RC–9 photography, it can be used to view an area in three-dimensional perspective or stereo. The stereo effect, though exaggerated, reveals the nature of an area's topography and the relative heights of objects. This set of photographic materials and equipment makes available to the ethnographer a massive collection of data concerning his area of interest.

The Harvard Chiapas Project aerial photo laboratory became fully operational during 1965–1966, and its facilities were made available to Chiapas field workers from other universities as well. In November 1965, George Collier and I presented a paper on "Aerial Photography and Computers in the Analysis of Zinacanteco Demography and Land Tenure" at the meetings of the American Anthropological Association in Denver. A week's training program for field workers was provided by Itek in February 1966 at their laboratories in Palo Alto, and in October of that year, Itek produced "A Manual for Users of Aerial Photography of the Highlands of Chiapas, Mexico," by Richard M. Kroeck, which was distributed to Chiapas field workers.

During the third phase (1967–1969), while continuing to operate the aerial photo laboratory at Harvard, we obtained additional ground control surveys and photogrammetric work from the Compañía Mexicana Aerofoto. They provided maps with a scale of 1:10,000 and contour lines of 10-meter intervals for settled areas and 50-meter intervals for farming areas, in order to test hypotheses concerning the influence of topography on land use and settlement. They also requested to borrow the original film of our 9 × 9 coverage in order to complete a photomosaic of Chiapas that they were preparing for the Mexican government. We complied, so that it is now possible to purchase excellent copies of rectified aerial photomosaics of any part of Chiapas directly from them.

The use of aerial photography in the Harvard Chiapas Project turned out to have two major aspects. First, there were the uses that we anticipated and planned for in advance. Second were the unexpected uses, which emerged in the course of the project operations over the six-year period.

Evon Z. Vogt

Five major uses of the aerial photographic data were planned for in the original research designs. They are discussed here briefly, to provide a kind of inventory of the research.

Analysis of Settlement Patterns. The mapping and analysis of settlement patterns is in the long run perhaps the most fundamental use of aerial photography in ethnographic research. If settlement patterns are defined as "the patterned manner in which household and community units are arranged spatially over the landscape" (Vogt, 1956), one can not only map and describe settlement patterns with precision for both prehistoric and contemporary societies, but can also utilize them as a focus for the analysis of certain ecological and cultural factors that enter into and maintain particular cultural systems (Steward 1955).

More specifically in the case of the Maya, of which the Tzotzil-Tzeltal of highland Chiapas are an important branch, a major continuity has been observed in their settlement pattern (Vogt 1961; 1962; Willey 1956; Bullard 1960). The basic type of Maya settlement pattern is described as one of dispersed hamlets, where the bulk of the population lives. These sustain ceremonial centers of various types and sizes, which are either occupied or controlled by religious officials (priests), or at least serve as the foci of ritual activity for the people living in the dispersed hamlets. It is assumed that this settlement plan evolved early in Mayan cultural history and that the Mayas have tended to follow it in essence ever since. In the concept of ceremonial center are included the large centers containing pyramid temples, the minor ceremonial centers, the *cabeceras* (town centers) of the modern municipios that now contain Catholic churches rather than pyramid temples, as well as a variety of waterholes, caves, cenotes, and other sacred places that function as the foci of ritual activity for smaller units of Maya society.

Two extreme positions have been taken to account for the development and persistence of this type of settlement pattern among the Maya. The plan is said to have evolved as a systemic pattern early in Maya prehistory, and the Maya have tended to follow it ever since —geographical and historical circumstances permitting; or the pattern is said to reflect important ecological conditions and to have little or nothing to do with basic cultural patterns that have persisted from the prehistoric past. For the Maya area there has been a paucity of data on which to choose between these two extreme positions, a basic cultural hypothesis versus an ecological hypothesis, especially for contemporary communities. The recent efforts of the ethnographers have lagged behind those of the archaeologists, the ethnographers having produced little that compares with the precise and elegant settlement pattern maps that the archaeologists have drawn for sites in the Maya area.

The data derived from the aerial survey combined with continuing ethnographic research were utilized to study selected municipios where the ecological and cultural conditions vary in specifiable ways. We now have photomosaics and maps of Aguacatenango and Tenejapa in the Tzeltal area and of Zinacantan in the Tzotzil area. We also have more detailed photomosaics and settlement pattern maps of three hamlets of Zinacantan—ʔApas, Nabenchauk, and Pasteʔ (ranging from compact to very dispersed)—and of the ceremonial center of Zinacantan (Figs. 19, 20, 25), as well as settlement pattern maps of three hamlets of Chamula—Lomo, Peteh, and Bautista Chico (likewise ranging from compact to very dispersed) —which are being used for a comparative analysis of settlement patterns in order to factor out both ecological and cultural determinants that are operative. Not surprisingly, we have discovered that the determinants of the settlement patterns of any given municipio or hamlet are an intricately interwoven set of ecological and cultural factors (Frake 1962). But it seems clear that two factors in the ecological setting are decisive: microtopography, and the availability of household water during the critical dry season.

We are also in the process of trying to develop a uniform grid, for up to this point, the comparative analysis of settlement patterns has been based on either descriptive phrases, such as "compact" and "dispersed," or

Fig. 19. Aerial photomosaic of Zinacantan Ceremonial
Center, constructed from HyAc photos.

Evon Z. Vogt

CENTER

METERS

Fig. 20.   Aerial oblique of Zinacantan Ceremonial Center,
showing the grid pattern of roads and trails, Church of San
Lorenzo (center), and Church of San Sebastián (upper left).

Evon Z. Vogt

individual maps (differing in scale) of each contemporary community or archaeological site. Comparative studies should be vastly enhanced by a uniform grid that will make it possible to present settlement pattern data in a quantified, graphic form.

Census-Taking. In the early years of the Harvard Chiapas Project we learned how difficult and time-consuming it is to take a precise census of a Tzotzil community by going from house to house. Not only does the ethnographic census-taker run into the usual suspicion found in closed corporate communities throughout Middle America as to what he plans to do with the census, but in traditional Tzotzil society it is customary to engage in ritual drinking when any kind of delegation goes from house to house on a mission, such as collecting contributions for the annual fiesta for the patron saint. Suffice it to say that even the most experienced drinker is not likely to cover many houses in a single day before he has been drunk under the table. This difficulty can be avoided by using a sample of informants to tell one who lives in which houses on a set of aerial photos. We found it possible to reach nearly 100 percent accuracy in a fraction of the time and effort that is required for the traditional method of taking a census. The ʔApas census collected by Frank Cancian and George Collier is an excellent example of what can be done along these lines.

Mapping Land Use and Land Ownership. The aerial photographs provided a wealth of data on land use and land plots. We discovered that land use can be determined quite exactly by ground checking sample areas with Indian informants. The land plots can be precisely mapped, since each small plot has some kind of border, such as brush or pole fence, which shows up in the aerial photos. Present ownership and inheritance can be studied by presenting the photos and maps to Indian informants, who will describe the details of transmission of land in the case of each plot used for either a house or a field. A study of land tenure should include, where possible,

the analysis of cemeteries where previous owners are buried, since we found that the graves can be identified in ground photos and that they provide an excellent check on informant's memories about preceding generations, about the determination of the present owners, about details of how the plots were acquired, and about stated expectations as to who will acquire the plots in the future. These three steps are linked to a household census and to a set of genealogical plates on each community. The data were collected in a manner that permits computer handling.

Study of Sacred Geography. Another use of the aerial photographs that proved to have great potential for Tzotzil-Tzeltal ethnography concerned what is called sacred geography. By this term is meant the location and mapping of sacred shrines that are visited by ritual processions performing complex ceremonies for curing illness, for making rain, and for worshiping the ancestral gods who are believed to live inside the mountains and hills, as well as the earth god who lives below the surface of the earth. The major mountaintop shrines show up clearly in the photographs (Fig. 21), and with the aid of informants we were able to pinpoint the shrines at the foot of mountains, as well as the location of sacred caves on the sides of mountains.

Two aspects of this sacred geography are of special interest. The first concerns the precise orientation of the shrines with reference to the ceremonial centers and with reference to the cardinal or intercardinal directions. These orientations provide data for the study of directional symbolism in Maya society. It has long been assumed by Maya authorities such as J. Eric S. Thompson (1934) that the Maya recognize four cardinal points (north, east, south, west) in the same manner as these directions are reckoned by compass. But it is possible that both the early Spanish chroniclers and the more recent Maya scholars elicited data from Maya informants with a European model of compass points in mind and that Maya directional symbolism does not in fact correspond with this model.

Fig. 21. Aerial oblique of two important sacred mountains in Zinacantan Ceremonial Center: Kalvario (lower right), including cross shrine with six crosses, and Sisil Vits (upper left).

Evon Z. Vogt

It is known that most Maya groups believe in gods who are located at the four corners of the world. But what is not clear is whether the locations correspond to Western conceptions. There is suggestive evidence from Quintana Roo (Villa Rojas 1945) that the four corners are not the cardinal points of the compass but rather are closer to the four intercardinal points (northeast, northwest, southeast, southwest).

Careful mapping of the directional orientations of houses, fields, churches, sacred mountains with reference to ceremonial centers, major waterholes, and cross shrines should eventually solve the problem as to whether the Tzotzil-Tzeltal communities are following certain rules about directional orientation. Preliminary work has revealed that directional placement is not random, nor is it related in any obvious way to topography. Neither are informants systematically explicit about these matters, except that in some communities the dead are buried with heads to the setting sun, ritually used tables are oriented with the "head" to the rising sun, and houses ideally face the rising sun. The orientation of ceremonial centers with reference to the sacred mountains surrounding them is even more of a problem, since these orientations were established in the past, when it is suspected that the rules were more explicit.

As the research proceeds, three hypotheses for the Tzotzil-Tzeltal are currently being explored. First, the four directions of the *vashakmen* or "four-corner gods," as they are called in Zinacantan, are not reckoned according to Western cardinal points, but rather are calculated according to the solsticial points as follows:

(X) Sunset at Summer Solstice	Sunrise at (X) Summer Solstice
West	East
(X) Sunset at Winter Solstice	Sunrise at (X) Winter Solstice

The sacred mountains around a ceremonial center were selected to conform approximately to this orientation.

Second, and alternatively, the four directions are reckoned according to the intercardinal points of the compass, and sacred mountains were selected to represent these points. Theoretically, the placement of square houses or square pyramids could just as easily be oriented facing east if the conceptions of the important directions are the intercardinal points as they could if the important directions are the cardinal points. However, if houses, for example, are oriented to the "rising sun," then a systematic variation would appear in their orientation, depending on the time of year they were constructed. Third, even if further field work disclosed that the four cardinal directions are reckoned according to compass directions, as assumed by Thompson and others, then two alternatives exist for the orientation of square houses and fields:

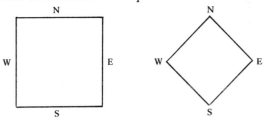

The second aspect of sacred geography under investigation is the relationship of social units to the ceremonial circuits made by ritual processions. The hamlets that share in the use of a large ceremonial center are made up of waterhole groups, which in turn are composed of localized lineages. In each of these groups, ritual processions make counterclockwise circuits to the sacred places. Maps of these circuits show how new groups are formed from the fission of old ones while maintaining ritual relations with the larger groups and the ceremonial center. They also pinpoint the size and structure of the social units in relation to the land and waterholes they control.

Good examples include our mapping of the sacred geography of Zinacantan Center and of the ceremonial circuit followed by the *K'in Krus* ceremony performed for *Sna Akovetik* in the hamlet of Paste? (Figs. 22, 23). Much more sophisticated use of the aerial photos in the study of sacred geography was undertaken by Robert M. Laughlin of the Smithsonian Institution, who used the aerial photographs to elicit a complete inventory of place

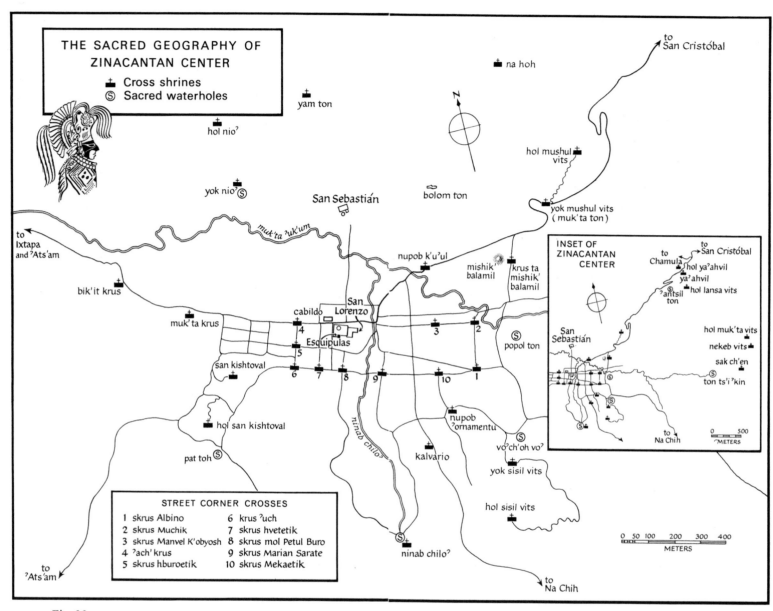

THE SACRED GEOGRAPHY OF
ZINACANTAN CENTER

✝ Cross shrines
Ⓢ Sacred waterholes

na hoh

yam ton

hol nio⁷

hol mushul
vits

yok nio⁷ Ⓢ

San Sebastián

bolom ton

yok mushul vits
(muk'ta ton)

to
Ixtapa
and ⁷Ats'am

muk'ta ⁷uk'um

nupob k'u⁷ul

mishik'
balamil

krus ta
mishik'
balamil

to
San Cristóbal

bik'it krus

cabildo

San
Lorenzo

muk'ta krus

4

Esquipulas

3

2

popol ton

5

san kishtoval

6   7   8   9

10   1

hol san kishtoval

ninab chilo⁷

nupob
⁷ornamentu

pat toh Ⓢ

kalvario

vo⁷ch'oh vo⁷

yok sisil vits

hol sisil vits

ninab chilo⁷ Ⓢ ✝

to
Na Chih

INSET OF
ZINACANTAN
CENTER

to
Chamula

to
San Cristóbal

hol ya⁷ahvil

ya⁷ahvil

⁷antsil
ton

hol lansa vits

San
Sebastián

hol muk'ta vits

nekeb vits

sak ch'en

ton ts'i ⁷kin

to
Na Chih

0   500
METERS

STREET CORNER CROSSES

1 skrus Albino   6 krus ⁷uch
2 skrus Muchik   7 skrus hvetetik
3 skrus Manvel K'obyosh 8 skrus mol Petul Buro
4 ⁷ach' krus   9 skrus Marian Sarate
5 skrus hburoetik   10 skrus Mekaetik

to
⁷Ats'am

0 50 100   200   300   400
METERS

Fig. 22.

Evon Z. Vogt

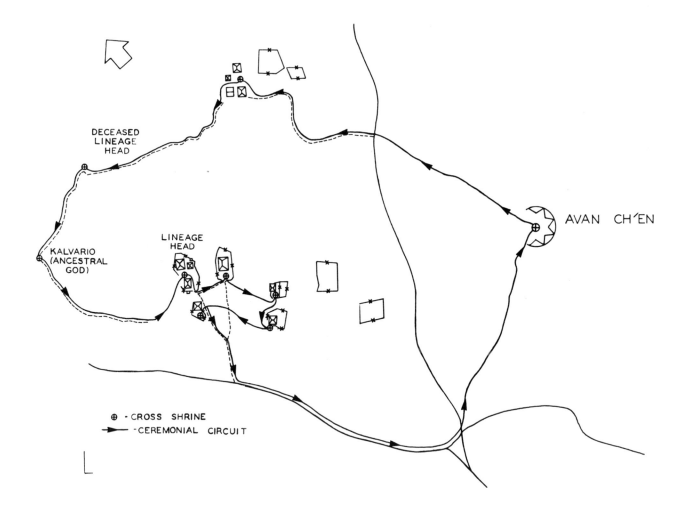

DECEASED
LINEAGE
HEAD

KALVARIO
(ANCESTRAL
GOD)

LINEAGE
HEAD

AVAN CH'EN

⊕ · CROSS SHRINE
➤ -CEREMONIAL CIRCUIT

Fig. 23. Map of sacred places visited by the ritual procession for the K' in Krus ceremony for Sna Akovetik in the hamlet of Pasteʔ. The counterclockwise circuit links the house shrines with each other, with a shrine in a cave (*ch'en*) devoted to the Earth Lord, with another shrine dedicated to the deceased head of the lineage, and with a third shrine dedicated to the ancestral god of the lineage. The map was drawn with the aid of aerial photos covering the houses and lands belonging to this Akovetik lineage.

names (sacred, civil, and so forth) in the municipio of Zinacantan (Fig. 21). I have described additional results elsewhere (Vogt 1966, 1969b, 1970, 1970, n.d.).

Indices of Cultural Change. From the beginning of the aerial photography project, we also planned to map certain kinds of data that would provide objective indices of cultural change. It would be ideal to have a succession of aerial photos of the same municipios taken at intervals of one, five, or ten years. Photos taken in 1954 of selected areas of the Chiapas highlands by the Compañia Mexicana Aerofoto compared to the same areas covered in the 1964 photos provide useful comparative data on such matters as change in settlement pattern, demographic growth, and new roads.

Other evidences of change can be studied from the 1964 photos, especially from the HyAc large-scale (1:10,000) coverage. A critical index of change is the shift going on from the traditional thatch roofs to more modern Ladino-style tile roofs. By means of the HyAc photos we were able to count and map the distribution of the shift in roof style from thatch to tile for parts of Zinacantan, Chamula, and Aguacatenango (Johnson 1967). However, the shift is a complex one, involving such factors as the distance of the hamlet from a tile factory, the relative wealth of the families in a hamlet— for tile costs much more than thatch—and the ceremonial uses—for example, tile-roof houses can be larger than thatch-roof houses and hence can accommodate large groups of Indian ritualists during ceremonies.

Unexpected Uses of Aerial Photography

I turn now to the five unexpected uses of aerial photography that emerged in our project operations. They are discussed here briefly; more details will be found in the articles by members of the Harvard Chiapas Project which follow.

More Precise Ethnographic Data. Although we had anticipated that mapping of such features as settlement patterns from aerial photos would result in much better ethnographic information, we were startled by the extent to which this proved to be the case. Two dramatic examples are a settlement pattern map of the hamlet of Paste? and a settlement pattern map based on the 1964 aerial coverage (Vogt 1961; 1969b—Figs. 24, 25). The 1961 data were based on an enlargement of the 1954 RC–9 coverage, while the 1969 data were based on the HyAc coverage flown in 1964. Some of the difference is attributable to changes that occurred over the ten-year period, but since the 1954 photo data were brought up to date by field work in 1959, there is really only a five-year gap. More important is the fact that the HyAc coverage permitted much clearer data for the location of houses with reference to waterholes and to major hilly areas that are uninhabited. Further, the HyAc coverage provided for much more precise identification of lineage and waterhole groups. With the better photos, the same informants that had been used in 1959 were forcibly reminded of lineage groups and waterhole affiliations they had previously overlooked. Thus, Paste? proved to have six waterhole groups rather than five, and the large waterhole group at the south (VI in Fig. 25) proved to have thirteen localized lineages (or *snas*) rather than six.

The second example was the discovery that the municipio of Zinacantan has fifteen rather than eleven outlying hamlets. This ethnographic error derived from having taken the Mexican census as the basis for the count, since the Mexican government groups the hamlets into eleven units. Once we had the aerial photos, it was possible to re-examine the whole municipio in detail and to pick out clusters of houses tucked away in remote places and to ask informants about them. They would respond, for example, "Oh, yes, that's Potovtik, we forgot to tell you about that group before!" It is now clear that from a Zinacanteco point of view, and judged by the operational presence of municipio officials representing the hamlets, Zinacantan has fifteen hamlets rather than the eleven used in the Mexican census (Fig. 26).

Saving Research Time. Although we had anticipated that the aerial photos would save us time in such matters

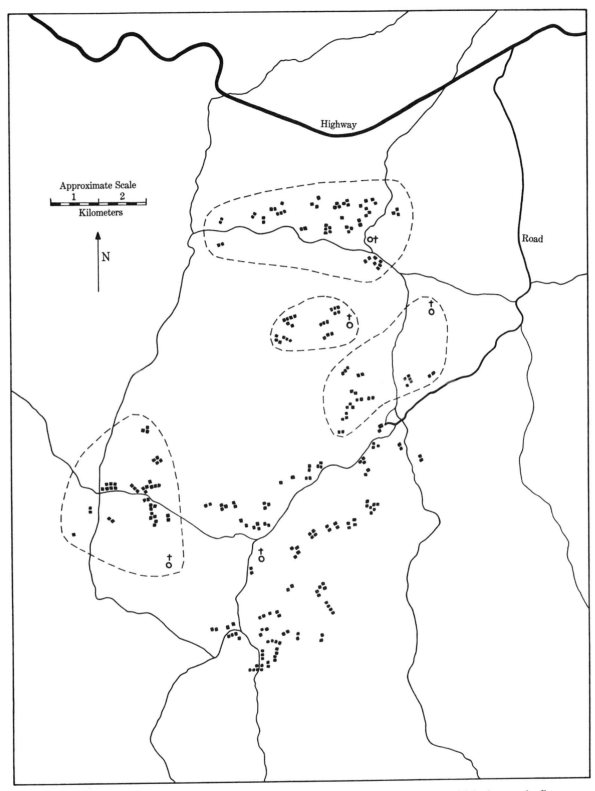

Fig. 24. Map of the settlement patterns in Pasteʔ, based on data collected in 1959, which show only five waterhole groups.

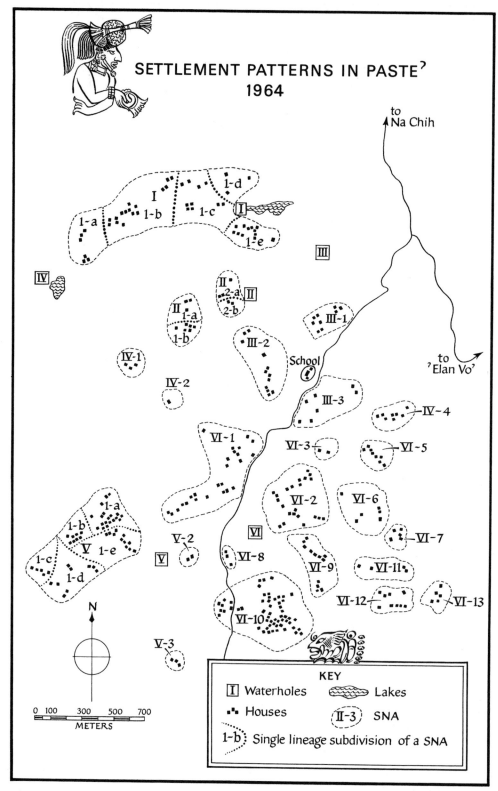

SETTLEMENT PATTERNS IN PASTE'
1964

to
Na Chih

to
'Elan Vo'

I
1-d
1-b   1-c   I
1-a   1-e

III

IV

II
2-a   II
2-b

II
1-a
1-b

III-1

IV-1

III-2

School

IV-2

III-3

IV-4

VI-1

VI-3   VI-5

VI-2   VI-6

VI-7

1-a
1-b
V   1-e
1-c   1-d

V-2

VI

V

VI-8

VI-9

VI-11

VI-12   VI-13

N

VI-10

V-3

KEY

I Waterholes   Lakes

Houses   II-3 SNA

1-b Single lineage subdivision of a SNA

0 100   300   500   700
METERS

Fig. 25.

74   *Evon Z. Vogt*

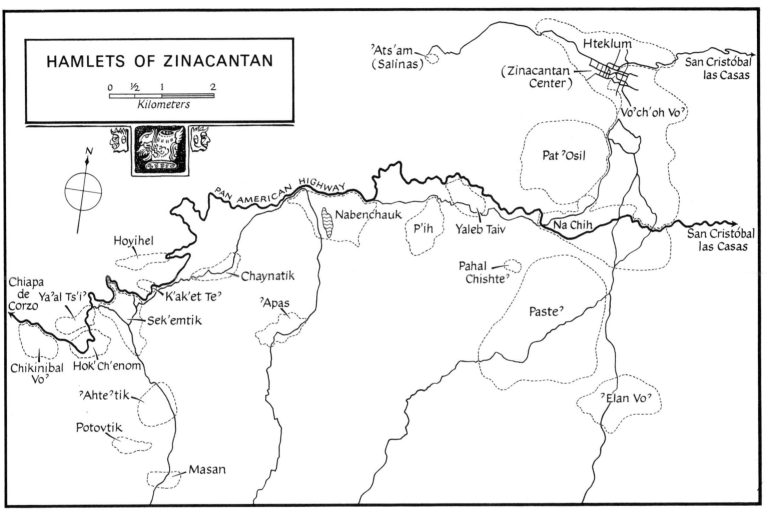

HAMLETS OF ZINACANTAN

0 ½ 1 2
Kilometers

N

ʔAts'am
(Salinas)

Hteklum

(Zinacantan
Center)

San Cristóbal
las Casas

Voʔch'oh Voʔ

Pat ʔOsil

PAN AMERICAN HIGHWAY

Nabenchauk

P'ih

Yaleb Taiv

Na Chih

San Cristóbal
las Casas

Hoyihel

Chaynatik

Pahal
Chishteʔ

Chiapa
de
Corzo

Yaʔal Ts'iʔ

K'ak'et Teʔ

Sek'emtik

ʔApas

Pasteʔ

Chikinibal
Voʔ

Hok'Ch'enom

ʔAhteʔtik

ʔElan Voʔ

Potovtik

Masan

Fig. 26.

as taking a census or mapping and studying land use, we were again startled by the extent to which this proved to be the case. A good example is provided by Richard Price's study of land use in the ejido of Muktahok, a project on which he accomplished the field work in less than a month. Price estimates that comparable work without the aid of the aerial photos would have required many months. I would judge at least six months, or a ratio of 1 to 6 in the saving of research time.

General Ethnographic Use of Aerial Photos. Each season I introduce a new crop of students to the aerial photo laboratory and ask them to think of ways to use reader-printer prints, or other photos, on their particular projects. During the 1968 field season, for example, two-thirds of the field party used aerial photos in their projects: George and Jane Collier in their analysis of large-scale ecological problems in Chamula; Gary Gossen in his study of mythology and the world view in Chamula; Francesco Pellizzi in his study of the structural organization of shamans and their uses of sacred shrines in ceremonies in Zinacantan; Carolyn Pope Edwards in her study of Zinacanteco cemeteries and funeral ceremonies; Jonathan Hiatt in his study of the social organization of the Ladino ranch in the valley of Zinacantan; Maxine Warshauer Baker in her study of the patterns of courtship and marriage in Chamula; Jan Rus in his study of pottery making in Chamula; Susan Levine Kaplan in her study of the social organization of the barrio of La Merced in San Cristóbal; and Phyllis Kazen in her study of the first factory in San Cristóbal and its impact on that Ladino town. It is clear that aerial photos have become as crucial to many of our students as notebooks and typewriters.

Large-Scale Ecological Analysis. From the beginning we talked about trying to use the aerial photos for a larger scale of problem than that involving such matters as settlement patterns and land use in given communities. We asked ourselves, "What kinds of questions suggest themselves if one looks at the aerial photos of a large region, such as all of Chamula?" With George and Jane Collier, I began to scan our coverage of Chamula with a view to detecting things that one does not notice either in looking at photos of smaller areas or in traveling over the country on foot or by jeep. We began to notice that certain areas of Chamula, especially near the ceremonial center, appeared to be unusually treeless and barren; and that other areas, which seemed inhabitable, were still almost completely devoid of houses. This led the Colliers to propose a detailed study using the RC–9 frames as samples running across the municipio, which would systematically classify each frame with respect to such features as tree cover, degree of erosion, presence or absence of houses and fields, and presence or absence of trails and roads. This kind of systematic analysis provided a series of hypotheses about long-range cycles in ecological relationships that might otherwise have been missed and which are now being tested. One example is the following hypothetical cycle in six stages:

1. Pure slash and burn farming.
2. Slash and burn farming with the beginnings of settlement.
3. Diminished slash and burn; increased intensive horticulture with pickax land preparation; introduction of sheep, requiring the fencing of land parcels; increased settlement.
4. Exhaustion of land for swidden agriculture; conversion of larger tracts to grazing for sheep.
5. Abandonment of settlement; fences giving way to open grasslands for sheep grazing.
6. Heavy erosion along trails, aggravated by sheep grazing, rendering the area unusable.

Trail Patterns in a Nongrid World. During the course of a Harvard Freshman Seminar on the Maya during 1966–67, a group of students were given suggestions about problems to explore, utilizing the aerial photos on the highlands of Chiapas. Linnéa Holmer Wren selected the topic of communications networks in Zinacantan and began to study the networks of roads and trails that appear on the aerial photos of the municipio. It was clear

Evon Z. Vogt

that one kind of pattern prevails in the ceremonial center, which is laid out in a grid pattern (Figs. 19, 20), but that quite a different pattern characterizes the network of trails in the nongrid world of the outlying hamlets. Her research disclosed that in Zinacanteco hamlets without grid patterns, the trails fork at an average of sixty degrees. The problem then became one of explaining this surprising regularity. I am confident that it would never have occurred to us to explore this interesting problem without the aerial photographic coverage. This piece of research is an excellent example of the kinds of novel discoveries that can be made in ethnographic research with the aid of aerial photos.

This project was supported by Grants GS–262, GS–976, and GS–1524 from the National Science Foundation and, in Mexico, by the Instituto Nacional Indigenista. I am grateful to George and Jane Collier for their perceptive comments.

George A. Collier

The Impact of Airphoto Technology on the Study of Demography and Ecology in Highland Chiapas

Research is a multifaceted endeavor, involving the flow and feedback of information through a system of processual stages including conceptualization, data collection, and analysis, linked together as a research strategy. Research strategies differ in design. A theorist begins with a conceptual scheme, devises an analytic procedure to test its validity, and collects data to deny or confirm his hypothesis; whereas an empiricist is interested in reconceptualization only as the end product of a sequence that begins with data collection and analysis. Both, however, include in their strategies a projection of the information flow through their research designs, recognizing that concepts and the available techniques of data collection and analysis place constraints on both the kind and the amount of information they can handle. The availability of air photo coverage of highland Chiapas has affected each stage of the design of our research on demography and ecology in that area. We have developed techniques

not only for using air photos in data collection but also for removing unanticipated bottlenecks in the flow of data at the stages of analysis and conceptualization.

The ʔApas Farmland Survey

It is too often blithely assumed that air photos facilitate the immediate collection of data on a large scale. The role that air photos can play in data collection is more accurately indicated in the statement: "It is through perception, largely visual and auditory, that we respond to the humanness that surrounds us. Our recognition of cultural phenomena is controlled by our ability to respond and to understand. The camera is an optical system—it has no selective process—and alone it offers no means of evading the need for perceptive sensitivity" (John Collier 1967:xiii).

Thus, anthropologists exploiting aerial photography for field research must confront the fundamental problem of training themselves and their informants to relate their knowledge of the "real" world both to the photo medium and to one another. In our research on modes of land use in ʔApas, a hamlet of the Tzotzil-speaking municipio of Zinacantan, we developed a number of techniques that permit the researcher and his informants to develop a shared understanding of and vocabulary for speaking about photographic evidence of land use—techniques that in turn facilitated a very rapid and exhaustive collection of land use data.

The ʔApas farmland, according to the map, consists of a portion of the escarpment rising from the northern edge of the Grijalva River basin into the central

Chiapas highlands (Fig. 27). From the crest of the escarpment, like fan segments, radiate a series of erosion-cut valleys sloping toward the lowlands. The land is a patchwork of field plots in various stages of regrowth except for rare, untouched cloud-forest stands on steep, nearly inaccessible ridge faces between the valleys. A network of major trails follows these ridges down from the ʔApas settlement, to take Zinacanteco farmers and their beasts of burden to their lowland rental farms. Smaller trails link valley to valley. Within this area, bounded on the west by a deep gorge, on the south by rocky badland pine forests, and on the east by an important highland-to-lowland trail, are three zones of differing tenure history, including communal and purchased land held as private property and ejido land acquired under recent land reform. In all three zones the principal exploitation is corn farming.

Although many of these features can be illustrated with the photo coverage of ʔApas land, little of it would be self-evident to a newcomer to the area equipped only with the evidence of the photographs. Thus, I began the research on ʔApas land use with a series of procedures to train myself and my informants to relate to the photo coverage as though we were relating directly to the land itself, and only then did we turn to systematic data collection on land tenure and use.

Nothing can substitute for the researcher's direct, first-hand experience of the land area under study. My first goal, therefore, was to gain knowledge of the land area and its forms, and to define its boundaries. I hiked with informants up and down the major mountain ridges with the photo coverage in hand, taking additional still photographs to piece together into panoramic sweeps of the countryside. In this way I discovered from informants that the areas they farmed had discrete boundaries, which we could pinpoint on the photographs so as to define the study area. Coupled with the site inspection of fields in cultivation and in fallow, a systematic interviewing of informants on Tzotzil concepts of the farming cycle and its technology isolated significant features of land use and tenure. These steps established part of the framework needed by both the informants and myself for later photo interpretation.

The cultural labels for locations within the study area were our next focus. An informant typed a list of more than 150 place names encountered on hypothetical tours of study area trails. Identification of these locations on the photo coverage then fixed them in our minds. Informants then assisted in the task of putting together a photomosaic of the study area, on which was placed an acetate overlay, scribed with a grid pattern permitting coordinate location of points within the coverage.

Despite these efforts, I found myself still incapable of facile communication with the informants about land use features that were evident in the photographs. I lacked an adequate three-dimensional conception of the study area topography comparable to that implicit for the informants. To better orient myself, we began construction of a scale model. Lacking planimetry or ground control for the photographs, I trained an informant to read a pocket altimeter to record the altitude at each of the named locations in the study area. We converted these readings into scaled vertical displacements, marked by plastic straws of appropriate length, at corresponding points on a horizontal base map. We constructed a mirror system (Fig. 28) permitting full-frame stereo viewing of the study area from stereo photo pairs, a capability with which informants were fascinated. By constant reference to the stereo imagery, we were able to model finer detail into a plaster surface. Although we painted paths, trails, and many other cultural features onto the plaster model, I later found that informants were nevertheless confused by surface irregularities in the model and could relate much more easily to the photomosaic. Thus, construction of the scale model served primarily to force me to assimilate the microgeography of the study area, a knowledge that could be taken for granted on the part of the informants.

My knowledge of and ability to communicate about the study area with informants were now adequate to the task of photo interpretation. Subsequently, systematic interviewing of informants generated a year-by-year

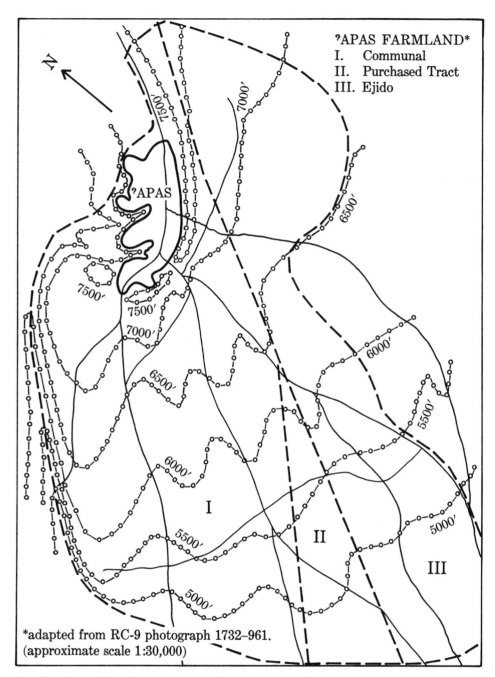

'APAS FARMLAND*
I. Communal
II. Purchased Tract
III. Ejido

*adapted from RC-9 photograph 1732–961.
(approximate scale 1:30,000)

Fig. 27. Map of the 'Apas farmland, showing communal
land (I), purchased tract (II), and ejido (III). Adapted from
RC-9 photograph, approximate scale 1:30,000.

George A. Collier

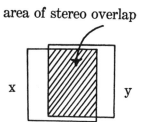

area of stereo overlap

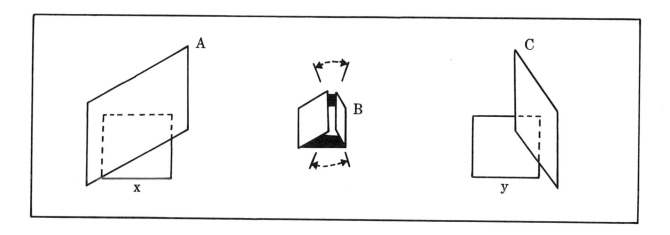

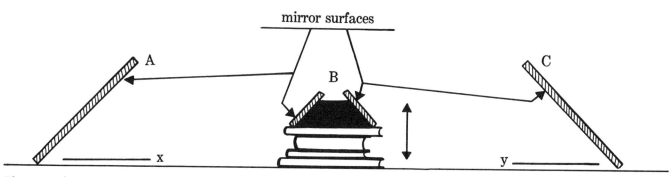

Fig. 28.   Mirror system for full-frame stereoscopic viewing of a study area from stereoscopic photo pairs. Two photographs with overlapping imagery, *X* and *Y,* may be arranged for stereoscopic viewing in a system of mirrors, *A, B,* and *C.* Mirrors *A* and *C* are supported at a 45° angle over the photographs so as to reflect their images toward the central mirror component *B.* In turn, the two mirrors on *B* reflect their images upward at the center of the system, maintaining stereo separation and permitting the user to view the imagery by looking down into *B*, one eye to each side, both eyes functioning simultaneously. A slight rotation, raising, or lowering of *B* facilitates the visual superimposition of images from the photos.

synopsis of land use and tenure of each of several hundred property parcels, relying exclusively on the air photos as a data base. Because the interviewing took place in a laboratory setting, the data could be transferred to indexed cards, permitting parcel-to-parcel comparisons and cross-checking of information sources. Later spot-checking of data on the ground proved the photo interpretation process to have been accurate as well as efficient. Indeed, it is hard to imagine how a comparably exhaustive survey of parcel use and tenure could have been collected by on-site techniques alone.

The conclusion to be drawn from the ʔApas land survey is perhaps self-evident. Aerial photographs can enormously enhance the data collection process only after an initial investment is made by both researcher and informants not only in photo interpretation but also in developing a vocabulary for discourse about both the photo image and the subject photographed. Air photos, while greatly enhancing data collection within a conceptualized framework, do not relieve the researcher of this initial and fundamentally ethnographic task.

Facilitating Tools for Census Materials

At its inception, those involved in the Chiapas air photo survey were concerned with developing techniques for analysis of the substantially increased volume of data on social organization that the air photos would afford. Evon Vogt and A. Kimball Romney (1971) anticipated direct use of the photo coverage for collection of anthropological census materials. Photographs of human settlements would provide an immediately interpretable data base for elicitation of exhaustive household-by-household censuses focusing on genealogical, economic, and other information. Romney (in press) was the first to formulate a system for the annotation of genealogical census materials that would be amenable to computer processing in a system which he illustrated with an exhaustive genealogical census of Aguacatenango. His system of algebraic notation of kinship relations proved to be instrumental to devising methods for the componential analysis of terminological systems then developing (Romney and

D'Andrade, 1964). Thus, there was a healthy awareness that air photo technology, by removing constraints on data collection, required new techniques of data analysis to permit the efficient flow of information through the analytic stages of research design.

The actual advent of the Tzotzil area photo coverage justified this early concern with the need for new analytic methods and tools, particularly in the study of demography and settlement patterns, as will be shown by a recapitulation of our first experiences in using air photos. From the beginning, we found that the air photos were most useful in ethnography when examined carefully with the Tzotzil informants, who helped to construct maps as accurate and complete as those we might have constructed by surveying and sketching on-site with a much greater expenditure of time and effort. We found the highly detailed vertical photos, such as that of ʔApas (Fig. 29), particularly useful for our research. In them we could see houses, trails, and cultivated lands, which led to the facile production of a sketch map of the hamlet (Fig. 30). Several additional days' work with a few selected informants from ʔApas allowed us, on the basis of the photo, to compile an exhaustive house-by-house census, to catalog ownership of several hundred garden plots, and to identify most of the community's sacred waterholes, mountains, caves, and cross shrines. This task for a village of 670 residents would otherwise have taken many weeks' time.

Impressed with the relative ease of census collection from air photos of ʔApas, we could contemplate research on more general problems of social organization in the Chiapas highlands. One such problem is the variation in settlement patterns that is characteristic of Tzotzil communities. The pattern in ʔApas, for instance, is much more compact than that of other Zinacanteco hamlets, and the relation of settlement variations to ecological factors, such as availability of land and water, and to sociological factors, such as local descent-group solidarity, is amenable to study by the method of controlled comparison. To this end, the air photos could provide a uniform basis for collecting large bodies of

George A. Collier

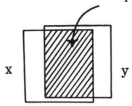

area of stereo overlap

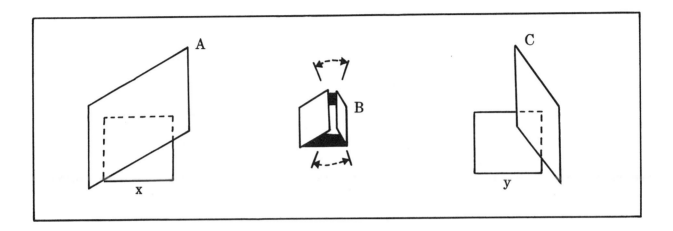

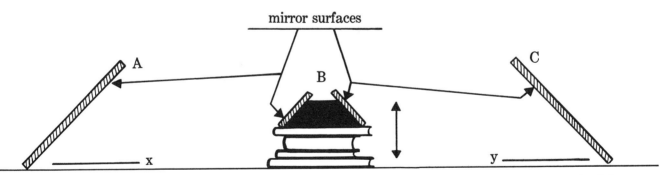

mirror surfaces

Fig. 28. Mirror system for full-frame stereoscopic viewing of a study area from stereoscopic photo pairs. Two photographs with overlapping imagery, *X* and *Y,* may be arranged for stereoscopic viewing in a system of mirrors, *A, B,* and *C.* Mirrors *A* and *C* are supported at a 45° angle over the photographs so as to reflect their images toward the central mirror component *B.* In turn, the two mirrors on *B* reflect their images upward at the center of the system, maintaining stereo separation and permitting the user to view the imagery by looking down into *B,* one eye to each side, both eyes functioning simultaneously. A slight rotation, raising, or lowering of *B* facilitates the visual superimposition of images from the photos.

synopsis of land use and tenure of each of several hundred property parcels, relying exclusively on the air photos as a data base. Because the interviewing took place in a laboratory setting, the data could be transferred to indexed cards, permitting parcel-to-parcel comparisons and cross-checking of information sources. Later spot-checking of data on the ground proved the photo interpretation process to have been accurate as well as efficient. Indeed, it is hard to imagine how a comparably exhaustive survey of parcel use and tenure could have been collected by on-site techniques alone.

The conclusion to be drawn from the ʔApas land survey is perhaps self-evident. Aerial photographs can enormously enhance the data collection process only after an initial investment is made by both researcher and informants not only in photo interpretation but also in developing a vocabulary for discourse about both the photo image and the subject photographed. Air photos, while greatly enhancing data collection within a conceptualized framework, do not relieve the researcher of this initial and fundamentally ethnographic task.

Facilitating Tools for Census Materials

At its inception, those involved in the Chiapas air photo survey were concerned with developing techniques for analysis of the substantially increased volume of data on social organization that the air photos would afford. Evon Vogt and A. Kimball Romney (1971) anticipated direct use of the photo coverage for collection of anthropological census materials. Photographs of human settlements would provide an immediately interpretable data base for elicitation of exhaustive household-by-household censuses focusing on genealogical, economic, and other information. Romney (in press) was the first to formulate a system for the annotation of genealogical census materials that would be amenable to computer processing in a system which he illustrated with an exhaustive genealogical census of Aguacatenango. His system of algebraic notation of kinship relations proved to be instrumental to devising methods for the componential analysis of terminological systems then developing (Romney and D'Andrade, 1964). Thus, there was a healthy awareness that air photo technology, by removing constraints on data collection, required new techniques of data analysis to permit the efficient flow of information through the analytic stages of research design.

The actual advent of the Tzotzil area photo coverage justified this early concern with the need for new analytic methods and tools, particularly in the study of demography and settlement patterns, as will be shown by a recapitulation of our first experiences in using air photos. From the beginning, we found that the air photos were most useful in ethnography when examined carefully with the Tzotzil informants, who helped to construct maps as accurate and complete as those we might have constructed by surveying and sketching on-site with a much greater expenditure of time and effort. We found the highly detailed vertical photos, such as that of ʔApas (Fig. 29), particularly useful for our research. In them we could see houses, trails, and cultivated lands, which led to the facile production of a sketch map of the hamlet (Fig. 30). Several additional days' work with a few selected informants from ʔApas allowed us, on the basis of the photo, to compile an exhaustive house-by-house census, to catalog ownership of several hundred garden plots, and to identify most of the community's sacred waterholes, mountains, caves, and cross shrines. This task for a village of 670 residents would otherwise have taken many weeks' time.

Impressed with the relative ease of census collection from air photos of ʔApas, we could contemplate research on more general problems of social organization in the Chiapas highlands. One such problem is the variation in settlement patterns that is characteristic of Tzotzil communities. The pattern in ʔApas, for instance, is much more compact than that of other Zinacanteco hamlets, and the relation of settlement variations to ecological factors, such as availability of land and water, and to sociological factors, such as local descent-group solidarity, is amenable to study by the method of controlled comparison. To this end, the air photos could provide a uniform basis for collecting large bodies of

Fig. 29. Aerial photomosaic of ʔApas, taken with HyAc panoramic camera.

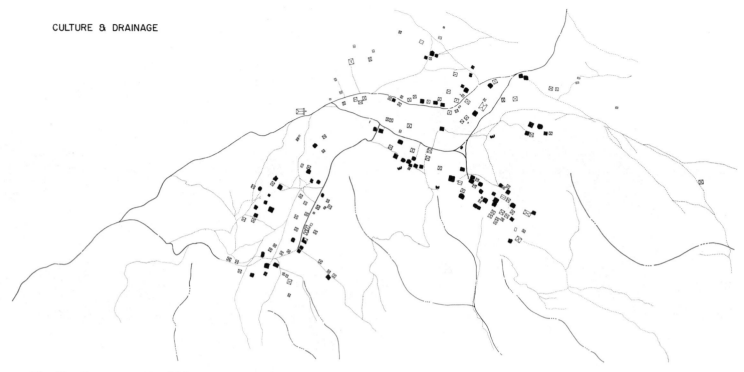

Fig. 30. Computer map of ʔApas.

data, which must be comparable from community to community in order to make statements about the determinants of settlement pattern and land use.

However, while the air photos hastened and improved data collection, they also produced the bottleneck of having to sort and analyze new masses of detail on demographic and settlement patterns. Hence, we turned to the computer to streamline this stage of the research, developing the Kinprogram to process census materials and to construct settlement pattern maps (George Collier 1969). A revised and expanded version of the Kinprogram for use on the IBM 360 system is available at Stanford University.

Anthropologists have made extensive use of genealogical trees to study the structure of kinship. Because kinship systems differ in their fundamental concepts of what kinship relations are, the methodology of kinship study has concentrated on techniques for elucidation of these concepts. To this end, genealogies representing biological kinship relations have functioned as a grid onto which native conceptions can be projected, and by which ancillary information on household composition and demography can be studied. Unfortunately, however, the complexities of genealogical tree construction have hampered anthropologists' attempts to collect such information for populations numbering more than a few hundred. The principal feature of the Kinprogram, the automatic construction of genealogical trees, made possible research utilizing such information for populations numbering up to three thousand.

The representation of biological kinship relations to the computer for processing was by means of a simple algorithm, suggested to me by Romney, focusing on the biological tie of a child to his parents. If all the individuals in a census corpus are numbered uniquely during census collection, it is easy to specify for the computer the number of each individual's father and mother, thereby completely cataloging the parent-child ties. From this specification other kinship relations involving strings of parent-child connections can be inferred. Siblings, for instance, will share in their specification of one or both parents, and the linkage of an individual to his parents

combined with the linkage of his parents to theirs connects that individual to his grandparents. Actually, all marital unions with offspring can be identified as the coincidence of the spouses' numbers in the parental specification of their children. Childless marriages can be symbolized by giving the couple a fictitious child whose number the computer can ignore except for the purpose of inferring marriage. Finally, specification of biological kinship by the algorithm is completed by assignment to individuals whose parentage is unknown—whose ancestors are long dead, for instance—dummy numbers for their father and mother.

Such a specification permits the total reconstruction of genealogies when tracing descent either patrilineally or matrilineally. Consider the problem of tracing patrilinial descent. As each individual has a real or a dummy father, one can trace *ascent* from him through the male line until encountering the unique dummy father defining the limits of knowledge of his patrilineal ancestry. Reversing the process, by tracing patrilineal *descent* from each dummy father, one is assured of including every individual of the census corpus in one, and only one, tree of patrilineal descent. The same logic applies to the problem of tracing matrilineal kinship.

The Kinprogram accepted as a data input this economical representation of biological kinship relations and from it produced as output genealogical trees made up of print characters selected to approximate best the highly redundant symbols that anthropologists are accustomed to using, as can be seen by comparison of a traditional hand-drawn genealogy with its Kinprogram counterpart (Fig. 31). In the first case, the redundant imagery facilitates comprehension of the genealogical tree. Siblings who are connected by a horizontal line also share at least one parent. Parents of a child may be married, as indicated by the = symbol. Generational differences appear both implicitly in the vertical array and explicitly in the parent-child connections. In the second case, however, it is the computer that has created the redundant imagery from the simplified data input, freeing the anthropologist for more productive chores.

Other Kinprogram features permitted the correlation

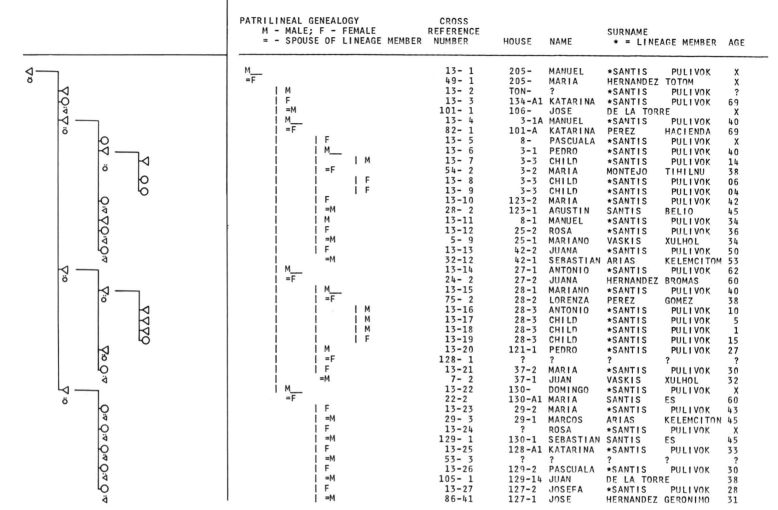

PATRILINEAL GENEALOGY M - MALE; F - FEMALE = - SPOUSE OF LINEAGE MEMBER	CROSS REFERENCE NUMBER	HOUSE	NAME	SURNAME * = LINEAGE MEMBER	AGE
M	13- 1	205-	MANUEL	*SANTIS PULIVOK	X
=F	49- 1	205-	MARIA	HERNANDEZ TOTOM	X
| M	13- 2	TON-	?	*SANTIS PULIVOK	?
| F	13- 3	134-A1	KATARINA	*SANTIS PULIVOK	69
| =M	101- 1	106-	JOSE	DE LA TORRE	X
| M	13- 4	3-1A	MANUEL	*SANTIS PULIVOK	40
| =F	82- 1	101-A	KATARINA	PEREZ HACIENDA	69
| | F	13- 5	8-	PASCUALA	*SANTIS PULIVOK	X
| | M	13- 6	3-1	PEDRO	*SANTIS PULIVOK	40
| | | M	13- 7	3-3	CHILD	*SANTIS PULIVOK	14
| | =F	54- 2	3-2	MARIA	MONTEJO TIHILNU	38
| | | F	13- 8	3-3	CHILD	*SANTIS PULIVOK	06
| | | F	13- 9	3-3	CHILD	*SANTIS PULIVOK	04
| | F	13-10	123-2	MARIA	*SANTIS PULIVOK	42
| | =M	28- 2	123-1	AGUSTIN	SANTIS BELIO	45
| | M	13-11	8-1	MANUEL	*SANTIS PULIVOK	34
| | F	13-12	25-2	ROSA	*SANTIS PULIVOK	36
| | =M	5- 9	25-1	MARIANO	VASKIS XULHOL	34
| | F	13-13	42-2	JUANA	*SANTIS PULIVOK	50
| | =M	32-12	42-1	SEBASTIAN	ARIAS KELEMCITOM	53
| M	13-14	27-1	ANTONIO	*SANTIS PULIVOK	62
| =F	24- 2	27-2	JUANA	HERNANDEZ BROMAS	60
| | M	13-15	28-1	MARIANO	*SANTIS PULIVOK	40
| | =F	75- 2	28-2	LORENZA	PEREZ GOMEZ	38
| | | M	13-16	28-3	ANTONIO	*SANTIS PULIVOK	10
| | | M	13-17	28-3	CHILD	*SANTIS PULIVOK	5
| | | M	13-18	28-3	CHILD	*SANTIS PULIVOK	1
| | | F	13-19	28-3	CHILD	*SANTIS PULIVOK	15
| | M	13-20	121-1	PEDRO	*SANTIS PULIVOK	27
| | =F	128- 1	?	?	? ?	?
| | F	13-21	37-2	MARIA	*SANTIS PULIVOK	30
| | =M	7- 2	37-1	JUAN	VASKIS XULHOL	32
| M	13-22	130-	DOMINGO	*SANTIS PULIVOK	X
| =F	22-2	130-A1	MARIA	SANTIS ES	60
| | F	13-23	29-2	MARIA	*SANTIS PULIVOK	43
| | =M	29- 3	29-1	MARCOS	ARIAS KELEMCITON	45
| | F	13-24	?	ROSA	*SANTIS PULIVOK	X
| | =M	129- 1	130-1	SEBASTIAN	SANTIS ES	45
| | F	13-25	128-A1	KATARINA	*SANTIS PULIVOK	33
| | =M	53- 3	?	?	? ?	?
| | F	13-26	129-2	PASCUALA	*SANTIS PULIVOK	30
| | =M	105- 1	129-14	JUAN	DE LA TORRE	38
| | F	13-27	127-2	JOSEFA	*SANTIS PULIVOK	28
| | =M	86-41	127-1	JOSE	HERNANDEZ GERONIMO	31

Fig. 31. Two genealogical trees, traditional hand-drawn, flipped sideways (on the left), and computer. The Kinprogram also constructs a cross-referencing number to index nonlineage individuals to their own genealogical trees.

of genealogical with other kinds of census data, the construction of settlement pattern maps, and automatic searches through the genealogical corpus. In their input, program users could specify information on name, age, and socioeconomic characteristics in addition to identifying an individual and his parents. The program would generate in the genealogical printout and on cards punched for each individual a label for him, including both the number of his genealogical tree and his sequential position within that tree. Lists of individuals' punched cards sorted by the additional variables were linked through this cross-referencing number to the genealogies and permitted the indexing of the genealogical corpus by alphabetized name, age, house number, and so forth.

The ʔApas census illustrates the Kinprogram feature of plotting settlement pattern maps. A base map of ʔApas was drawn using print characters to simulate the line-drawn map (Fig. 32; cf. Fig. 30). House locations within the base map, fed into the computer on punched cards, were specified by their coordinate position, permitting the computer to project onto the base map selective residential patterns. For instance, the map of a patrilineage of ʔApas is achieved with a computer-projected pattern of houses belonging to that lineage. The computer automatically constructed such a map for each lineage that it treated.

Finally, the Kinprogram user could ask the computer to generate lists of persons in certain kinship relations to each of several individuals by means of an algebraic notation adapted from Romney (in press). In the study of ʔApas farmland tenure, for instance, I could test the empirical validity of inheritance rules calling for the equal distribution of farm property by a man to his sons, by relying on the program to generate exhaustive lists of father-son sets.

To date, the full potential of the Kinprogram to facilitate analysis of the data on Tzotzil demography and settlement patterns collected from the air photo data base has not been realized. But it has been possible to arrive at some fundamental explanations of settlement pattern variations within hamlets such as ʔApas. There,

the degree of clustering of localized residential groups has been shown to be related to the process of patrilineage fission, causing the formation of local descent groups based on economic factors deriving from land inheritance (Collier and Bricker 1970; George Collier 1968). Yet the success of this study, to which both aerial photography and the Kinprogram were integral, has shown that our research plan for studying these patterns in the Tzotzil highlands by controlled comparison is practical, in spite of our limited human resources as researchers.

In the case of ʔApas, the Kinprogram serves as an example of an analytic tool designed to remove the constraints of conventional data-processing techniques that are incapable of the efficient transformation of the volume of information afforded by the air photo base. Exciting possibilities exist for the development of comparable tools for the study of other problems amenable to air photo interpretation. For instance, the potential of the Tzotzil highland photo coverage for the study of Tzotzil economic communications networks is marked, comparable to Skinner's study of Chinese market systems (1964, 1965), and the photo coverage should stimulate the development of appropriate programs for network system analysis. Thus, the aerial photographs, by demanding that we restructure our research designs, serve as a lodestone to challenge us to explore new anthropological frontiers.

The Problem of Scale in Ecological Analysis

In many of the hard-science disciplines, technological innovations are the initial stimulus for new concepts and new bodies of theory. In the last three decades, for instance, information theory, dealing with information sources and communication channels (Abramson 1963), developed in direct response to the needs of the burgeoning communications industry. The limited experience with air photo technology for ethnography has not resulted in new bodies of theory, but there are a few areas in which the use of photographs to cope with seemingly restricted research problems has brought into

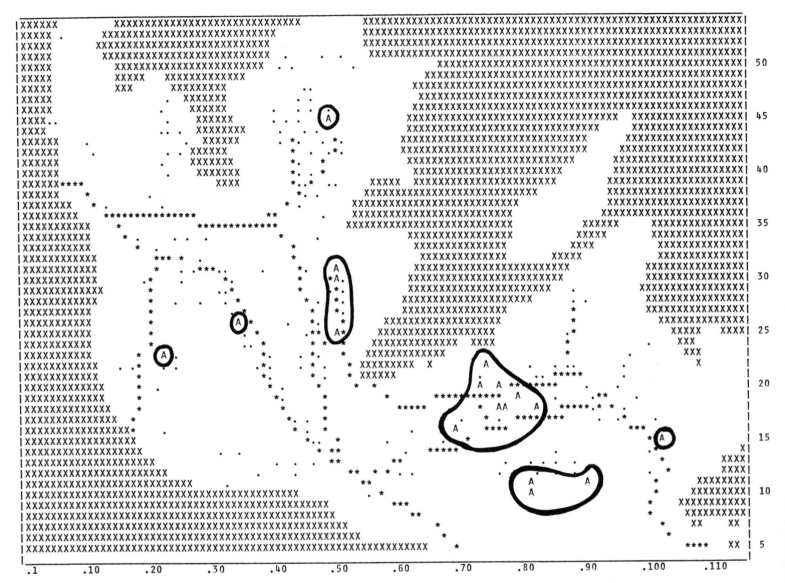

MAP OF APAS. SYMBOLS: XX = UNINHABITABLE AREA; . = HOUSES; ** = TRAILS; HOUSES OF THE PRECEDING LINEAGE LISTED ARE REPLACED BY THE CHARACTER A.

Fig. 32. Computer map of settlement patterns of ʔApas. When the Kinprogram is supplied with a base map of characters illustrating the settlement area, and the houses are identified by their coordinates on the map, the Kinprogram prints a map for each genealogical tree, showing where lineage members live by inserting an *A* at the location of their house. This map represents the lineage appearing in Fig. 31.

George A. Collier

sharp focus conceptual problems of a more general nature. An example comes from an ecological survey of the Tzotzil municipio of Chamula, which my wife and I recently completed. We discovered that a positive relationship between two variables characterizing survey units of one size might be negated or reversed when the size of the survey unit was changed. In other words, we had to confront the problem that in ecological analysis, statements of interrelation are dependent on scale, a problem that has its analogue in other fields as well, as in linguistic, economic, and cross-cultural analysis.

The aerial photos offered a unique opportunity to make an exhaustive study of ecological patterns in Chamula. Using enlarged high-resolution prints of the entire municipio, we laid onto them a grid pattern dividing the region into squares of roughly ten-acre size. We examined and rated each square on the photos as to the percentage of tree and scrub coverage, the number of houses, the intensity of trails, the placement of property boundaries, and the amount of erosion. The ratings were spot-checked on the ground for accuracy. Although the process of data collection was mechanical and time consuming, it would have been impossible without the use of aerial photographs to make an exhaustive evaluation of these variables over the Chamula landscape.

Because the data units were of an arbitrarily small size, they numbered in the thousands. To facilitate preliminary analysis, we contemplated the construction of variables for larger data units by consolidating the data of several smaller constituent units. But the question arose as to how large these larger data units should be. The beauty of the data collected from the small units was that they provided an almost photographic evaluation of the microvariations of Chamula ecological features over space. By combining the small data units into larger ones, microvariations would be averaged out, and important microenvironmental relationships might be obscured. The disadvantages of averaging would be proportional to the size of the analytic unit selected: the larger the unit, the more microenvironmental features it would obscure.

This realization led us to consider more carefully the problems implicit in ecological analysis. We recognized that the questions we wished to broach were both macroenvironmental and microenvironmental. Yet if we selected analytic units that were too large, we would obscure microenvironmental variations in the ecology. Generalizations about large environmental blocks would ignore important microvariations within blocks. In effect, we would be looking at the woods but not the trees. Conversely, data units that were small enough to capture the important microenvironmental variations would not allow us to focus on macroenvironmental variations of intrinsic importance. We would not be seeing the woods for the trees.

That these problems are real can be illustrated by the results from a preliminary analysis of a portion of the Chamula data using analytic units of varying size (Fig. 33). The largest analytic unit is called the matrix, each matrix corresponding to the rectangular block containing thirty-six of the smallest data units. The unit of intermediate size is the matrix quadrant, each quadrant containing nine of the smallest data units. The smallest unit is the original data unit itself.

In the original survey, each small data unit had been rated as to the number of houses it contained, the density of its trees, and the intensity of its trails. For each matrix and each quadrant, three variables were recomputed from their values for the small constituent units by simple addition. Contingency tables were constructed for each of the analytic scales to show the interrelationships between house density, on the one hand, and tree and trail intensity, on the other (Table 1).

The contingency tables show that at the microenvironmental level, using the smaller data unit for analysis, tree and house coverage are negatively related. Houses appear overwhelmingly in data units where tree coverage is minimal. This relationship holds true at about the same strength when the quadrant is used for analysis. But when the matrix is the analytic unit, the relationship almost disappears. Apparently Chamulas eliminate forest growth in the environments immediately around their settlements, but not necessarily over the landscape at large.

Demography and Ecology in Highland Chiapas

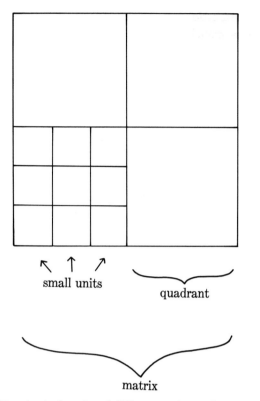

small units

quadrant

matrix

Fig. 33. Analytic units of different scale employed in preliminary examination of Chamula survey data.

Conversely, the relationship between houses and trails is almost nonexistent when sought out at the level of the smallest analytic data unit. But at the quadrant scale of analysis it appears that houses and trails are moderately correlated, and when the matrix-size data unit is analyzed, this relationship is strong. It would appear that the networks of trails facilitate the relation of human settlements to their broader environment, not just to the nearby lands. The relationship between tree and house coverage, then, appears to be a microenvironmental feature, which emerges only when microenvironmental units are examined, while the relationship between houses and trails is a macroenvironmental feature, which would not be perceived by examining the smallest data units.

To generalize, the interrelations between any two given variables may be scale-related; in other words, they are best perceived when one, not another scale of analysis is selected. The scale of analysis that is optimal for the interrelation of any two variables may not be optimal for perceiving the interrelation between any other pair of variables. Methodologically, the problem of ecological analysis is inherently complicated by the problem of scale. The only discovery procedure which guarantees that all the important variable interrelations implicit in an ecological survey will be found is the very cumbersome one of searching for each possible variable interrelation at every possible scale of analysis.

Conceptually, this means that there is no easy route to an adequate ecological description which will necessarily encompass complex statements of variable interrelations at a number of analytic scales. Statements about variations in regional agricultural productivity, for instance, must be cognizant of both macroscale phenomena, such as altitude and rainfall, and microscale phenomena, such as erosion, proximity to human settlements, and fertility.

This methodological problem is not confined to the study of cultural ecology. In linguistics, it is possible to interpret the analytic construct of the phoneme as a scale-related construct. By analogy, the early studies of

90

Table 1. Interrelationships between house density and tree and trail density.

	Analytic unit used								
	Small			Quadrant			Matrix		
	Tree coverage				Tree coverage				Tree coverage	
	0–25%	26% or more			0–10%	11% or more			0–10%	11% or more
0	1184	398	0–3		78	48	0–7		7	9
	(−73)[a]	(+73)			(−9)	(+9)			(−1)	(+1)
Houses			Houses				Houses			
1 or more	562	55	4 or more		58	13	8 or more		9	7
	(+73)	(−73)			(+9)	(−9)			(+1)	(−1)
	$\varphi = 0.184$				$\varphi = 0.206$				$\varphi = 0.125$	

	Trail intensity score				Trail intensity score				Trail intensity score	
	0	1 or more			0–8	9 or more			0–29	30 or more
0	752	830	0–3		89	34	0–11		11	5
	(+22)	(−22)			(+8)	(−8)			(+2.5)	(−2.5)
Houses			Houses				Houses			
1 or more	259	356	4 or more		39	32	12 or more		6	10
	(−22)	(+22)			(−8)	(+8)			(−2.5)	(+2.5)
	$\varphi = 0.048$[b]				$\varphi = 0.182$				$\varphi = 0.312$	

a. Parentheses indicate deviations from expected values computed from margins.

b. φ = four-fold point correlation = $\sqrt{\dfrac{\chi^2}{N}}$

phonology were microenvironmental studies, which failed to perceive the woods for the trees. The construct of the phoneme was a breakthrough in macrophonological perception. In economic description, to give another example, it is all too often glibly assumed that an area is marginal for agriculture, forgetting that the concept of marginality is necessarily scale-related. Land that may be marginal to a regional economy may be brought under productive cultivation within the context of a local economy nested within the broader regional one. Thus, the concept of marginality may again confuse the woods for the trees. Finally, the methodology of cross-cultural comparison that seeks validation of cross-cultural inferences from controlled comparison and from intracultural data has given implicit recognition to the problem of scale.

In retrospect, it may seem that the problem of scale in ecological analysis should always have been obvious. However, it became obvious only when the luxury of efficient data collection from aerial photos permitted microvariations in ecology to be plotted over an entire region. Thus, just as the computer revolutionized the field of statistics by eliminating the burdens of data manipulation, aerial photos are permitting methodological and conceptual advances, freed from preoccupation with adequate data collection.

During my first seasons of field work in Chiapas, I traveled frequently on the Pan-American Highway, which traverses Zinacantan by a serpentine climbing route. Many times I noticed from a distance of several miles a small, ranchlike cluster of dwellings, which seemed linked to the highway by a secondary road, but I was never able to locate the actual road junction. When aerial photographs became available in 1964, I was astonished to discover that the cluster was on the highway itself, and that I had traveled through it thirty or forty times without ever connecting its image at close quarters with that from afar. This minor experience mirrors the general impact of air photography on our research in ecology and demography. In both cases, the mental maps of the routes traversed have been transformed by the new vantage points afforded by photography. Moreover, the transformation is still taking place, as we gradually adapt our research strategies to the air-photo medium.

In addition to the specific instances where data collection techniques, analytic devices, and concepts were pushed in new directions by the Chiapas photo coverage, such coverage has an important general characteristic of influence on demographic and ecological research. This is the stimulus of photography on the researcher to collect total samples, which exhaust the universe of data under study. The reason that air photos facilitate the collection of total samples is obvious. Once data collection tools have been adapted to the photo medium, data collection is extremely rapid, and the additional increment of effort required to exhaust the universe, after a sample adequate in size for a given research goal has been collected, is small.

Yet the collection of universe-exhausting samples has special implications. For one, a sample that exhausts a data universe can stand as a resource against which to project a variety of research problems, not just the one for which research was conceived. Second, the existence of exhaustive sample data eliminates the need for certain kinds of statistical inference. For instance, the researcher can be concerned directly with statistical measures of the strength of the relationship between variables characterizing the universe, thereby avoiding the inferential use of significance tests to determine whether characteristics of a partial sample are likely to pertain to the universe.

In the same vein, exhaustive samples offer the potential for research into the validity of statistical inference from populations whose parameters do not clearly match those assumed by a given statistical model. By simulating the selection of partial samples from known total samples, one may gain fundamental knowledge about the permissible limits of inference from classical statistical models when their underlying assumptions are not fully met.

Finally, the possibility of collecting exhaustive data samples will encourage the development of formal models for describing whole systems, not just parts of systems. Because so many anthropological models for whole systems do not stand up to the requirements of formalization, this channel may be the most significant one by which aerial photography ultimately influences developments in the field of anthropology.

This research was facilitated by a National Science Foundation predoctoral fellowship and, later, by United States Public Health Service Predoctoral Fellowship MH–32,736.

Richard Price
Aerial Photography in the Study of Land Use: A Maya Example

During the summer of 1965, my wife and I conducted field research on the social organization of Muktahok, a community of Tzotzil-speaking highland Maya Indians in Chiapas, Mexico (Price and Price 1970). In the following summer, we brought this background knowledge of the community to bear on an investigation of local patterns of land use. With the aid of detailed air photos, it proved possible to complete a rather comprehensive survey of land use practices in a relatively brief time.

The community of Muktahok lies on a mountain ridge at an elevation of 5,400 feet, facing the Grijalva lowlands to the south and the Pan American Highway, a precipitous twenty-minute walk away, to the north (Figs. 34, 35). In 1965, Muktahok had a population of two hundred—all Zinacanteco Indians—and included thirty-nine households, a one-room school, and a chapel. Surrounding the community are 1,224 hectares of rugged ejido—land taken from large landowners and given to landless communities in a reform program with origins in the Mexican Revolution (see Edel 1966). The ejido provides the people of Muktahok with their water sources, wood for cooking fires, grazing land for horses, most of their farmland, and house plots (Fig. 36).

Our technical resources for the study included two kinds of photographic coverage provided by the Harvard Chiapas Project: RC–9 cartographic print enlargements at an image scale of approximately 1:20,000, each of which covers an area about eight times that of the Muktahok ejido, and high-acuity panoramic (HyAc) contact prints at a scale of approximately 1:1,250, of which eight strips along each of two flight lines are necessary to cover the ejido. After several days of familiarizing myself and a Muktahok informant with photo analysis by walking large tracts of land with HyAc contact prints in hand, we moved indoors to a makeshift office where we charted the boundaries of the ejido and its various zones on the HyAcs and RC–9s, a task that took another several days. We then began estimating the current state of each field (one year fallow, two years fallow, and so forth) on the basis of enlarged HyAc prints and HyAc contact prints viewed through portable stereoscopic glasses. These estimates from photos were then systematically checked by walking the fields with informants, often the farmer himself, and judging their current state from the ground. Thirty-two of the thirty-five estimates made from the photos in different parts of the ejido were within one year of the ground estimates. Given these encouraging results, I decided to proceed with an enumeration of the state of every field in the ejido on the basis of photos.

Including occasional ground checks in areas with unusual terrain, this program was completed in less than a week, working full time with a highly competent informant. I must stress that my own abilities to make accurate discriminations were far inferior to those of my principal

Fig. 34. Stereogram of part of the Muktahok ejido, constructed from two HyAc contact prints, showing the
community of Muktahok (top left of left-hand strip).

Aerial Photography of Land Use

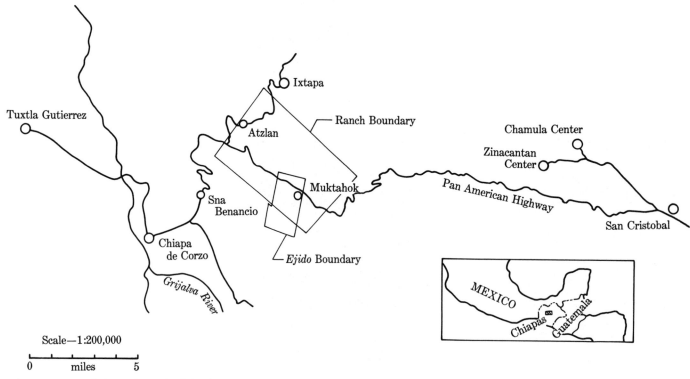

Scale—1:200,000

0   miles   5

Fig. 35. Map of the Muktahok ejido, former ranch boundaries, and nearby towns.

informant. Fields that to me looked alike in the photos seemed "obviously" different to him as soon as he had noted through the stereo viewer differences in slope, rockiness, and so forth. However, looking at photos without the stereo viewer, he was as unable as I to make consistent discriminations. An intimate knowledge of the ecology of the different zones of the ejido helped him greatly. Often, for example, a field of wild grass was distinguishable from maize only because of his prior knowledge of the area. Without stereo pairs and an intelligent informant who was also a successful local farmer, this whole project could not have been carried out.

To move from the completed estimates, written out on enlarged HyAc prints of the ejido, to numerical analyses of the current stage of cultivation of fields required correcting in a rough-and-ready way for the considerable distortion in the photos, owing to such factors as slope and camera angle. These adjustments were facilitated by engineers' surveys made at the time when the lands were granted to the community. Although for present purposes the inexactness of these corrections does not seem serious, a more detailed analysis of land use would require that corrections be based on better ground control.

Without air photos, estimates of the state of Muktahok ejido fields would have required many months, and in the end they might well have proved less accurate. Many fields in the ejido are set in extremely rugged terrain and covered with thick growth; to distinguish boundaries and shapes or judge areas, not to mention mere walking, are

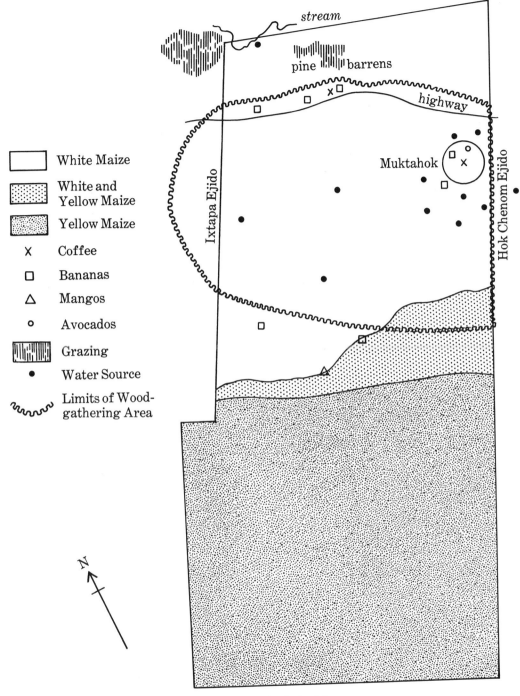

Legend

	White Maize
	White and Yellow Maize
	Yellow Maize
X	Coffee
□	Bananas
△	Mangos
o	Avocados
	Grazing
•	Water Source
	Limits of Wood-gathering Area

stream

pine barrens

highway

Ixtapa Ejido

Muktahok

Hok Chenom Ejido

N

Fig. 36. Patterns of land exploitation in the Muktahok ejido.

often remarkably difficult. Aerial photos, then, provided a relatively simple means of gathering data that with more traditional methods would probably have had to remain untouched.

Types of Land Exploitation

Maize completely overshadows in importance every other crop grown in Muktahok. Eaten at every meal and figuring importantly in ritual, it is also marketed in San Cristóbal, Chiapa de Corzo, and Tuxtla, and provides the only source of income to most local families. At least 75 percent of the annual harvest, and in some years more than 95 percent, is reaped in the Muktahok ejido; the rest is grown in Hot Country, on lands rented from Ladinos in the plain near Chiapa de Corzo. Maize prices fluctuate greatly during the course of the year, but the average is about $8 US per *fanega*—approximately 130 kilos (Cancian 1965b:295). The mean gross annual income from maize is approximately $85 US per farmer, with the most successful men grossing about $300 US.

Coffee, which is grown close by the houses of Muktahok, is the only other crop regularly marketed for cash. However, most men sell no more than $8 US annually, with the bulk of the harvest saved for home consumption. The other foods grown in the ejido—squash, mangos, avocados, bananas, and formerly beans—are sold only rarely.

Muktahok women draw their water supply from eleven waterholes, situated at five- to twenty-five-minute walks from the houses, as well as from the stream that flows below the Pan American Highway. Waterholes belong to the community as a whole. When all but one dry up in late autumn, water is rationed, with an equal share being given to each married woman every other day. From February until May or June, the waterholes are all dry, and women must carry their entire water supply from the stream, which is an hour away.

Firewood is the only cooking fuel in Muktahok, and women must replenish the household supply several times each week. During January and February, when the secondary growth in the fallow fields is felled prior to burning, the women are allowed to gather wood anywhere in the ejido. At other times, however, a woman may gather only in her husband's plots or in those belonging to the husband of a woman with whom she is gathering wood. By the time a woman is married, she has learned to stagger her woodcutting activities and to cut only the large, dry pieces, so as to avoid depleting any one area.

Many families own a horse or two, which may be staked temporarily in the patches of hay surrounding the community. Normally, however, small horses are kept in the sparse pastures of the ejido pine barrens, while larger ones roam in pasture rented in the ejido of Ixtapa, at $0.40 US per horse per year.

The Agricultural Cycle

The maize cycle in the ejido begins in late December or early January, when men fell the secondary growth with axes and billhooks. This work requires approximately twelve man days per hectare (hereafter mdph). During the second week in April, when the stumps and brush have dried thoroughly, the men burn each field, keeping the blaze from spreading by a firebreak two meters wide (about 2 mdph). They seed the fields during the first week in May, and reseed if necessary after the rains have commenced, eight or ten days later (4–6 mdph).

By mid-June, the men begin to weed the *planada* fields with hoes (12–13 mdph). Planadas in the Muktahok ejido are the particularly flat areas, never very large, which are used relatively intensively, and in which the growth of wild grass frequently poses a threat to productive maize farming. Although they are distributed throughout the ejido, they are treated as a single zone by the Muktahok farmers, because of such factors as their similar terrain, fallow cycle, and yield (zone X in Fig. 37).

In August, the men move on to the more extensive rocky fields, which can be cleaned only with billhooks (9–10 mdph). This is the most intensive period of work in the agricultural cycle, for the weeding must be completed before the end of the month if the crop is to grow well. Men with many hectares planted often must hire wage labor to finish the job in time. Once the rocky

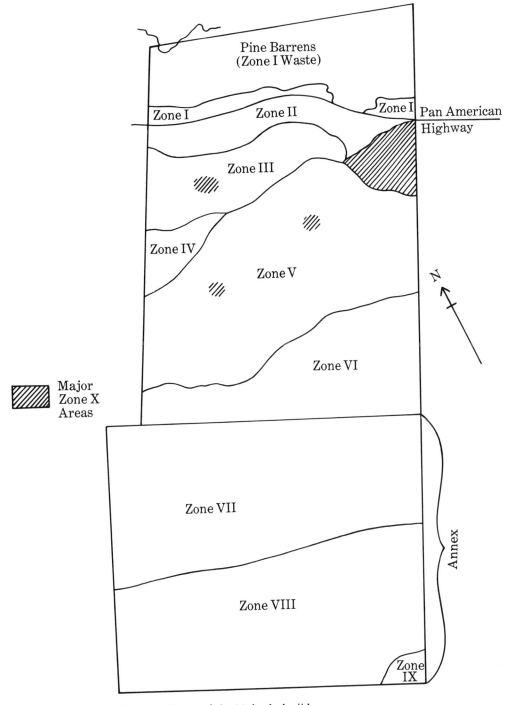

Fig. 37. Zones of the Muktahok ejido.

Within the figure:

Pine Barrens
(Zone I Waste)

Zone I   Zone II   Zone I   Pan American Highway

Zone III

Zone IV   Zone V

Zone VI

N

Major Zone X Areas

Zone VII

Annex

Zone VIII

Zone IX

terrain has been cleaned, the flat planada areas need a quick second weeding, often with billhooks rather than the more time-consuming but more effective hoes.

In September, when the weeding is finished, farmers usually hold a ceremony in each field of a hectare or more in size. A ritual specialist is hired, and a ceremonial meal is offered later in the house. In October, they "double" the stalks of maize to speed drying and to keep them from rotting (2 mdph). In late December or early January, the cycle begins again, with the felling of secondary growth for the next year's fields. When the moon reaches the first quarter in February, this task is interrupted for the harvest, which goes on intensively until the waning moon reaches the third quarter. The men then go back to felling secondary growth until the moon again reaches the first quarter, when they may complete the harvest (3–4 mdph). In zones VII, VIII, and IX (Fig. 37) the maize is shelled in the fields (3 mdph) and transported by horses (2 mdph). In nearer areas, the whole ears are taken back to each farmer's storage bin.

The agricultural calendar for maize in the rented fields in Hot Country differs slightly from that for the ejido lands. Because Muktahok men farm only those Hot Country fields nearest the community, they must be willing to plant the same land year after year. Each April, after burning their ejido fields, groups of men clear the stubble and weeds in their Hot Country fields with billhooks (2–3 mdph). Several days later, they return to burn the piles of refuse, which can be done in a single day, since firebreaks are rarely necessary. In late May, after the ejido planting has been completed, the same seeding procedure is used in Hot Country (only 2 mdph, because the land is flat and relatively free of rocks). In mid-June, men weed these fields, first with hoes (12 mdph), and later usually with billhooks, as in zone X of the ejido. In October the stalks are doubled, and in November or December, men harvest the crop, following the moon's phases, as in the ejido, unless the field is particularly small. The harvest never requires more than a few days' work, and the maize is transported by truck to Muktahok.

Coffee trees demand minimal care, requiring only an occasional weeding with hoe or billhook. Men pick the berries in late January and early February, without following the phases of the moon. They gather 25–30 kilos of unhulled coffee per man day. Formerly, they hulled the coffee by pounding it with rocks, but now they use a hand-powered machine, bought second-hand by one of the men. The coffee is then soaked in water for three days, washed carefully in the river, and laid out to dry on mats in the sun for five to six days.

Three varieties of beans used to be planted at the same time as the maize, with one variety in zone X areas, a second variety in zone III, and a third in zones VII and VIII under the tall trees. All were harvested in December, however, before the maize was ready to be picked. Beginning several years ago, bean yields fell off suddenly, and no beans have been planted for the past two years. Squash, which grows only in ant hills, is also planted in May, and it ripens in November or December.

The Recent History of the Land

Pre-1935 Farming Patterns. Until 1935, Muktahok was one of a number of hamlets that belonged to a vast ranch (Fig. 35). Each man gave one week's labor per month to ranch agriculture under the supervision of Ladino overseers employed by the owner. In return, the men were free to grow maize on any of the marginal lands not used for the profit of the ranch, which concentrated more on sugar cane, coffee, and livestock, and only secondarily on maize. The land that was later granted to Muktahok as an ejido was never farmed by the ranch, and the men of Muktahok planted their maize both there and in the richer bottomland around Aztlan. The current ejido was farmed less intensively then than it is now, and the presence of high secondary growth contributed to much better yields. Although men were free to farm as much land as they wished, the total area

Richard Price

planted per man was approximately the same as it is today. Very little coffee was grown by individuals before the expropriation of the ranch, apparently because the possible profits were outweighed by the risk that, in the wake of fighting, alleged laziness, or insubordination and before the crop was in, the owner would send the worker back to Zinacantan, whence the men had originally come because of the availability of better land, and that the worker would thereby lose his investment.

The Original Ejido. In 1935, after all the official documents had been signed and stamped and the surveyor's map deposited in the care of the president of the local Ejido Commission, the thirty ejido members faced the task of dividing their 696 hectares. Walking the area as a group, they first marked off five main zones of relatively homogeneous land quality (Fig. 37). Then measuring with a 30-*brazada* (armspan) rope, except in zone I where plots were 20 brazadas wide, they marked off thirty parcels—one for each man—in each of the zones. In addition, the scattered flat areas or planadas throughout the ejido were apportioned as a separate zone, with each man receiving a 40 × 40 brazada piece. The operative principle here was to allot strictly identical portions to each man, a principle that is today carried to its greatest extreme in communal bull butchering. For example, should forty-seven men purchase and slaughter a bull together, not only each type of meat but every organ is divided into forty-seven pieces, which are painstakingly equalized on a balance amidst much good-natured altercation.

In three different areas of the ejido, blocks of land were left undivided for eventual distribution to sons, as they came of age. With the fields separated into five zones and only thirty men, it was apparently not difficult to balance such factors as land quality and proximity to the village, as well as to allow brothers, fathers, and sons, or others who wished, to have adjoining or nearby fields. Although the men of Muktahok now owned their own land

for the first time, its total area was somewhat less than that to which they had been accustomed on the ranch. It was at this time, then, that the practice of renting small fields in Hot Country began. In fact, the land that twenty years later would be annexed to the ejido was at this time among the more popular rented areas, because of its proximity.

The Annex. Beginning in the late 1940s, the men of Muktahok began petitioning for an addition to their original grant, since the number of ejido members had increased considerably. In 1954, after countless trips by the community's officials, often on foot, to Chiapa de Corzo as well as Tuxtla, an additional 528 hectares contiguous to the original ejido was granted. Because of the cost of sending delegations, securing legal advice, and so forth, several men from the nearby hamlets of Zinacantan were permitted to join the group. In addition, the names of several men who resided elsewhere and had nothing to do with the ejido were "borrowed" to dramatize Muktahok's land shortage to unsuspecting officials in Tuxtla.

At the time that the men set out once again to measure individual parcels on this new land, it was in a very uneven state, as it had been farmed by renters from Muktahok and elsewhere right up to the time of the grant. From the beginning, therefore, part of each plot in the new area was farmed one year, and part the next, depending on the height of the secondary growth. The new land was divided into three portions: two large zones, with most men receiving a 30-brazada width in each zone (though some received two plots in one of the zones instead), and one tiny area (zone IX), which was farmed in common the first year for the benefit of the school but has since been divided into 8 × 8 brazada plots.

The Ejido Today

Today the ejido is divided into the seven original zones and the three zones of the 1954 annex. As the original divisions were chosen to achieve maximal homogeneity of land quality within each zone, the considerable ecological variations in the total area are reflected largely in differences among zones (Table 2). Although a specialist could no doubt make many finer distinctions, some general observations should help to highlight the characteristics of each zone.

The elevations of the zones (Fig. 38) present perhaps the most dramatic variation, influencing, for example, whether white maize (grown above about 4,400 feet) or yellow maize (grown below about 4,800 feet) shall be planted. In fact, this distinction may be more cultural than strictly ecological, since both white and yellow maize are grown by some Zinacantecos in Hot Country (Frank Cancian, personal communication). The same distinction is nevertheless also made in the Zinacanteco hamlet of ʔApas (George A. Collier, personal communication.)

The number of limestone outcroppings and the degree of rockiness in general, both of which factors vary from one zone to another, not only influence the yield per hectare but also determine whether hoe or billhook is to be used for cultivation. The informants distinguished three degrees of rockiness in the ejido (Table 2).

Because of the overall ruggedness of the terrain, it proved more difficult to achieve homogeneity of slope when the zonal divisions were made than it did for other factors, such as rockiness. Nonetheless, certain distinctions are clear. Four of the zones are relatively flat or gently rolling; the planada zone is almost totally flat; the other five zones include extensive slopes of 30° or more, with zones VII and VIII being traversed by several deep gullies, along the sides of which the steepest fields of all are planted.

Finally, the percentage of unarable land varies by zone (Table 2). Large trees, particularly above the highway and along the beds of deep gullies in the annexed land, cannot be felled without the permission of the Department of Forestry, which is always withheld. And many patches of wild grass, which are particularly extensive at the lower elevations, are completely unusable for farming. Thus, for example, the partitioning of the annexed land, in spite of attempts to be fair, left many individuals with a high percentage of unusable land. These and no doubt other influences, such as soil composition, contribute to a definite variation in yield by zones.

The Fallow Cycle

A seven-year fallow cycle of one year of planting followed by six years of rest is the general rule in the Muktahok ejido. In 1963, for example, the community as a whole let only 3 percent of arable land lie fallow for more than six years (Table 3). Fields in zones VI, VII, and VIII may be planted when the secondary growth is only four years old with respectable yields, but these fields are almost always left fallow for five and usually six years before re-use, because of an increase in yield of approximately 50 percent with the extra two-year wait. Many men plant a second time small portions of a field that they have planted the year before, but only if the field originally lay fallow at least six years. Second-year yields in these cases are 60 percent lower than the previous harvest, but the work involved is minimal, since no clearing is necessary, and men often sow such small plots in addition to their usual first-year fields. In zones I–V, fields are always left fallow at least five years, and few areas are left more than six years. These fields are never planted for more than a single year. The scattered fields of zone X form an exception, being more intensively farmed. They may be used after only two or three years' rest and are often planted a second year, with a decrease in yield of 30–50 percent, if the soil has not been unusually exhausted and wild grass has not already taken over, in which case they may have to be left six years or more. Instead of farming their more fertile plots earlier, which would produce more uniform yields throughout the ejido, Muktahok men choose a uniform fallow cycle (with the exception of fields in zone X) in return for higher yields on the better lands. In fact, the current ratio of yield per hectare planted to number of years fallow in the annexed lands (approximately four fanegas after a four-year rest and six fanegas after six years) would quickly decrease with the repetition of a four-year cycle.

Table 2. Ecological features by zone.

Land feature	Zone									
	I	II	III	IV	V	VI	VII	VIII	IX	X
Slope	Steep	Steep	Flat	Flat	Flat	Steep	Steep	Steep	Flat	Flat
Rockiness[a]	Billhook	Billhook	Both	Both	Billhook	Billhook	Billhook	Billhook	Hoe	Hoe
Mean Elevation[b]	4850	5200	5375	5250	5100	4350	3800	3200	2675	5375
Wasteland	83%[c]	22%	0%	3%	6%	6%	22%	49%	87%	27%[d]
Mean yield[e]	3.5	3.5	3.5	3	4.5	5	5.5	5.5	3.5	3

a. The tool used in weeding was taken as the index of rockiness: hoes are used only in fields with relatively few rocks; billhooks are used in particularly rocky areas.

b. Altimeter readings were taken at forty points around the ejido that were located on the aerial photos. These were used in conjunction with stereoscopically viewed aerial photos to estimate mean elevations by zone.

c. This wasteland covers 149 hectares of pine barrens that were not divided for use. The area used for farming in this zone has no wasteland.

d. This "wasteland" cannot be farmed only because it is used for houses.

e. Yields are given in fanegas harvested per *almud* planted: a 4-fanega harvest represents a return of roughly 50:1 on seed (one fanega is equal to twelve almudes; see Cancian 1965a:65). Mean yields were estimated with yield figures for several plots in each zone and, because the sampling was not extensive, were further adjusted on the basis of discussions with informants.

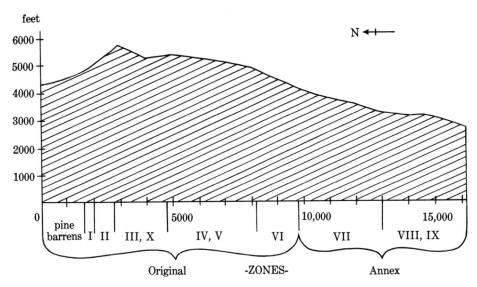

feet

Fig. 38. Elevations of zones of the Muktahok ejido.

Analysis of the aerial photos reveals that the acreage of maize planted in each zone varies considerably from one year to the next. For example, zone VI had only 6 percent of its area in maize in 1962, but 28 percent in 1963—and this is not atypical. I would suggest tentatively that this variation is largely a function of the diversity from one zone to another in readiness to be planted at the time of acquisition. It is even possible that the choice of zonal boundaries, intended to assure homogeneity of land quality within each zone, was also influenced by the differential readiness for planting. Given these variations at the time of acquisition, it is easy to see how a relatively uniform fallow cycle could have perpetuated them until the present.

There may also be significant though less marked annual variations in the *total* ejido acreage planted. In 1963, for example, the annexed land included a most unusual amount of land lying two years fallow (Table 3). Extremely heavy planting of the relatively fertile annex in its first year of operation, 1954, is clearly indicated by this figure. With a seven-year fallow cycle, these fields would have been planted a second time in 1961 and

would thus have been two years fallow in 1963, when the aerial photographs were taken. This eagerness to use the annexed land apparently resulted in a greater than 52 percent use of that area's arable land during the first two years, leaving only 5 percent ready for planting the third year.

In general, if a perfectly uniform fallow cycle of seven years is assumed, it is clear that the amount of land which is currently in maize, lying fallow one year, and so forth in any zone would be exactly the same as the amount seven years ago or seven years hence. The land use in zone VII in 1963 can be projected through time according to these assumptions (Fig. 39). The field data suggest that actual patterns of farming approach this hypothetical model. Fallow cycles are of course not always seven years long, but in eliciting data from informants on the number of years when fields in each zone were actually cut, I found no factors that would systematically bias the cycle by zone. For example, an individual often happens one year to have few plots that have been lying fallow for six years, so he decides to slash and burn prematurely one of his five-year fallow plots. He must choose among his

Richard Price

Table 3. Hectares in maize, one to ten years fallow, and wasteland in each zone, 1963.

Zone	M	1	2	3	4	5	6	7	8	9	10	W	Total
I	0	0	3	0	14	0	13	0	0	0	0	149	179
II	0	3	1	2	8	3	32	4	1	0	1	15	70
III	4	7	4	4	11	4	17	0	0	0	0	0	51
IV	2	3	5	1	6	2	0	2	0	0	0	0	21
V	23	21	25	28	29	44	34	4	8	0	0	14	230
VI	34	8	24	29	9	7	3	0	0	0	0	7	121
X	7	4	3	1	2	0	1	0	0	0	0	6	24
Total original ejido	70	46	65	65	79	60	100	10	9	0	1	191	696
VII	28	37	81	47	6	0	5	3	0	0	0	58	265
VIII	9	12	39	15	12	11	29	3	1	0	0	124	255
IX	0	0	0	0	0	0	0	0	0	0	1	7	8
Total annex	37	49	120	62	18	11	34	6	1	0	1	189	528
Total ejido	107	95	185	127	97	71	134[a]	16	10	0	2	380	1224

a. The variation in total fields lying five and six years fallow seems to be largely a function of the informant's tendency to favor the higher of the two numbers when in doubt, owing to his awareness of the general fallow cycle rule—one year in maize, six years fallow. These figures should probably be more evenly distributed between the two years.

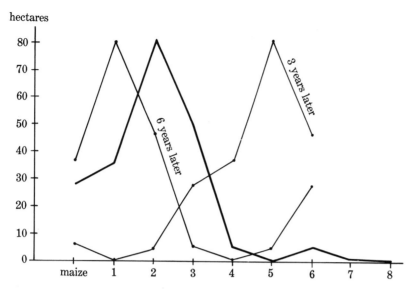

Fig. 39 Area of zone VII of the Muktahok ejido planted in maize or lying fallow for 1–6 years, 1963, with curves projected at three-year intervals thereafter.

five-year fallow plots on the basis of such considerations as proximity, expected yield based on rockiness and soils, or a plan to save time the following year by cutting a firebreak around a certain field in common with the adjoining farmers. It seems unlikely that these influences on yearly choice significantly affect the fallow cycle of each zone in any systematic way; that is, the fairly numerous deviations from a seven-year fallow cycle appear to be random by zone.

The stability of the system is further enhanced by its built-in flexibility from each individual's point of view. For example, rather than farm a plot that has lain fallow for only four or five years, most men will try either to rent a six-year fallow plot from someone else, or to rent that much more land for their small Hot Country holding. (Although renting ejido land is strictly forbidden by the government, men do in fact lease fields at $3.20 US per hectare, almost always in one-hectare plots.) The widespread adherence to a seven-year fallow cycle, coupled with the apparent randomness of the six-year or eight-year exceptions, thus permits the perpetuation of the intrazonal annual variations from one seven-year cycle to the next.

At the time of our study, the available aerial photos of the ejido did not permit a test of the fit between this model and actual farming patterns, since it was impossible to see when any currently farmed field was last farmed, and hence to read more than one cycle. Now, however, a test would be possible at any time in the field simply by sampling the state of plots in each zone. If the model represents the actual dynamics of the system, the curves drawn from the new field data should replicate my own, but be horizontally displaced by $n-7$ years, where n is the number of years elapsed since 1963. My own limited data, gathered from informants in 1966, are suggestive in this respect, but the numbers are unfortunately too small to be conclusive.

Land Tenure and Transmission

Although the last few years have witnessed a real land squeeze in Muktahok, leaving a few young married men with no ejido land at all, the average man, with the benefit of the annexed lands, still held in 1965 about as many hectares as the members of the original ejido had held in the late 1930s. Because of the system of zonal divisions, each man's total parcel includes a number of scattered plots. About half of all adult men have a full parcel in the original ejido ($\bar{x}$ = 7 plots) plus a full parcel in the annex ($\bar{x}$ = 2 plots); about one-fourth have a partial parcel in the original ejido ($\bar{x}$ = 2 plots) plus a full parcel in the annex; and of the others, several have two full parcels in the original ejido or in the annex, several have original ejido parcels but none in the annex, and a few who are still waiting to inherit parcels from their fathers have no land of their own at all (see also Price 1968:12). From the point of view of individual ejido members, the mean number of plots per man is seven, totaling about twenty-one hectares.

Most households, however, control more land than these figures would indicate, since two or three landholding men often live in a single household. Of Muktahok's thirty-nine households, thirteen hold a full parcel in the original ejido plus a full parcel in the annex (mean number of plots for these households is nine), twelve households have more than this, and only fourteen households have less. Households with less than full parcels usually produce less than ten fanegas of maize (in 1965, only one of the fourteen produced more), while about half of those households with more than full parcels regularly produce over ten fanegas. Thus, large landholdings seem to be necessary for large production, but they by no means assure it, for several men in households with twelve, fifteen, and eighteen plots annually produce only the five or six fanegas required to feed their families.

The transmission of ejido land in Muktahok follows several simple principles which, to conform to the legal indivisibility of parcels, depart from the traditional Zinacanteco inheritance pattern of division among all the sons. When an ejido member dies, his parcel passes in strict order of preference to: first, his oldest son without a parcel of his own, even if he is only an infant, the parcel to be held in trust; second, his widow; and third, the communal pool for redistribution. In this final circumstance, the new holder of the parcel must pay an entrance fee, and in case of competition, brothers of the deceased apparently receive preference. I have information on the immediate provenience of forty-eight of the fifty-one current parcels in the Muktahok ejido. Thirteen of the original parcels are still farmed by their first holders, eleven of these having since been supplemented by plots in the annex; eleven parcels were inherited from the holder's father; nine parcels consist of leftover pieces received after the original division of the 1935 ejido, usually supplemented by annex plots; three parcels were given to men who paid the first holder's debts after the latter had died without an heir or moved away; four were received from fathers who secured them for their sons before marriage; two are still being held in trust for unmarried sons; four are being farmed for widows whose husbands died without sons (two by the woman's second husband, one by her father, and one by her brother); and finally, two parcels were given to an ejido member's brother when that member died or moved away.

Annual Choice of Fields

Each year, the ejido member faces a choice of which of his fields to plant. (In discussing his options, I use the household as the unit of analysis, since land use is controlled by the household head, fields are worked in common by the men of the household, and the harvest is never divided among them.) The average household holds nine plots scattered throughout the farming area, most of which are further subdivided into two, three, or four pieces—each at a different stage in the fallow cycle. Apparently, these subdivisions are a result of both the mixed state at the time of acquisition and, perhaps, the risk of each year relying too heavily on one or two zones, which may be hard hit by winds, flooding, or drought. Many large maize producers habitually find themselves with fewer "ready" fields than they would like and therefore attempt to rent extra plots from other men. Today, there are always more potential lessees than willing lessors, and even those men fortunate enough to obtain some rental land are forced to strike a balance between the amount that they would ideally like to harvest and the number of their own five-year fallow fields that they are willing to use prematurely.

An examination of the actual choices facing one Muktahok maize farmer and his co-resident married son will illustrate the foregoing generalizations. In this case, the father held his son's parcel in trust until the son was married, and when the additional ejido land was annexed in 1954, they took contiguous plots. The current state of their fields in 1966, and which ones they expected to plant in 1967 and 1968, can be shown schematically (Fig. 40). Incidentally, none of the twelve men questioned on current and projected land use found it odd to discuss which pieces of their scattered plots they would use two or three years hence, and this propensity to plan ahead recalls a similar trait manifested in the Zinacanteco cargo system (Cancian 1965a).

In 1966, then, this informant selected for planting his only field planted seven years before, two of his fields planted six years before, a zone X field that had lain fallow for three years, and a small piece of a field planted the previous year that demanded minimal clearing. Instead of using his own remaining fields planted six years previously, he rented two fields last planted seven years before. In 1967, he planned to use both fields planted seven years earlier, four of the five fields planted six years earlier, a zone X field that had lain fallow for three years, and extra rented fields if they could be found. In 1968, he would take the only field planted seven years earlier, all three fields planted six years before, and a field in zone X; in addition, since no other fields were ideally ready for cultivation, he might—depending on rental possibilities—use a few fields planted four and five years earlier. He definitely planned to leave fallow one block of fields in zone VI planted four and five years earlier, which he intended to burn in cooperation with the surrounding landholders in 1969. This practice substantially reduces the amount of labor each man puts into a firebreak for his fields. In general, this informant left fewer fields fallow for the full six years than did any of the seven other farmers for whom there is comparable data, perhaps because he was particularly ambitious and anxious to use all available land each year.

It is notable that, no matter how few ready fields the Muktahok farmer possesses, he never attempts any extensive farming on rented fields in Hot Country. In contrast, the most successful farmers from the hamlets of

Zinacantan farm very little in their highland ejido plots and, instead, rent and plant, with the help of hired Chamula labor, large tracts in the Grijalva lowlands, sometimes netting $400 US annually (Cancian 1965a: 76). Muktahok men, however, almost never plant more than a hectare in Hot Country, working the land themselves or with wage labor from Muktahok. A tentative explanation for this phenomenon can be offered, although it may be overly influenced by the rationalizations given by the local farmers for their own behavior. The ejido of Muktahok gives each of its members about five times as much acreage as do the other ejidos of Zinacantan, such as ʔApas (Edel 1966; George A. Collier personal communication). Moreover, the land quality in the Muktahok ejido is considered better. For example, Sna Benancio, which is only an $0.08 US bus ride down the Pan American Highway (Fig. 35) and is the place where almost all Muktahok Hot Country farming is done, gives yields similar to those in the ejido annex, that is, below both the phenomenal 15–20 fanegas per almud reported for some Zinacanteco Hot Country operations and the more usual Hot Country yields of 8 fanegas (Cancian 1965a:66). Furthermore, the yields at Sna Benancio are much more variable than in the annex, with a total loss of the crop not uncommon. The men of Muktahok claim that the risks at Sna Benancio, as well as the added investment that it requires in rental fees and in transportation of the harvest, make this operation attractive only on a small scale. Believing correctly that large-scale Hot Country farming involves high risks (Cancian 1965a:78), they claim that only people who lack decent ejido land like theirs would undertake it.

Furthermore, the lack of normal contact with Chamulas may help to discourage large-scale Hot Country operations. A local tradition of not hiring Chamula laborers apparently stems from two sources: the location of Muktahok as the farthest Zinacanteco hamlet from Chamula and, more importantly, the fact that Chamulas are not considered skillful with the billhook, with which almost all of the ejido is cleared. Whatever the real reasons, most local men with a full parcel seem content

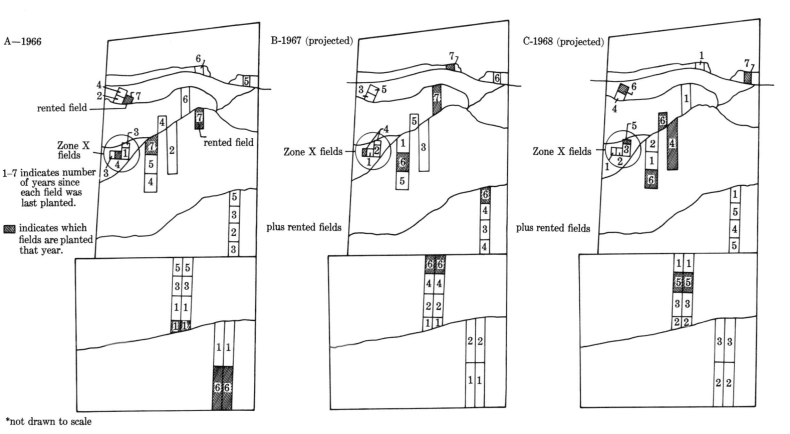

A—1966

rented field

Zone X fields

1–7 indicates number of years since each field was last planted.

▨ indicates which fields are planted that year.

rented field

B-1967 (projected)

Zone X fields

plus rented fields

C-1968 (projected)

Zone X fields

plus rented fields

*not drawn to scale

Fig. 40. Projected use of the Muktahok ejido fields for a household with two parcels.

to keep their farming operation within the ejido limits rather than to rent additional lands in Hot Country. A few of the most successful farmers, however, do seek wider economic horizons. For example, one owns an expensive coffee-hulling machine, several were making an attempt to acquire additional land in the ejido of Ixtapa, and during 1965–1966, a few men even tried to experiment with large-scale Hot Country farming in distant fields, although they subsequently returned to the more normal ejido pattern.

Contrasting Farming Strategies

In addition to decisions based on the current number of fields in maize and at different stages of the fallow cycle, each household makes certain farming choices that seem consistent from one year to the next, as in matters involving land rental or wage labor. Some households rent extra ejido plots yearly in an attempt to expand their potential for production, while others regularly rent out a plot or two that is ready for planting rather than farm it themselves. Similarly, certain households hire wage laborers periodically each year, while the men in others spend much of their time working for wages. Thus, although each of two given households may have nine ejido plots, one may rent extra land each year, pay workers to help farm it, and sell part of the harvest in the markets of San Cristóbal, Chiapa, or Tuxtla, while the other may choose to rent out some of the land, harvest only enough to feed the household, and earn what cash is needed by wage labor. These rental and labor practices are only two of a number of factors that reflect relative prestige in Muktahok. Men who rent land or hire laborers are generally those who also serve in civil positions, take senior religious offices, or lend money and maize to others. In contrast, those who rent out land or work for wages tend to serve in no civil positions, take subordinate religious offices, and borrow both money and maize (Price and Price 1970).

Recent Land Pressures

Traditionally, men with initiative, even when not inheriting land, were able to obtain ejido parcels. However, during the late 1960s, the situation of the young, small landholders had become critical. The population continues to increase, yet there is no possibility of annexing land in the future, since all private ranches within the legal distance of the community are too small to be expropriated. Furthermore, during the annual competition for rental land, large landholders, who tend to be the community's most powerful and influential men, are in a better bargaining position than are even the most ambitious small landholders, since they provide employment and various economic favors, such as loans of money and maize, to the lessors of ejido land. Thus, young men with small holdings today have little chance of either acquiring a parcel or renting sufficient land to become large producers. The only small landholder who is consistently able to rent land is a brother of men ranking second and sixth in maize production, one of whom is president of the Ejido Commission; he can apparently rent only because of their support and influence.

With the traditional agricultural avenues of success closed to them, many young men have turned to various kinds of wage labor. Of the fourteen men with small holdings, only four do not perform wage labor. Construction work on the Pan American Highway and in Tuxtla offers high wages, four times those for agricultural labor, as well as the chance to spend time in Ladino towns; accordingly, eight young men (mean age = 27.6) were earning much of their income in this way during 1966. One man has even bought a one-sixth share in a used truck in the state capital. All these activities help to change traditional values in the community, and some men in Muktahok, like many other Zinacantecos, already show signs of acquiring a consumer mentality. For example, two expensive transistor radios appeared in the community, about 1965, and many articles of non-Indian clothing are becoming popular as men begin to spend more time working in Ladino towns. Since the ejido is being farmed close to maximally today, it seems inevitable that more and more young men, as they come of age, will look to the outside world for incomes and, ultimately, new styles of life.

    An earlier version of this paper was published as "Land Use in a Maya Community," *International Archives of Ethnography* 51 (1968): 1–19. The project was supported by United States Public Health Service Fellowship MH–22,007 and by National Science Foundation Grant GS–976. For criticism and help in the field, I am grateful to Frank Cancian, George A. Collier, Sally Price, and Evon Z. Vogt.

Gary H. Gossen
Another Look at World View: Aerial Photography and Chamula Cosmology

The technique of aerial photography has proved to be a useful, fairly objective tool in the field investigation and analysis of spatial concepts and world view—topics that have traditionally been interpreted intuitively by anthropologists. Although aerial photography and maps will of course not remove the subjective dimensions from these studies—nor should they—they do make it possible to gather and present concrete data about an aspect of culture which is often imprecise and nebulous, even to the culture-bearers themselves.

Robert Redfield (1952:30) defined world view as being that which "attends especially to the way a man, in a particular society, sees himself in relation to all else. It is the properties of existence as distinguished from and related to the self. It is, in short, a man's idea of the universe. It is that organization of ideas which answers to a man the question: Where am I? Among what do I move? What are my relations to these things?" I shall attempt to demonstrate how the concepts of spatial relationships shared by a group of contemporary Maya answer some of these questions. (For excellent compara-

tive data on world view and cosmology from other contemporary Maya communities, see Alfonso Villa Rojas, 1968.)

Chamula is a Tzotzil-speaking municipio of approximately 40,000 modern Maya Indians. The municipio is a Mexican political and administrative unit analogous to a county, and in this part of Mexico it frequently coincides with ethnic boundaries. This is the case with Chamula. The population of 40,000, estimated from the 1960 census figure of 26,789 compounded by the explosive growth rate over the past few decades, includes both the main municipio and other Chamula hamlets located in municipios contiguous to Chamula. Although 92 percent of the Chamula population is monolingual in Tzotzil, most men know enough basic Spanish to deal with Ladino merchants and employers. Most women speak no Spanish whatsoever (Secretaría de Industria y Comercio 1963:25, 898).

Chamula lies at the top of the Chiapas highlands of southern Mexico and has an average altitude of 7,600 feet. All Chamulas engage to some extent in subsistence agriculture, with emphasis upon maize, squash, cabbage and beans. In addition, nearly all Chamula families keep a few sheep, whose wool is both used for their own clothing and, in smaller amounts, sold to Indians in nearby municipios. In the many cases in which limited land holdings result in inadequate food production, Chamulas engage in secondary economic activities, such as charcoal, pottery, or furniture manufacture. Others seek employment as day laborers in nearby San Cristóbal, the principal Spanish-speaking trade center for nearly all of the highland Indians. Still others travel to the tropical lowlands to work as day laborers on coffee plantations or in maize fields rented by the neighboring Zinacanteco Indians. A few Chamulas rent milpa land for themselves in the lowlands.

Chamulas live in dispersed patrilineal hamlets that belong to one or more of the three barrios of the municipio. The three barrios converge on a ceremonial center, which has virtually no permanent population (Fig. 41). Rental houses there provide temporary homes for the political and religious officials, whose terms range from one to three years. Chamulas are governed by a political organization in two parts. One body is the Ayuntamiento Regional, consisting of sixty-three positions or cargos; the other body is prescribed by Mexican law, the Ayuntamiento Constitucional, consisting of six positions, including that of the chief magistrate or presidente. A religious organization consisting of sixty-one positions supervises the complex ceremonial calendar and coordinates ritual activities with those of the political organization. At the local level, political and religious authority lies in the hands of past cargoholders, heads of segments of patrilineages, and shamans (Pozas 1959; Gossen 1970, 1974).

Contemporary Chamula is caught in a rapidly expanding web of outside contact and interaction. The relevant factor, in addition to the diversified economic activities, appears to be the rapid population growth. Chamulas, who are by far the most numerous group of Chiapas highland Maya, hold less land per capita than any other Indian municipio in the state of Chiapas. Population density is 74.5 persons per square kilometer (Secretaría de Industria y Comercio 1963:8). Population pressure has driven these Indians to use various means, legal and illegal, to secure new lands outside Chamula territory for maize production. The extent of Chamula expansion, both legal and de facto, into nearby and distant municipios is considerable (Fig. 42). Moreover, since only populations of over one hundred people have been con-

sidered in the figure, it understates the actual distribution of Chamulas throughout the highlands.

In conflict with these modern pressures to associate with non-Chamulas, the community has been traditionally characterized by a high degree of cultural conservatism. As a consciously ethnocentric Indian municipio, it has few, if any, rivals in all of the Chiapas highlands. Costume and speech distinguish it immediately from other groups. It permits no Spanish-speaking Mexicans to live permanently or to hold property within its boundaries, with the exception of one family, that of the Mexican secretary who assists the Chamulas in their dealings with the state and national governments. Overnight stays on a semiregular basis are permitted only of Ladino (Mexican) schoolteachers, the Ladino priest (who was temporarily banished in the fall of 1969), and a doctor who goes occasionally to the Instituto Nacional Indigenista clinic located in the ceremonial center. Any other non-Chamula must get explicit permission from municipal authorities to remain there overnight. In the same spirit, Chamulas who leave their home municipio in search of additional farmland do not, in most cases, become acculturated. Usually sufficient numbers relocate together to make it possible to create a microcosm of normal Chamula life, where traditional language, costume, and religious and political loyalties are maintained. For example, two generations have passed since the settlement of Rincón Chamula by Chamulas in 1910 and 1911 (no. 9, Fig. 42), yet the Tzotzil language and Chamula cultural patterns persist there to this day.

Chamula, then, offers a curious combination of modern and traditional orientations to the spatial nature of the universe. Chamulas are numerous and expanding, yet for the most part, their loyalties remain closely tied to Chamula. They take maximum advantage of the agrarian reform laws offered by the Mexican government to move into Spanish-speaking areas, yet no Spanish-speaking Mexican, with the one exception, is welcome to live in Chamula. Acknowledging their dependence on wages and goods of the Ladino world, they are neverthe-

Fig. 41. Oblique photograph of Chamula Ceremonial Center, showing Church of San Juan, churchyard with cross and kiosk, plaza for open-air market, town hall (*cabildo*) and school (right of plaza), and clinic (left of churchyard). Other buildings near plaza are small stores. Outlying houses belong to religious and political cargoholders.

Gary H. Gossen

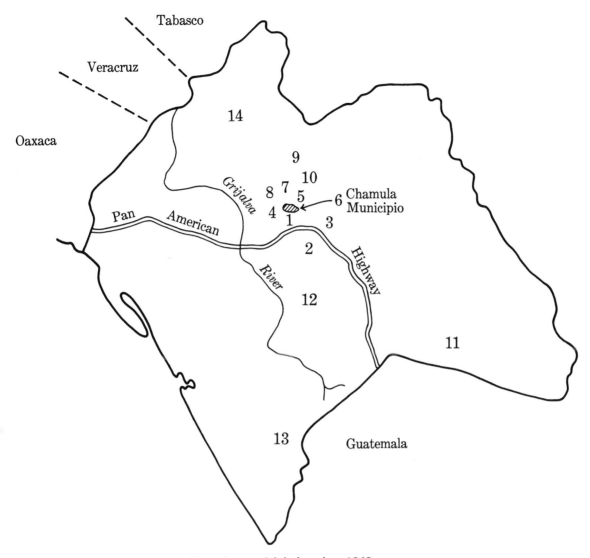

Fig. 42. Map of Chamula populations in Chiapas by municipio location, 1968.

1. San Cristóbal: four ejido colonies and various private plots.
2. Teopisca: two ejido colonies.
3. Huixtan: one non-ejido colony.
4. Zinacantán: small properties on a Ladino ranch in Zinacantan Valley, where workers receive homes and land rights in exchange for labor.
5. Chenalhó: one ejido and one non-ejido colony.
6. Chamula: four ejidos.
7. Mitontic: many small hamlets of squatters.

8. Larrainzar: several concentrations of squatters.
9. Solistahuacán: several colonies (ejido status unknown), comprising an *agencia* (submunicipio administrative unit).
10. El Bosque: founded entirely by a colony of Chamula refugees from the Caste Wars of 1867–1869.
11. Las Margaritas: one ejido colony.
12. Venustiano Carranza: agricultural plots privately purchased by Chamulas through National Indigenous Institute.
13. Tapachula: one new center of population to become an ejido.
14. Tecpatán: one new center of population, ejido status unknown.

less hostile to most elements of that culture. What is the basis—the Chamula justification—for ethnocentrism in the face of their increasing interaction with the outside? What, in fact, is their "idea of the universe" and their alloted place within it?

The Chamula Spatial Universe

In trying to discover the nature and extent of the Chamula universe, I first tried to get a general idea of where Chamulas go in work and travel. One difficulty in this undertaking was to agree on geography, for reports on the number of hamlets within Chamula territory are not consistent. For the 1960 census, Chamula authorities reported 90 hamlets within the municipio boundaries (Secretaría de Industria y Comercio 1963:70–71); Ricardo Pozas (1959:31–32) reported 111 hamlets officially recognized in 1944; and as of 1968, authorities claimed that there were only 76 hamlets. However, informants helped me to locate 109 traditional hamlets on the photomosaic of Chamula in 1968. The variation is partially explained by shifting demographic patterns caused by deforestation, erosion, and land exhaustion. As hamlets lose population, they merge with other hamlets for purposes of administration, tax collection, and representation. The hamlet names nevertheless persist long after the location has ceased to be a population center. All of this basic geographic and demographic information was central to my research, and the photomosaic of the community was instrumental in providing me with a relatively quick elementary education in these matters.

In my study of the extent of the Chamula universe, I employed twenty-seven informants to answer a series of questions about themselves and their travels. All of them (fourteen children, thirteen adults) came from two contiguous hamlets of the seventy-six that officially lie within Chamula territory. Both Milpoleta and Peteh (Fig. 43) are characterized by poor land and timber resources and dense populations, which factors drive the majority of men to seek day labor in San Cristóbal or in the lowlands in order to support their families. I asked

Fig. 43. Map of places used in relative distance interviews.
1. Bisombat: stone landmark near Peteh.
2. Chamula Ceremonial Center: ceremonial and political center of the municipio.
3. Saklamanton: hamlet east of Peteh, with a school, where cane liquor is made.
4. Ichinton: stone landmark and also a hamlet west of Peteh, on the truck road from Chamula Ceremonial Center to San Cristóbal.
5. San Cristóbal: Ladino town south of Peteh, the principal trading center of the central Chiapas highlands.
6. Zinacantan: Tzotzil-speaking municipio contiguous to Chamula.
7. Muken: liquor- and charcoal-making hamlet east of Peteh.
8. YaᵖaIchitom: hamlet west of Peteh, close to the Zinacantan-Chamula boundary.
9. Behbakhó: important bridge and landmark on the footpath to Chenalhó, northeast of Peteh.
10. Larrainzar: Tzotzil-speaking municipio northwest of Chamula.
11. Tzontevitz: highest mountain in the central Chiapas highlands and an important place for rain-making rituals. Chamula patron saint San Juan and the earth gods are believed to live inside the mountain, and the corral for the animal souls of Chamulas is believed to be there also.
12. Magdalena: Tzotzil-speaking agencia of the municipio of Chenalhó.
13. Chenalhó: Tzotzil-speaking municipio north of Peteh.
14. Pistik: charcoal-, furniture-, and liquor-making hamlet of Chamula, on the truck road to Tenejapa.
15. Tenejapa: Tzeltal-speaking municipio, which has many Ladinos residing in its ceremonial center.
16. San Pablo Chalchihuitán: Tzotzil-speaking municipio northwest of Chamula, beyond Larrainzar.
17. Ixtapa: important salt-producing town inhabited by Ladinos and Zinacantecos.
18. Chanal: Tzeltal-speaking municipio.
19. Amatenango del Valle: pottery-making, Tzeltal-speaking town south of San Cristóbal, where the water jugs used by Chamulas are made.
20. Chiapa de Corzo: Ladino town in the lowlands, near the point where the Pan American Highway crosses the Grijalva River.
21. Grijalva River: flows west of the highlands through a large, lowland valley where maize farming is done.
22. Venustiano Carranza: lowland Ladino and Indian town, regarded in Chamula as an important source of shamans and witches, and near a mountain sacred to Chamulas.
23. Tuxtla Gutiérrez: capital of the state of Chiapas.
24. Comitán: Ladino town south of San Cristóbal, near the Guatemalan border.

Gary H. Gossen

25. Guatemala

26. Arriaga: lowland Ladino town on one of the main routes to the coffee plantations.

27. Pacific Ocean: where the sun, *htotik,* is believed to sink at night.

28. Huixtla: Ladino town in the lowlands, in the region of the coffee plantations.

29. Tapachula: main town in southwestern Chiapas, also near the Ladino coffee plantations.

30. Oaxaca

31. Gulf of Mexico: from which the sun is believed to rise every morning.

32. Veracruz

33. Puebla

34. Campeche

35. Mexico City

36. United States

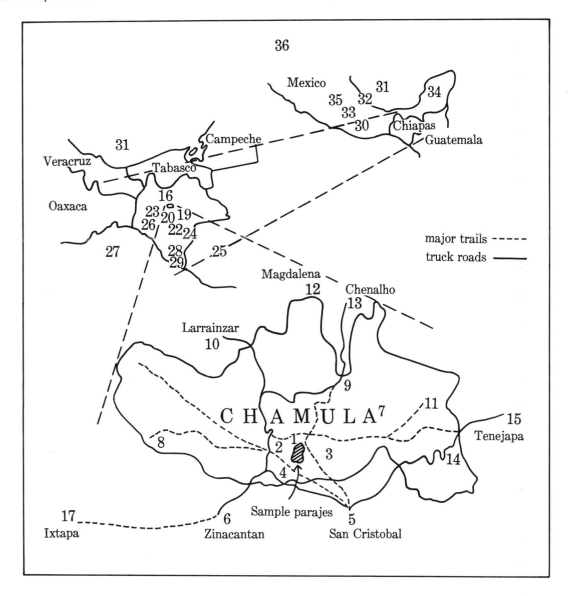

the twenty-seven informants to tell me the most distant place that each had visited in his life.

Although the sample was neither sufficiently large nor well enough distributed between the sexes to offer conclusive evidence, the results gave a general indication of the very limited Chamula knowledge of the outside world. None of the informants had been out of the state of Chiapas, nor did they know much about Indian communities of the highlands other than those contiguous to Chamula territory. Several women, in fact, had never visited any municipios other than San Cristóbal and Chamula. By far the most commonly known "distant" places were the lowlands of the Pacific Coast, where the coffee plantations are located, and the Grijalva River valley, where lowland maize fields are rented.

Given these general limits to the extent of Chamula travel, I wanted to determine their own concepts of "near" and "distant." Their home municipio seemed the obvious place to start. The location of Chamula place names and hamlets could best be achieved, I thought, by constructing a photomosaic of Chamula and then working with informants to plot locations on acetate overlays. The photomosaic was constructed from RC 9×2 prints from the 1964 Harvard Chiapas Project aerial coverage of the highlands, commissioned by Evon Z. Vogt through Compañía Mexicana Aerofoto, S.A., of Mexico City. Once the mosaic had been constructed, I innocently proposed the project of finding all hamlets in Chamula, hoping that this would be an easy task. I worked with individuals and with groups of men and boys of all ages, from twelve to sixty. It turned out that no Chamula from either of the hamlets that interested me could locate with any certainty population centers and the boundaries of more than five hamlets of the 76–110 which actually exist. The hamlets they located lay understandably close to their home hamlet. Some knew the relative positions of as many as sixty hamlets, but these they knew only vaguely and in relation to principal trails. Even the most knowledgeable of my informants, a tax collector for the municipio, could roughly locate only those hamlets in his barrio where he had collected taxes. To my surprise,

it appeared that Chamulas' knowledge of their own municipio was quite limited. Informants readily located the ceremonial centers of Indian municipios bordering on Chamula, such as Tenejapa and Larrainzar, but much of their own territory remained unfamiliar to them.

Since my first two efforts showed only tendencies in the way that Chamulas thought about small parts of their world and about distances within it, I wanted to get an idea of how they conceived of relative distances within a whole range of places of varying degrees of familiarity to them. I wondered whether criteria other than actual travel time and true distance would be relevant to them in "ordering" place names from the "closest" to the "most distant." To test informants in a uniform fashion, I prepared a set of thirty-six cards, which carried a written place name on one side and a coded number on the other. Informants who could read were asked simply to arrange them in order from the nearest to the most distant. Informants who did not read were allowed to work with a Chamula assistant, who elicited from them verbally the order that they believed to be correct. Fourteen children between six and fifteen years old, twelve of them boys and two girls, and thirteen adults between twenty-seven and forty, six of them women and seven men, were interviewed from the hamlets of Milpoleta and Peteh.

Thirty-six places were selected, ranging from those through which Chamulas from the sample hamlets passed every day to places about which they had heard but had never seen (Fig. 43). The inhabitants of these thirty-six places included most types of human and supernatural beings with whom the Chamulas deal on occasion: other Chamulas, Ladinos, non-Chamula Tzotzil speakers, Guatemalans, Tzeltal speakers, Americans, lowland Mexicans, earth gods (associated with Tzontevitz Mountain), and even the sun itself (associated with the Eastern and Western Seas). Within the coverage of the Chamula photomosaic (nos. 1 to 15, Fig. 43), trail distances from Peteh hamlet were calculated by tracing on the photomosiac the routes preferred by informants. Distances to places not covered by the photomosaic

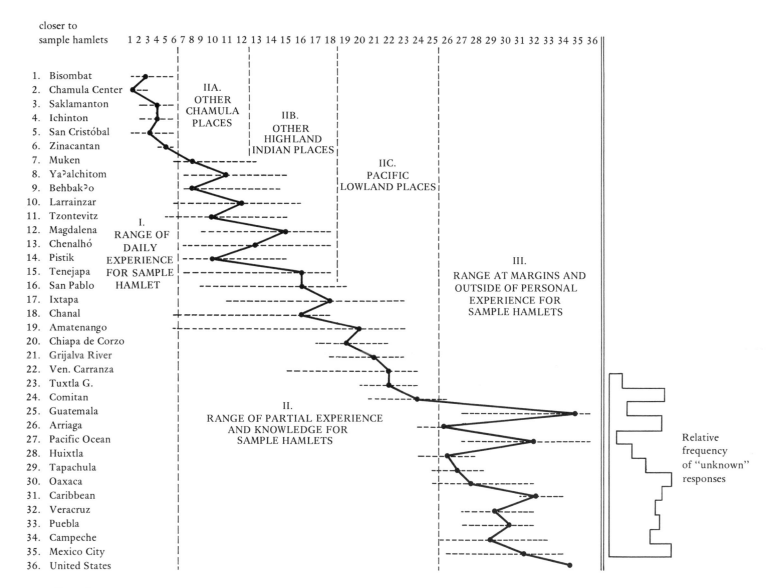

closer to
sample hamlets

1 2 3 4 5 6 7 8 9 10 11 12 13 14 15 16 17 18 19 20 21 22 23 24 25 26 27 28 29 30 31 32 33 34 35 36

1. Bisombat
2. Chamula Center
3. Saklamanton
4. Ichinton
5. San Cristóbal
6. Zinacantan
7. Muken
8. Yaʔalchitom
9. Behbakʔo
10. Larrainzar
11. Tzontevitz
12. Magdalena
13. Chenalhó
14. Pistik
15. Tenejapa
16. San Pablo
17. Ixtapa
18. Chanal
19. Amatenango
20. Chiapa de Corzo
21. Grijalva River
22. Ven. Carranza
23. Tuxtla G.
24. Comitan
25. Guatemala
26. Arriaga
27. Pacific Ocean
28. Huixtla
29. Tapachula
30. Oaxaca
31. Caribbean
32. Veracruz
33. Puebla
34. Campeche
35. Mexico City
36. United States

IIA. OTHER CHAMULA PLACES

IIB. OTHER HIGHLAND INDIAN PLACES

IIC. PACIFIC LOWLAND PLACES

I. RANGE OF DAILY EXPERIENCE FOR SAMPLE HAMLET

III. RANGE AT MARGINS AND OUTSIDE OF PERSONAL EXPERIENCE FOR SAMPLE HAMLETS

II. RANGE OF PARTIAL EXPERIENCE AND KNOWLEDGE FOR SAMPLE HAMLETS

Relative frequency of "unknown" responses

more distant from
sample hamlets

Fig. 44.   Results of relative distance interviews. Dotted lines indicate the horizontal spread of rank order responses, and ● indicates the median point in these distributions. Bar graph on the right shows frequency of the inability of informants to respond to the corresponding place names.

were calculated along preferred Chamula routes, when specified and applicable, by kilometer indications on existing maps. This means, for example, that although air and foot path distances in kilometers from Chamula to Tapachula are shorter than road distance between the same two points, I used the longer route, for it is the easiest way to get there by truck and is certainly the route used by most Chamulas today. In this way it was possible to arrange the thirty-six places in order of increasing actual distance from the sample hamlets, Peteh and Milpoleta (vertical axis on Fig. 44). Informants' responses in order of increasing distance (horizontal axis on Fig. 44) were plotted against the actual order. When informants were unable to respond to a place name (indicated on the bar graph to the far right of Fig. 44), their reply was most often "I don't know" or "I never heard of it."

Several patterns are apparent in the distributions. A curve drawn through the median values for order of increasing distance shows that the respondents had a generally accurate view of relative distance. Notice, however, particularly within the first fifteen place names, that informants consistently responded conservatively (that is, brought the places "closer" to home than they actually were) on hamlets that they knew to be inhabited by Chamulas (especially nos. 9, 11, and 14, Fig. 44). The bordering non-Chamula municipios of Larrainzar (no. 10), Chenalhó (no. 13), and Tenejapa (no. 15) were pushed slightly outward in the universe from their true relative positions. The only exception to this tendency was Zinacantan, which was correctly placed with those locales closest to the geographic sample area of the study. Chamulas from Milpoleta and Peteh saw Zinacantecos every day, traded and worked with them often, and visited the Zinacantan Ceremonial Center "just over the mountain" on special ritual occasions. Zinacantecos belonged very definitely to the everyday social universe of Chamulas from this part of the municipio (group I, Fig. 44).

In the middle range of the sample (group II, Fig. 44), the place names of the Pacific lowlands (group IIc) were judged with striking accuracy. Other Chamula places

(group IIa) and other highland Indian places (group IIb) were ordered with considerable inaccuracy and a wide range of variation from respondent to respondent. There was a tendency to bring distant Chamula places closer to home than they really were in terms of travel time. This offered further evidence that Chamulas actually knew relative distances along the routes to the lowland coffee plantations and maize fields better than they knew relative distances in parts of their home highlands. Further along in the sample (group III) was a clear change in evaluation of places. "Unknown" responses began abruptly here among the girls and women, with a few Pacific lowland places, and with increasing relative distance they became more generalized and frequent, characterizing children and adults of both sexes. A major break in the overlap of range of responses occurred at rank positions nos. 24–25, which clearly distinguished group II from III. Moreover, other countries (Guatemala and the United States) and the seas were considered to be roughly equidistant in the sample, even though Guatemala and the Pacific Ocean are actually closer to Chamula than are certain places in the Pacific lowlands. The places included in group III for the most part shared only negative attributes: Chamulas in the sample did not want to go there and had few reasons ever to do so. They thought of these places (the seas, Mexico City, the United States, Guatemala, and Oaxaca) as the origin of rich Ladino coffee planters, peculiar tourists and other strange beings, war makers, and deities.

To test further how Chamulas thought about spatial relationships in their world, I decided to ask informants for freehand maps of the world. I wanted to compare relative distances of places on these maps, drawn by Chamulas, with the results of the relative distance experiments, which I had devised. The informant whose work is reported briefly here, Marian López Calixto, came from Peteh, one of the sample hamlets of this project. Marian was not unfamiliar with maps, for at the time he was in his fifth year of school in Chamula Ceremonial Center. I gave him a large rectangular piece of cardboard, three feet by four feet, and asked him to draw a detailed map

Gary H. Gossen

of the "knowable" world; that is, where one might travel if one wished. I gave him no instructions except that he should use a consistent set of symbols to identify rivers, roads, boundaries, and land forms such as caves and mountains. While working on this project, he occasionally consulted his older brother, who also lives in Peteh but who had not gone to school. The map itself was too large and detailed to reproduce here in an appropriate scale. However, trails were well enough indicated on the freehand map to allow the measurement of distances between selected places and the sample hamlets of Milpoleta and Peteh.

Although five of the thirty-six place names used in the card test for relative distance were missing from Marian's map, fruitful comparisons could be made. In general, the map results dramatically confirmed tendencies suggested by the card test: the conceived physical proximity of a place was directly related to the degree of social similarity it shared with traditional Chamula culture.

Having a general idea of where Chamulas traveled and what they meant by the words "near" (*nopol*) and "far" (*nom*), I nevertheless felt that I still understood very little about their world as a whole. In tales and myths they used repeatedly the nebulous expression *ta skotol banamil*, meaning "in all the earth" or "everywhere." If Chamula were the center of the moral universe, as it is purported to be by Chamulas, then how did it fit into the more inclusive *skotol banamil*? I again commissioned a map of Marian, asking him simply to draw Chamula as it lay within *skotol banamil*, "all of the earth." I requested only a numbered code for place names on the map (Fig. 45).

The map shows that Chamula, for Marian, is the center not only of the moral universe but also of the physical universe. Chamulas insist that their ceremonial center is "the earth's navel" (*smišik banamil*), which would not be an unreasonable assumption if Marian's map actually mirrors how Chamulas picture their universe. Chamula looms enormous in the extent of the "whole earth." Only Chamula among all the place names receives a boundary. Within Chamula, even the three barrios are

delimited. These boundaries represent only an ideal conceptualization of Chamula, for work with the photomosaic has shown that not all hamlets belonging to a barrio form a continuous extension of territory. Neither do all hamlets belong only to one barrio. Some hamlets belong to all three barrios. This is only one feature of the map that shows it to be a highly stylized and ideal representation of the universe. Marian divides the world into three major regions: Cold Country (*sikil ʔosil*), Hot Country (*k'išin ʔosil*), and the unknown (*mu hnaʔtik*). These general categories of the spatial universe were shown in the relative distance interviews to have some significance for most Chamulas with whom I worked.

Two places have special characteristics. These are the shores of the Eastern and Western Seas (nos. 18 and 19), or the Caribbean and the Pacific. They represent extremely important points of orientation in Chamula cosmology, for they are the limits of the earth, which is like a huge island. From these vantage points, devils, witches and people who live nearby, such as Americans (no. 15), can see the awesome spectacle of the sun emerging and sinking into the sea each morning and afternoon. As the burning sun (*htotik*, "our Lord," the principal deity of Chamula) passes through the sea on his way to the heavens (day) and the underworld (night), he turns the seas into a boiling mass and evaporates them, causing a flow of water around the earth to refill the empty ocean basin, which explains the tides. These points at the edge of the earth are also important in that they are points of contact between the earth and the other two principal realms of Chamula cosmology, the Heavens (*vinahel*) and the Underworld (*lahebal*). All of the heavenly bodies (stars, moon and saints) and the inhabitants of the Underworld (the dead) have close access to the earth at these points. The edges of the earth, therefore, play an important conceptual role in Chamula cosmology; since the shores lie only a step away from the paths of the sun and the moon, they are situated at key points in the universe. These distant shores lie at the portals of that which is at the same time ancient and sacred, evil and unknown. They are the logical opposite of the navel of the earth, the center, the home of Chamulas.

In summary, Chamula concepts of spatial relationships are derived both from individual work or travel experience and from traditional beliefs. Both spheres of data demonstrate the tenacity of the Chamulas' perception of their municipio as the focal point of contemporary existence. In projective tests, such as Marian's map, they consistently located distant Chamula settlements closer than they actually were and, conversely, pushed other ethnic groups toward the margins of the universe to the degree that they were dissimilar from themselves. The encroachment of the modern world does not appear to be changing their outlook.

Despite the current phenomena of expansion and increasing interaction with the outside, the Chamulas continue to maintain a high degree of cultural conservatism. Their spatial concepts consistently emphasize the importance of Chamula's focal place in the universe. Although the form and content of the municipio may be altered by population growth and by relocation in non-Chamula areas, the basic relationships between spatial categories remain more or less constant. Thus, when Chamulas answer such questions as "Where am I? Among what do I move? What are my relations to these things?" from a spatial point of view, they gravitate unfalteringly toward the municipio, the navel of the earth, and the traditional patterns that their culture postulates.

In the absence of adequate maps of the area, the photomosaic of RC 9×2 prints and acetate overlays helped me to locate and establish relatively objective distances for places in the near and safe reaches of the Chamula universe. As such, aerial photography proved to be an exceptionally useful field tool and timesaver, as well as an objective control for the study of the inherently vague and elusive concept of world view. A project similar to the one described here could have been done without aerial photographic coverage, but only if adequate mapping of trails, hamlets, and geographic features were done beforehand. Yet such mapping is a kind of data that is seldom available in areas where

Fig. 45. Map of the whole earth, by Marian López Calixto. Explanations appear here only if places not given in Fig. 43.

1. Guatemala
2. Comitán
3. San Cristóbal
4. Zinacantan
5. Simojovel
6. Chiapa de Corzo
7. Grijalva River Bridge: on Pan American Highway near Tuxtla Gutiérrez.
8. Tuxtla Gutiérrez
9. Arriaga
10. Huixtla
11. Tapachula
12. Puebla
13. Mexico City
14. England
15. United States
16. Campeche: capital of Mexican state of the same name.
17. Mérida: capital of Mexican state of Yucatán.
18. Place where the sun comes up from the eastern ocean.
19. Place where the sun sinks into the western ocean.
20. Larrainzar
21. Chenalhó
22. Chamula Ceremonial Center.
23. Pujiltik: Ladino town in the Pacific lowlands.
24. Suyitán: Ladino town in the Pacific lowlands.
25. Venustiano Carranza
26. Lansavitz: sacred mountain near Venustiano Carranza, used for Chamula rain-making ritual.
27. Oshyoket: sacred mountain overlooking the valley of Zinacantan.
28. Calvario San Juan: sacred mountain near Chamula Ceremonial Center.
29. Calvario San Pedro: sacred mountain near Chamula Ceremonial Center.
30. Teopisca: Ladino town on the Pan American Highway near Comitán.
31. Calvario San Sebastián: sacred mountain near Chamula Ceremonial Center.
32. San Cristóbal mountains: range separating the municipio of San Cristóbal from Chamula.
33. Zinacantan mountains: range separating Zinacantan Ceremonial Center from the Pan American Highway.
34. Chamula boundary.
35. Sacred waterhole for Chamula barrios of San Pedro and San Sebastián.
36. Sacred waterhole for Chamula barrio of San Juan.
37. Nachih: hamlet of Zinacantan, located on the Pan American Highway.
38. Nabenchauk: hamlet of Zinacantan, located on the Pan American Highway.
39. Mispía: sacred mountain near Venustiano Carranza, used for Chamula rain-making ritual.
40. Tzontevitz: sacred mountain in Chamula, dwelling place of the patron saint San Juan and home of the earth gods and of the Chamula soul animals.
41. Ojovitz: sacred mountain in Chamula, home of the earth gods.

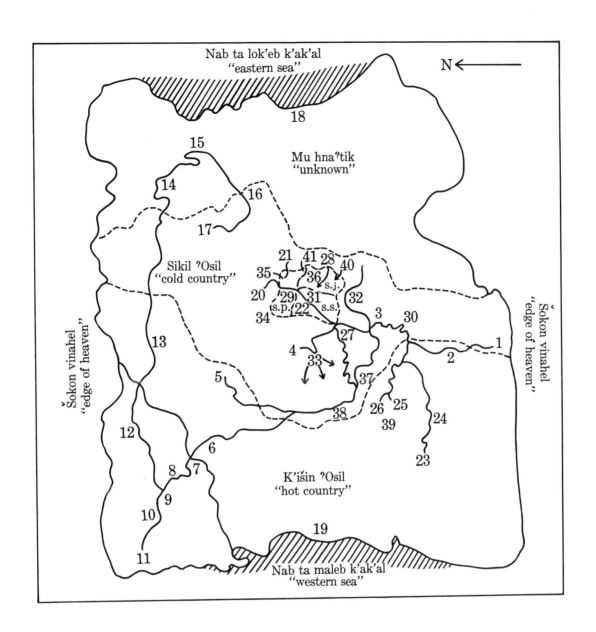

Nab ta lok'eb k'ak'al
"eastern sea"

N ←

18

15

14   16

Mu hna?tik
"unknown"

17

Sikil ?Osil
"cold country"

21 41 28
35   36   40
         s.j.
20 29 31 32
   (s.p.)22 s.s.
34

3   30

27

4

33

37

5

13

Šokon vinahel
"edge of heaven"

Šokon vinahel
"edge of heaven"

2   1

38   26 25
     39   24

12

6

23

8 7

9

K'išin ?Osil
"hot country"

10

19

11

Nab ta maleb k'ak'al
"western sea"

anthropologists do field work. Thus, in spite of the initial cost and the inevitable distortions, aerial photographic coverage of a community may, for projects similar to mine, prove to be an invaluable investment for the social anthropologist.

This research was supported by a National Institutes of Mental Health predoctoral fellowship and an attached research grant. I would like to thank Victoria R. Bricker, Robert Laughlin, George A. Collier, Elizabeth M. Dodd, and Richard Price for their advice and help.

Gary H. Gossen

Linnea Holmer Wren

Aerial Photography in the Investigation of Settlement and Trail Patterns in Highland Chiapas

In Zinacantan, density figures seemingly record an astonishing difference between hamlets. In ʔApas, the density figure for the inhabited area is twelve houses per one hundred square meters (Figs. 17, 29); in Nabenchauk, it is six houses per one hundred square meters (Figs. 46, 47); and in Pasteʔ, it is two houses per one hundred square meters (Hinton 1967:15). But the impression of the three hamlets conveyed by these figures is misleading, for they suggest that the hamlets, although supposedly of the same cultural composition, are characterized by very different settlement patterns. The density figures emphasize clearly the population differences between certain areas, but they obscure any similarity in the manner in which the three hamlets are settled.

Density in Zinacanteco Settlement Patterns

George A. Collier showed that conclusions about the relationships between ecological factors are in large part dependent on the size of the scale used in the survey. The determination of density figures may also be considered "scale-related." The standard method of obtaining a house density figure is to divide the total area under consideration by the number of dwellings it includes. The result provides some very general information about the dwelling pattern for the total area, but also proves misleading if construed to yield information on a more specific level.

The hamlets in Zinacantan are organized into three basic social units of ascending size: "the domestic group living in one or more houses in a compound; the *sna*, consisting of two or more domestic groups; and the waterhole group, composed of two or more snas" (Vogt 1969b:127). The domestic group is composed of kinsmen who live together in a house compound and who share a single maize supply. Each such group is characterized by a house cross, the *krus ta tiʔna*, which is erected on the terrace outside the door of the principal house in the domestic unit. A house cross always indicates a functioning domestic group.

The sna is composed of one or more localized domestic groups, varying in size from less than fifteen people to over one hundred and fifty people (Figs. 48, 49). Usually both patrilocal and patrilineal, the sna consists of members who live on adjacent lands inherited from their ancestors. Each May and October the K'in Krus ritual, ostensibly performed for the ancestral patrons of a lineage, serves also to link the descendants together as a group.

Fig. 46.   Aerial oblique photograph of the hamlet of Nabenchauk.

Linnéa Holmer Wren

Fig. 47. Aerial photomosaic of Nabenchauk, constructed
from HyAc photos. The settlement pattern is more scattered
here than in ʔApas.

Settlement and Trail Patterns in Highland Chiapas

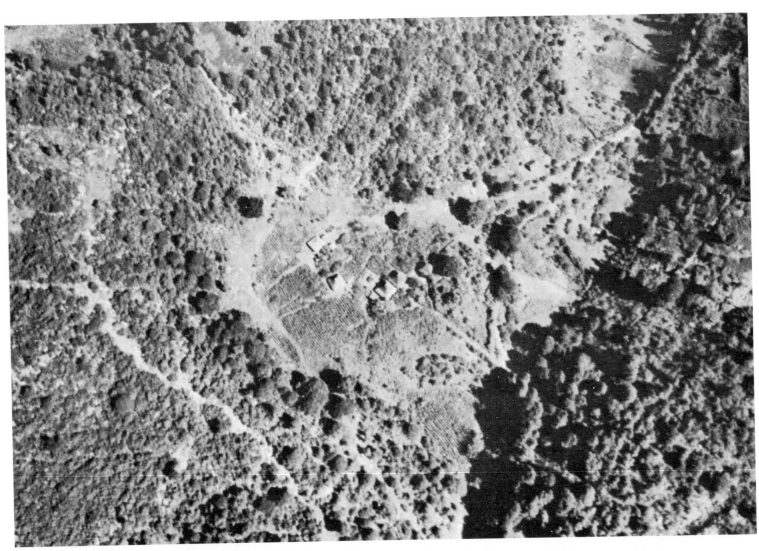

Fig. 48.   Aerial view of a small sna in Paste?.

Linnéa Holmer Wren

Fig. 49.   Aerial view of a large sna in Paste?.

The waterhole group may be composed of between two to thirteen snas, depending on the size and reliability of the water supply. Each waterhole group is also an important ceremonial group and maintains cross shrines as a means of communication with the group's ancestral gods. A K'in Krus ceremony, much like that of the snas, is performed every year by all the shamans living in the waterhole group. By including rituals for ancestral deities, the ceremony links together the snas and identifies the waterhole group as another structurally significant segment of Zinacanteco society.

This social structure is a major determining factor in the settlement pattern of all the hamlets. For the most part, domestic groups are patrilineal and patrilocal families; snas are localized patrilineages; and waterhole groups are further extensions of these two principles. Because the density figures are misleading in appearing to indicate different settlement patterns for the hamlets, I measured the density of houses in terms of the structural units of the society. By observing the location of the house crosses and the areas bounded by house fences, I identified the domestic groups in ʔApas, Nabenchauk, and Pasteʔ. Unfortunately, snas are not always identifiable from aerial photographs, and ethnographic data are not available for the sna groupings in Nabenchauk. However, information on the size and composition of waterhole groups does exist for all three hamlets. I measured and tabulated the distances between the houses within the domestic groups and the distances between the houses within the waterhole groups.

To measure these distances, I used mosaics made from enlarged HyAc photographs. Within the domestic unit, I measured and recorded all the distances between the dwellings. Measurements demonstrate strikingly that in all three hamlets the distance between houses within the domestic groups remains remarkably constant. The mean of these distances lies in each case within the 11 to 15 meter range.

However, when the distances between houses within the waterhole groups are considered, this similarity vanishes. Within the waterhole groups, I measured and recorded the distances between the houses in each domestic group, on the one hand, and the houses in every other domestic group, on the other hand. In ʔApas, the substantial majority of compounds are located between 26 and 175 meters apart, with the greatest single number located from 51 to 75 meters from each other. The mean of the distances between dwelling compounds is 112 meters. In Nabenchauk, the majority of compounds are located between 28 and 297 meters, with the greatest single number being located between 82 and 108 meters, while the mean is to be found at 224 meters. In Pasteʔ, the majority of compounds are situated between 51 and 1,150 meters apart, with the greatest single number falling in the range of 251 and 300 meters, while the mean is 550 meters.

This shows clearly how density figures can mislead one about the actual patterns of settlement. A comparison of the density figures for ʔApas (12 houses per 100 square meters) and for Pasteʔ (two houses per 100 square meters) seemed to indicate that in ʔApas people built their houses much closer to their neighbors than in Pasteʔ. But this is not the case at all. The distance between a Zinacanteco's house and his immediate neighbors' houses in all three hamlets remains virtually the same. What does change is the distance between these house clusters. The domestic compounds are built at greater or lesser distances from each other. For example, though the distance between the houses within the domestic compound is the same in ʔApas, Nabenchauk, and Pasteʔ, the average mean distance between domestic compounds within waterhole groups is five times as great in Pasteʔ as in ʔApas, and twice as great in Nabenchauk as in ʔApas. It is not that the whole settlement pattern changes in ʔApas or Pasteʔ; rather, the distance between the structural units in the Zinacantan social system expands or contracts, and this is reflected in the overall settlement pattern.

Describing and comparing settlement patterns in terms of varying density figures might seem to imply that changes in the ratio of houses to land are accompanied by changes in the social organization of the

Linnéa Holmer Wren

builders. But approaching settlement patterns in terms of the distances between structural units leaves open the question of the extent to which changes in those distances are accompanied by changes in social organization. The Maya are basically small-hamlet dwellers who, having developed patterns of social organization geared to hamlet dwelling, transfer these to different settings. Whether in the more intensely built-up hamlet of ʔApas or in the more dispersed hamlet of Pasteʔ, the Maya Indians of Zinacantan continue to practice their traditional patterns of domestic group behavior. The astonishing uniformity in the distance between houses within the domestic group compounds reflects the strength and continuity of Zinacanteco cultural patterns.

Slope As a Determinant of Settlement Patterns in Zinacantan

Aerial photographs of Zinacantan present an impressive dramatization of the rugged nature of this terrain. But more important, the quantity and quality of topographical detail revealed by aerial photographs can help to determine the extent and manner to which the Zinacanteco settlement pattern is dictated by ecological forces. The range of information made possible by aerial photographs, combined with a knowledge of the society, begins to make the settlement pattern decipherable in terms of a set of interwoven determinants, both ecological and cultural in nature.

The most striking feature of the terrain is the precipitous slope, which can drop as much as 2,000 meters over a distance of 15,000 meters. In order to investigate the importance of slope as a factor in the location of both entire settlements and individual dwellings, I chose two hamlets for study, ʔApas and Nabenchauk. These were chosen because in them the areas of settlement are clearly bounded: in ʔApas, by a barranca to the north and west, a steep cliff to the south, and a cemetery to the east; in Nabenchauk, by a ring of precipitous hills. From stereo pairs of RC–9 photographs, contour maps were made of the terrain by the Compañía Mexicana Aerofoto. Each contour line marks off a ten-meter change of elevation.

On each map, a grid was superimposed, which marked off areas of one hundred square meters. In each of these squares, I calculated the degree of slope and counted the number of houses. This made it possible to determine the percentage of land that falls within each slope range and the percentage of houses built on each slope range. A comparison of the expected number of houses with the observed number of houses indicates a high clustering of houses in the 3° to 11° slope range in ʔApas, and in the 3° to 8° slope range in Nabenchauk (Table 4).

The degree of slope is clearly a strong determinant, within a settlement area, of where people build their houses. The figures reveal that no houses are to be found on slopes of more than 33°. If at all possible, Zinacantecos will build their houses on an area with a low degree of slope. But the figures also reveal that people do not tend to build houses on land with a slope of two degrees or less. Field interviews with Zinacanteco informants indicate that this land is deliberately reserved for fields of maize. Because of the rotation required by swidden agriculture, the large lowland fields leased by Zinacantecos can only be farmed for three out of every ten years. But the use of fertilizer allows the small highland plots, lying near the houses and within the hamlets, to be intensively farmed for a generation or more (Vogt 1969b:36). To prevent the fertilizer, chiefly sheep manure, from being washed away in heavy rains, the Zinacanteco cultivators have carefully set aside the flattest land for their farmland. Thus, in terms of slope preference, it seems that the Zinacantecos decide what slope range is optimal for settlement by compromising several factors. The desire for a level house location is weighed against the prerequisites of farming, to determine which range of slope can best be utilized for each purpose.

The Zinacantecos themselves do not have a notion of "settlement pattern" in the sense of "an image of spatial relationships . . . to which they must conform" (Frake 1962). What is termed a settlement pattern by the anthropologist is the result not of conscious adherence to a formal design but of a large number of decisions made by

Table 4. A comparison of the expected number with the observed number of houses in ꞌApas and Nabenchauk.

Slope	Percentage of area		Number of houses in ꞌApas[a]			Number of houses in Nabenchauk[b]		
	ꞌApas	Nabenchauk	Expected	Observed	Difference	Expected	Observed	Difference
2°	1	16	2	1	+1	63	60	+3
3	2	9	4	19	−15	35	85	−50
4	2	5	4	11	−7	20	50	−30
5	4	5	8	22	−14	20	38	−18
6	3	2	6	19	−13	8	11	−3
7	3	4	6	16	−10	16	15	+1
8	2	2	4	13	−9	8	9	−1
9	1	2	2	3	−1	8	8	0
10	2	3	4	15	−9	12	10	+2
11	9	3	17	21	−4	12	6	+6
12	7	5	13	10	+3	20	25	−5
13–14	7	7	13	10	+3	27	34	−7
15–16	7	10	13	8	+5	39	15	+14
17–18	7	7	13	5	+8	27	13	+14
19–22	14	10	27	16	+25	39	10	+29
23–26	14	7	27	2	+18	27	4	+23
27–33	10	3	19	1	+18	12	0	+12
34–45	5	0	10	0	+10	0	0	0

a. Chi-square = 254.87; probability < 0.005
b. Chi-square = 738.57; probability < 0.005

Linnéa Holmer Wren

each individual. Nor are these decisions made at random; instead, they are made "by an evaluation of the immediate circumstances in terms of a set of quite explicit principles" (Frake 1962) concerning the desirability of relationships established by building in a certain area and the suitability of the land available. Therefore, no map or aerial photograph that simply locates and identifies house sites, snas, and hamlets can adequately describe the Zinacanteco settlement pattern. A description must also include the considerations in each individual's mind when he determines where to live.

For Zinacantecos, the primary considerations are the availability of land, the need for social groupings, the proximity to a water supply, and the nature of land. With these considerations in mind, the average Zinacanteco has little room for choice. The place he will build his house is largely predetermined by intermeshing social and ecological factors. It remains for the Zinacanteco to find the most suitable location available within his limited range of possibilities.

Trail Patterns in Zinacantan

Aerial photographs of the municipio of Zinacantan reveal a startling uniformity in the pattern of travel. This uniformity appears in even the most geographically dissimilar hamlets and on all levels of travel, from the major arteries connecting markets and towns to the minor footpaths surrounding individual houses.

In Zinacantan, the business of life flows daily over the trails. Every Zinacanteco makes daily use of the network of crisscrossing trails. Every man must be able to move with ease between his house, his fields, and the marketplace, as well as to participate in the ceremonial life of the community, including the ritual meals, ceremonial circuits, and fiestas in Zinacantan Ceremonial Center.

A woman, equally active in her daily life, must go to the waterhole daily and bring back the household water supply. She must also travel daily to the outlying wooded areas to collect fuel. Often she visits friends' houses within the sna group to gossip, and every week, together with a group of women, she journeys to the nearby markets to

buy and exchange household items. A Zinacanteco woman participates, although not as actively as her male counterpart, in the ceremonial life in Zinacantan Ceremonial Center. The trails and their patterns reflect the living patterns of the community at all levels, from the most personal tasks of each individual to the activities of the entire Zinacanteco society.

In studying the trail networks of Zinacantan, I worked for the most part with mosaics made from HyAc aerial photographs and the rolls of RC–9 photography in the reader-printer and in the stereoscopic viewer. I wanted to test whether the intersections of trails were predominantly forking or intersecting, and whether there was a consistent pattern. In order to obtain a measurement of the angles formed by the trails at their forks and intersections, I assumed the following: a straight line would have described most trails if there were no geographical or topographical hindrances; such straight lines would be most significant if drawn between points connected by the trails; and to provide an approximate measure of angles of the trails, it would be legitimate to superimpose on the trails a pattern of straight lines connecting the adjacent points from which and to which the paths proceed.

The points at which trails form or intersect were chosen as the termini of the straight lines, because these points are the termini for the person who travels along the trails. The traveler moves to a junction, turns, and proceeds to another junction, until he reaches his point of destination. On the basis of these principles, the trail pattern as it exists on the ground was then schematized to make possible the measurement of angles at the junctions (Figs. 50, 51).

My first interest was to discover if the pattern of junction was one of forking or of intersection. Zinacantan Ceremonial Center and one portion of a small hamlet exhibited a grid pattern, but they appeared to be the only settlements in the municipio to do so (Fig. 20). The rest, from a glance, seemed to follow a more random pattern of forking (Fig. 47). In compiling these figures, I first made a distinction between the main trails and minor

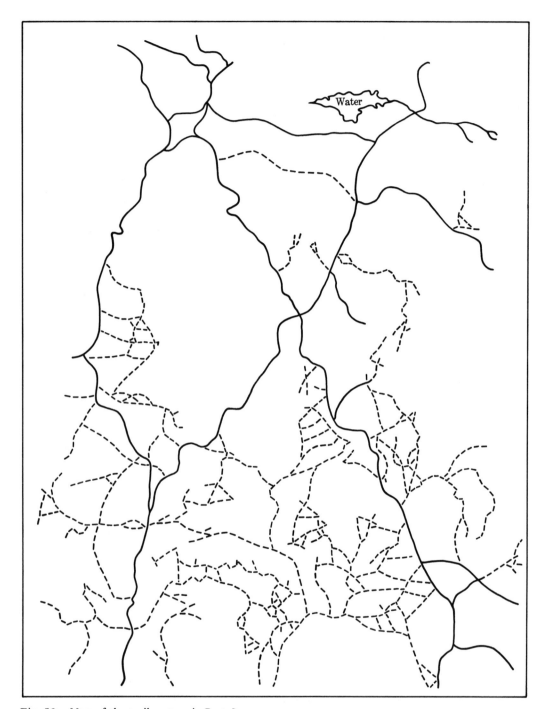

Fig. 50. Map of the trail system in Pasteʔ.

Linnéa Holmer Wren

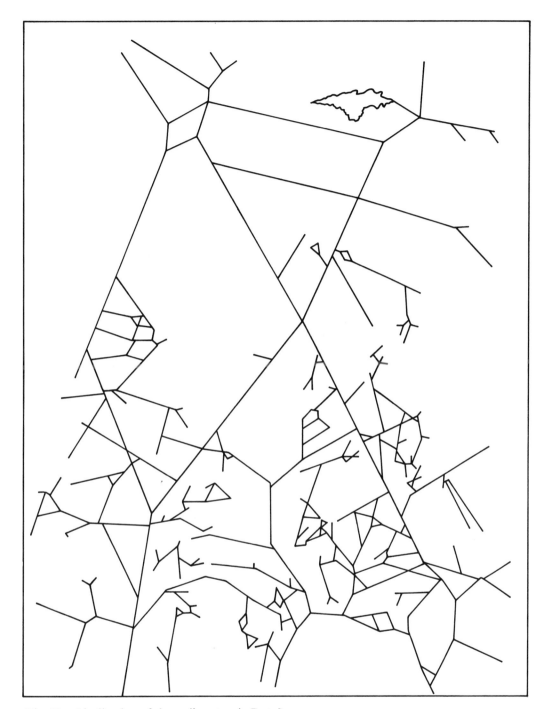

Fig. 51. Idealization of the trail system in Paste?.

trails, based on the amount of usage, and then combined both figures to arrive at a single percentage figure for the hamlet. In Pasteʔ, on the main trail system, there were no intersections but fifty-seven forks; that is, 100 percent of the junctions were forks. Along the minor trails, there were nineteen intersections but two-hundred and seventy-nine forks; that is, 93.2 percent of the junctions were forks. The total percentage of forks for both trail systems was 94.4 percent forks and 5.6 percent intersections. Following the same procedure, I investigated the trail patterns of the three hamlets of ʔApas, Nabenchauk, and Nachih. In Nachih, the information is only partially complete, because a mosaic has not yet been made for this hamlet, and data are available only for the main trails. The total percentages for the four hamlets combined, including both main and minor trails, are: 6.2 percent of the junctions in the form of intersections, and 93.8 percent in the form of forks. The pattern is clearly and consistently one of forking rather than of intersection at the junctions.

The next data I compiled concerned the angles of the junctions. My purpose was to determine whether there was any consistent pattern in the number of degrees in the angles formed by the trails. Using the schematized drawing, I measured either the inside angle of a fork or the two smallest vertical angles at an intersection.

In Pasteʔ, I found that the average angle on the main trails was 60° and on the minor trails was 61°. The combined average was an angle of 60.9°. In ʔApas, the average angle for the main trails was 63.4°, for the minor trails was 61.5°, and for the trails combined was 61.8°. For Nachih, data were available only for the main trails, where the average of the measured angles was 68°. The overall average in the four hamlets for the main trails was 67.9°, for the minor trails was 63°, and for all trails it was 63.8°.

From these figures there seems to appear another consistent pattern, namely, that the angles at junctions (which are overwhelmingly forks) have an average measurement of slightly over 60°. This average holds true for the main trails in the hamlets, the minor trails in the

hamlets, and the two combined. It also holds true for the main trails of all four hamlets, the minor trails of all four hamlets, and for all of the trails in all of the hamlets combined.

Finally, I charted the angles to find out whether the 60° average was statistical magic or was indicative of a large percentage of angles falling near that number. Using 10° ranges, I graphed the number of angles falling within ranges beginning with 1–5°, 6–15°, 16–25°, and so forth. For these data, I drew a graph for each hamlet that combined the measurements for the angles on the main trails and minor trails, and another graph that included all the angles for the three hamlets. I excluded Nachih, because the insufficient data do not include any of the minor trails (Fig. 52). The graphs seem to build to a peak at the 56–65° range, remain high at the 66–75° range and drop off rapidly afterward. The most dramatic example of the median occurring in the 56–65° range is in ʔApas. The total median also shows a dramatic peak in the 56–65° range.

This evidence reveals three consistent elements in the trail network of Zinacantan: the trails fork rather than intersect: the degree of the angles formed at the junction averages near 60°: and the median of the angles at junctions also lies near 60°. There are several possible explanations for these findings. One hypothesis is that these averages reflect the dispersion of houses and the density of population of the hamlets. However, a comparison of the figures for the spread of houses and for population density eliminates this possibility. Pasteʔ is a widely dispersed hamlet, with an average distance of 555 meters between domestic groups, while ʔApas is an extremely compact settlement, with an average distance of 112 meters between domestic groups. Nabenchauk lies somewhat between these extremes, with an average distance of 224 meters between domestic units. It is therefore unlikely that the uniformity in the trail pattern is closely linked to population density or house dispersion.

Another hypothesis requires consideration. Could the relative positions of the hamlets to the ceremonial

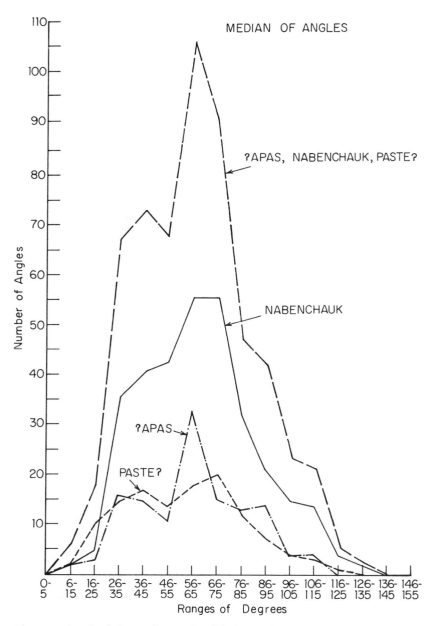

MEDIAN OF ANGLES

?APAS, NABENCHAUK, PASTE?

NABENCHAUK

?APAS

PASTE?

Number of Angles

Ranges of Degrees

Fig. 52. Graph of the median angle of forks on the trails in Zinacanteco hamlets.

center, the market, and other important sites determine the pattern of trails? In this case, the hypothesis would apply only to the main trail system connecting those important places and would not explain the pattern also evidenced in the minor trail system. Furthermore, the relative positions of the hamlets to the important sites are very different in each case. Pasteʔ lies to the south of Zinacantan Ceremonial Center and southwest of San Cristóbal; ʔApas lies to the southwest of Zinacantan Ceremonial Center and San Cristóbal; Nabenchauk lies to the southwest of Zinacantan Ceremonial Center and west of San Cristóbal; and Nachih lies to the south of Zinacantan Ceremonial Center and west of San Cristóbal. Thus, the relative positions of the hamlets in relation to major towns and markets do not explain the uniform findings even on the main arteries of travel.

A third possibility is that a similarity in geographical conditions would explain the similarity in trail patterns. But even a casual consideration of the geographical settings of the hamlets shows the diversity of the terrain in each hamlet. Pasteʔ is located in high terrain with an elevation range of 7,000 to 8,000 feet. The land is too rocky and mountainous for habitation on the western side. The rest of the land slopes gently, forming small hills. ʔApas is lower in elevation than is Pasteʔ. Located on a relatively flat bench, ʔApas is wedged between a rim of limestone mountains to the south and a series of precipitous barrancas on the north. Nabenchauk is concentrated in a mountain valley that drains into a lake. Around the perimeter of the valley are a number of precipitous limestone hills. In the dry season the lake is small, but during the wet season it overflows much of the surrounding flat land. In consequence, only the eastern upper side of the valley and the steep hill to the west are habitable year-round. Finally, Nachih is located in a mountain valley which, unlike the valley of Nabenchauk, is open to the west and drains into a barranca. Such dissimilar geographic factors do not offer a very plausible explanation for the remarkably similar trail patterns.

A hypothesis I would like to suggest is that this pattern of 60° forks has been developed by Zinacanteco travelers to save themselves time, energy, and resources. It is a compromise, made for efficiency's sake, between having no common paths and having an intersection pattern. Ideally, in completely flat and smooth terrain, the most efficient way for people to travel would be to go directly from their point of departure to their point of destination in one continuous, straight line. If this were done, there would be no common paths at all, for everyone would be following a slightly different direction. Even if a group of people started off at the same point and headed for places only slightly apart, they would all pursue somewhat divergent courses.

But in Zinacantan, this pathless mode would be a very inefficient manner in which to travel. The countryside is rugged, rocky, and often overgrown. For everyone to beat his individual path every time he went anywhere would take a tremendous outlay of time and energy, and would prove wasteful. Then, too, women walk barefooted, so that for them a journey through the brush and over limestone rocks would be extremely difficult.

During field interviews about trail patterns, it became apparent that the Indians had cogent explanations as to why common trails were absolutely essential. The factor reiterated by the Zinacantecos was that of "resource management" (Vogt 1967). Individually used trails to each house (the shortest possible travel distance) are never established, because such trails would take strangers through the fields and living sites. The Zinacantecos fear that travelers who are unrelated to the owner of each site would feel free to "acquire" the unguarded resources (corn, fruit, and vegetables) in the fields. When the trails fork off at approximately 60° to lead people to their individual house compounds, these individual trails are well within the boundaries of related kinsmen, who can be trusted not to pick corn, fruit, and vegetables that do not belong to them.

But while the Zinacantecos have found it advantageous to develop a system of paths, they have not found it advantageous to develop a grid pattern. A grid pattern is unnecessary in most of Zinacantan. Unlike city dwellers and government officials, the Zinacantecos are not strongly motivated by a desire for simplicity of design nor ease of management, which a grid offers. Instead, for the Zinacantecos, the paramount consideration is to reach one's destination with the least possible effort. A network of branching paths and trails is therefore far preferable to a grid, for a route that proceeds along trails that fork at 60° angles will be significantly shorter than a route that is confined to the parallel and perpendicular roadways of a grid. For example, if a Zinacanteco woman goes from her house to the waterhole on her normal route, she may walk approximately 620 meters, but if she were to use a grid pattern, she would walk approximately 800 meters, or 30 percent farther. This difference becomes even more significant on the return journey, when she is carrying a day's supply of water. It is also significant for the men, who serve as their own beasts of burden, carrying their corn and equipment on their backs.

The Zinacantecos are explicitly aware of their patterns of forking trails. For example, I questioned the Zinacanteco informants as to which of the following three trail patterns would be preferred:

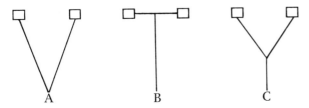

Each informant explicitly chose trail pattern *C* as being preferable.

Zinacantan Ceremonial Center, which became the outpost from which the Spanish and later the Mexican authorities governed the Indians, is the only large Zinacanteco settlement in which the grid pattern has persisted. The only other example of a grid pattern in Zinacantan occurs on the outskirts of the small hamlet of Yalebtaiv. This grid pattern was established at the time of the construction of the Pan-American Highway, and it was built for the use of the Ladino highway workers. But for most

of Zinacantan, a multitude of small decisions made every day by travelers as they walk has resulted in a consistent network of forked trails.

To summarize my results, the accurate measurements obtained from the aerial photos, combined with the ethnographic statements of informants, provided explicit answers in depth on the question of settlement and trail patterns in Zinacantan. These answers broadened knowledge and understanding of the interdependency of ecological and cultural factors determining settlement patterns, showed the importance of degree of slope in the selection of land for house sites or small nearby fields, and provided an explanation of the prevalence and efficiency of the forking trails throughout the municipio of Zinacantan.

In the preparation of this paper I received much help and encouragement from Evon Z. Vogt, George A. Collier, John B. Haviland, and John Sodergren.

Harold C. Conklin
Ethnographic Research in Ifugao

Ifugao, a subregion of the northwestern Luzon cordillera, exhibits a remarkably high degree of cultural and environmental interdependence. The inhabitants of this mountainous area have long been known for their astonishing feats of engineering in the construction and maintenance of extensive rice terraces, which are visually the most impressive aspect of the intricately patterned landscape (Molano 1801; Keesing 1962; Scott 1965). Surprisingly, however, detailed descriptions of this terracing and of related economic activities are conspicuously lacking. Even the rich anthropological accounts of legal, ritual, and social behavior (Barton 1919, 1922; Lambrecht 1932–1951) do not include precise land-use data or other forms of ecological documentation. To some extent, this situation reflects the general unavailability of environmental information on the area, for when I began my research, there were no published weather records, reliable hydrologic data, accurate large-scale maps, or cadastral surveys covering any part of Ifugao.

This unevenly chronicled but highly imageable arena of extraordinary hydraulic and agronomic performance presents the ecologically oriented field investigator with a considerable challenge. High-relief, dispersed settlements and densely but irregularly clustered agricultural holdings contribute to the observable complexity (Fig.

53). Among the hundreds of thousands of terraced fields in central Ifugao, for example, no two fields have the same form or dimensions, except by accident. In surface area, each of these individually controlled inundated plots range from as little as two or three square meters to more than ten thousand square meters (one hectare).

In order to describe and evaluate the allocation and utilization of resources in such an uncharted indigenous system of tropical agriculture, it is helpful to consider a number of general questions. How does an ethnographer approach an unfamiliar landscape, determine its conceptual and observable components, and record the changes that may affect these elements and their interrelationships through time? How can meaningful measurements and comparisons be made? How are the often complex data most effectively expressed? Without satisfactory answers to such queries and to their more specific derivatives (Conklin 1957; Frake 1962), one cannot hope to obtain precise or testable evidence of how a particular system has developed and how it is maintained, or to make statements about it that have analytic, comparative, or long-term relevance. In a very preliminary fashion, I shall document some recent attempts to cope with this type of ethnographic problem in Ifugao.

From July 1961 through 1965, during three short periods and throughout the academic year of 1962–1963, I was able to spend a total of eighteen months in the central part of Ifugao, which was then still a subprovince of the Mountain Province. Within a few kilometers of almost any inhabited point in this area, one can observe a wide range of agricultural activities that are obviously related within one larger pattern, but which also reflect

Fig. 53.   Low oblique aerial photograph of the agricultural landscape in Banaue, north-central Ifugao, looking north-northeast, Aug. 12, 1961.

local adaptations to contrasting biotic and physical components of the montane environment. Elevations above sea level range from less than 250 to more than 2,800 meters (about 800 to more than 9,000 feet), and water resources vary from abundant for all purposes to seasonally deficient.

Based on the first summer's ethnographic and aerial reconnaissance, I chose for regional study and detailed mapping a subarea of approximately 100 square kilometers (c. 40 square miles), roughly one-tenth of the agriculturally occupied part of Ifugao. In this survey area, which includes the upper reaches of two adjacent valley systems, live approximately 10,000 Ifugao settled in more than 300 dispersed hamlets. Some 25 discrete, agriculturally defined districts and several dialect areas are represented.

Within the central northern portion of this subarea, I later selected a much smaller sector of about five square kilometers for concentrated field study and larger-scaled mapping. One of the seventeen hamlets within the agricultural district of Bayninan included in this focal area became the site for the main field base. A check of practices recorded for test hamlets in four neighboring districts indicates that, at least in outline, the structure of the agricultural system revealed in my study holds also for other central and northern sectors. Wherever Ifugao terminology is cited, however, I use only forms checked in and for Bayninan.

After October 1962, ethnographic work was conducted almost exclusively in the local dialect. Extensive collections, records, and investigations of environmental factors ranging from soils to vegetation were facilitated by cooperation with visiting specialists and by the enthusiastic participation of Ifugao assistants.

The Agricultural System

For centuries, and with only the simplest of hand tools, the Ifugao have farmed the steep slopes and valleys of their mountainous territory. This firmly established, integral, and continuing agricultural pattern (Figs. 53, 54, 55) depends on many factors: the availability of water for irrigation and soil transport; suitable earth or stone for construction and repair of embankments; a variety of vegetational habitats as sources of fuel, fencing, and other construction materials; a large number of protected and cultivated plant types, including rice, sweet potatoes, legumes, and fruits; domesticated pigs, chickens, and ducks; the presence of mud fish, snails, and other aquatic fauna; sufficient labor to keep up the annual round of repairs, cultivation tasks, and associated rituals; and most important, the knowledge of how these and many other economic factors are interrelated and may be profitably utilized.

The farming system of Ifugao is complex. As in all integral agricultural systems, most of the settings, material components, participants, and routines serve multiple functions. For example, that which the Ifugao call *lūyoq*, the carefully puddled top layer of soil in an inundated field, not only provides a moist, fertile medium in which to grow rice and other wet crops, but this common agricultural artifact is also used for at least ten other purposes: as a source of clay for coating and lining dikes (Fig. 55); a smooth, unobstructed surface across which piles of unwanted or excavated earth can be easily transported on sledgelike drag boards; a substance for vegetable and spice cultivation, which after being mixed with an essential aquatic weed that grows in or just above the *lūyoq* layer, is formed into isletlike mounds; a convenient location for preserving the hollow-log sluicing troughs used in repairing and filling terraces; a muddy vat for soaking, loosening, and softening bast-fiber plant materials used in tying; a protective and decorative staining agent for carved bowls and other wooden implements; a place in which to set or manipulate a variety of basket traps for small pond fish; a source of many varieties of aquatic snails, whose flesh furnishes a continual supply of everyday food, the shells of some varieties also being burned to make slaked lime; a seasonal breeding ground for mole crickets and many other forms of amphibious or semiaquatic edible fauna; and a post-harvest mud pool for children's sports.

Other parts of the artificial terraces, including the lower layers of fill, waterworks, borders, and walls, serve similarly diverse functions. In the local ecosystem, such

Harold C. Conklin

Fig. 54. Closer view of a terraced slope in the Banaue hamlet of Panalngan (also visible in Fig. 53), showing features of the immediate and distant agricultural landscape, May 18, 1963.

Fig. 55. Grand photograph of the intercropping of rice and
taro in a pond-field terrace in Bayninan (field 1 in Fig. 59),
with a woman walking along the top of the terrace wall,
Mar. 14, 1963.

Harold C. Conklin

fields can hardly be treated as simple farm plots, leveled and watered solely for a single, seasonal foodcrop. In spite of the strong cultural bias emphasizing almost every aspect of rice farming, Ifugao "rice terraces" are in fact multipurpose pond fields (Wagner 1960:179; Spencer and Hale 1961:11–12; Geertz 1963:28–32; Leach 1961: 129–174). In order to study how these complex pond fields are constructed and maintained, measured and counted, assessed and exchanged, how their areas may be compared and the intricate overall land-use pattern made explicit, it is helpful to begin with some basic cultural data.

Pond Fields. In its most frequent and general sense, the Ifugao term *payo* means any type of irrigable farmland that is hydraulically leveled and artificially bunded. However, differing contexts, which are not necessarily obvious to the outsider, provide for this one label a wide range of semantic specificity and precision. Differences of regional extent, contiguity, and ownership of single fields or series of fields are indicated in the word. For example, in terms of economic and legal units, one or more adjoining pond field "plots" may comprise a "parcel"; and if privately owned and managed as a unit, one or more parcels in a district may constitute a "holding." Moreover, within any clustered parcel, the "main field" (largest in surface area and least attenuated) is distinguished from its subsidiary plots. Each of these last four English glosses translates an optional but determinable and specific sense of the term *payo*. In contrast with *puquŋ*, meaning a "small, insignificant pond field," *payo* also designates a "well-formed, large pond field." This distinction is relative only to the size and shape pattern of fields throughout a particular region. This instance of a common type of polysemy can be represented as follows:

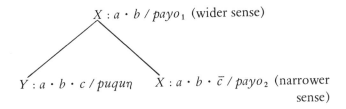

$$X : a \cdot b \: / \: payo_1 \text{ (wider sense)}$$

$$Y : a \cdot b \cdot c \: / \: puquŋ \qquad X : a \cdot b \cdot \bar{c} \: / \: payo_2 \text{ (narrower sense)}$$

The unmarked term, X, indicates the form of both the generic category "pond field," defined by a combination of semantic features symbolized as $a \cdot b$, as well as of the specific opposite of the marked term Y. Neither the added feature of the size limitation c, nor any expression of its absence $\bar{c}$, occurs at the more general level (Jakobson 1957:5). Subscripts distinguish different senses of the word.

There are many other locally recognized pond-field differences, such as soil depth and embankment construction (Spencer and Hale 1961). However, these general distinctions illustrate the basic point that, in locating, enumerating, and describing *payo* with respect to boundary disputes, inheritance rights, and similar problems, the kind of pond-field unit involved must be specified. Similarly, the relation between such units and other contrasting segments of the agricultural landscape should be established.

Land Forms. The Ifugao distinguish hundreds of terrain variations involving forms and combinations of rock, soil, water, vegetation, and the results of agronomic activity. The coverage of this folk classification ranges from broad polysemous concepts, such as *lūta*, "land," "earth," and *bīlid*, "mountainous slopeland," to such highly specific particulars as *quduŋo*, "limonite," and *qanul*, "underground drainage conduits." Like the latter examples, many terms refer to special qualities, aspects, or components of the agricultural environment rather than to contrasting types of land surface in general. However, one intermediate-level contrast set of eight categories, including *payo*, does cover in a mutually exclusive manner all major vegetationally and agriculturally significant land-surface types. A brief characterization of each of these locally distinguished land forms, listed in their general order of increasing agricultural involvement, follows:

mapulun, "grassland" (short, low, open grassland); often also *pulun*. Ridge and slopeland, untilled, covered with herbaceous grasses (*gūlun*, *Imperata* sp., *taŋlag*, *Themeda* sp., and others); public and unmanaged; open, unbounded, minimally valued; a source of outer roof thatch. Without new sources of irrigation water, such land is not normally brought under cultivation. The ridges and slopes of the most distant mountains visible in Figure 55 are largely "grassland."

qinalāhan, "forest" (public forest, distant forest). Slopeland, undisturbed soil, covered with various types of dense woody vegetation (from lower altitude mid-mountain climax forest to pine forest and mossy cloud forest types); public (for residents in the same general watershed area) and unmanaged; a source of firewood, other natural forest products, and game. See upper right of Figure 53, and the most distant slope in upper right of Figure 55.

mabilāu, "caneland" (cane grassland, high grassland, second growth, *runo* association). Mostly slopeland, unworked soil, covered with various stages of second-growth herbaceous and ligneous vegetation dominated by dense clumps of tall canegrass (*bilāu, Miscanthus* spp.); some protection and management (canegrass much used for construction, fencing, and so forth). See the higher uncleared slopes in Figure 54 and the closest background vegetation in upper right of Figure 55.

pinūgu, "woodlot" (private forest or grove); regional synonym, *muyuŋ.* Slopeland, unturned soil, covered with high tree growth (timber and fruit trees, erect palms, climbing rattans, and so forth); privately owned and managed (undergrowth clearance, selective cutting, and some planting of desired tree, vine, and bamboo types). Boundaries are definite and relatively permanent, though without artificial markers. Such groves are valued for timber and other products, as a nearby source of firewood, and for protection of lower farmland from excessive runoff and erosion. See tree growth areas in vicinity of hamlets in Figures 53 and 54 and the peaked rise in background, upper right of Figure 55.

bābal, "swidden" (slope field, camote field, kaingin); referential synonym, *qūma.* Slopeland, cultivated and often contour-ridged (especially for sweet potatoes).

Other highland dry-field crops (including taro, yams, manioc, corn, millet, mongo beans, and pigeon peas, but excluding rice except at elevations below 600–700 meters or 2,000 feet above sea level) are also cultivated in small stands or in moderately intercropped swiddens. Boundaries remain discrete during a normal cultivation cycle of several years. When fallow, succession is usually to a canegrass association. See the cleared patches on slopes in lower right of Figure 53 and in the background of Figure 54.

lattaŋ, "house terrace" (settlement, hamlet terrace, residential site); also *latāŋan.* Leveled terrace land, whose surface is packed smooth or paved but not tilled; serving primarily as house and granary yards, work space for grain drying, and so forth; discrete, often fenced or walled, and named. See Figures 53 and 55.

qilid, "drained field" (drained terrace, ridged terrace); often also *naqīlid.* Leveled terrace land, whose surface is tilled and ditch-mounded (usually in cross-contour fashion) for cultivation and drainage of dry crops such as sweet potatoes and legumes. Drained fields, though privately owned, are kept in this temporary state for a minimum number of annual cycles before shifting back to a more permanent form of terrace use.

payo, "pond field" (bunded terrace, rice terrace, rice field); ritual synonyms, *banāno, daluŋēne, lubog, bākah.* Leveled farmland, bunded to retain irrigation water for shallow inundation of artificial soil, and carefully worked for the cultivation of wet-field rice, taro, and other crops; privately owned, discrete units with permanent stone markers; the most valued of all land forms. See Figures 53–59.

From the contrastive properties noted in the first sections of each of these descriptions, one can derive a field-checked set of distinctive and minimal componential definitions for each of the eight land form categories:

Relevant oppositions (with respect to slope, soil, cover, and use)

$L : \overline{L}$	Leveled	:	Not leveled

Harold C. Conklin

$T : \overline{T}$	Tilled	:	Not tilled
$W : \overline{W}$	Wooded	:	Not wooded
$M : \overline{M}$	Managed maximally	:	Not managed maximally

Analytic definitions (symbols at left stand for Ifugao categories but are derived mnemonically from English glosses)

G	Grassland	$\overline{L}\ \overline{T}\ \overline{W}\ \overline{M}$
F	Forest	$\overline{L}\ \overline{T}\ W\ \overline{M}$
C	Caneland	$\overline{L}\ \overline{T}\ \overline{W}\ M$
W	Woodlot	$\overline{L}\ \overline{T}\ W\ M$
S	Swidden	$\overline{L}\ T$
H	House terrace	$L\ \overline{T}$
D	Drained field	$L\ T\ \overline{M}$
P	Pond field	$L\ T\ M$

Each formulaic transcription accounts for the essential features visually distinguishing one land form from the others in a unique, concise, and nonredundant statement. The use of the term S always refers to a farmed slope ($\overline{L}T$), term H to an untilled horizontal surface ($L\overline{T}$), and so forth. For ethnographic mapping of cadastral data and for many other recording tasks, these distinctions are crucial; and for most identificational purposes they are sufficient.

These land forms also represent many contrastive patterns of use and change. Each category thus embraces more than can be adequately covered by the synchronic combination of a small number of vegetational, cultural, and edaphic features. Additional parallel attributes and multidimensional contrasts abound. Many implied differences in Ifugao land-form classification relate only to past or potential changes in time and space determined by transitional restraints within the agricultural system. To analyze these alternatives and the restrictions governing them, it is helpful not only to focus on precise definitions (Malinowski 1935:79–87; Conklin 1962) but also to consider patterns of succession from one differential stage of land usage to another.

Time and Space. After the examination of many records of changing terrain characteristics through seasonal, annual, and longer cycles of agricultural activity, similarities and connections as well as contrasts and oppositions obtaining among the eight Ifugao land-form types are easily discerned. They may often be expressed in diagrammatic form. In fact, all essential, ethnographically attested, sequential links interconnecting these eight categories can be represented in the form of a finite directed graph (Busacker and Saaty 1965), where vertices stand for the eight land forms, and directed arcs represent possible changes through time (recursive loops indicating "internal" cyclic progressions) (Fig. 60). Special markings include the shape of the labeled nodes (square vs. triangular, for leveled vs. slope land); solidity of the node enclosure (broken vs. solid line, for nondiscrete vs. discrete status); thickness of node base (extra thick vs. normal line, for preferred terminal vs. less preferred or nonterminal status); loop symbols (m vs. ∞, for desired minimization of cycles [one season for D; c. three years for S] vs. desired perpetuation of normal cycles); and form of feedback arcs (broken vs. unbroken line, for indefinite vs. definite duration of cycles).

A large number of relational inferences are derivable from this network. C, for example, is the only articulation point in the network; its removal disconnects the graph and isolates the least involved pendant G. C is also the only node adjacent to all others. These clearly displayed features of the digraph underscore the nonrecursive, unbounded, central but intermediate position of this land form and reflect both its lack of sequential restrictions and its unique status as the normal extended fallow or second-growth association in the area. As abandoned terrace land loses its "shape," a former P, D, or H may shift rapidly to C. This is the most generalized, as well as the most frequently encountered, of the agriculturally involved land forms.

A multigraph expanding the partial bilateral symmetry of the network (Fig. 60) could easily be constructed to show additional paired sets of contrasts linking cor-

Fig. 56.   Aerial photographs of a terraced valley fifty years ago and today, showing a section of pond-fields, including the ritual field site for district II (Fig. 58), at Happe´, Kinnakin, Banaue. Left: portion of a photograph taken by Roy F. Barton a month or two after the July rice harvest, 1912 or 1913. Right: portion of a photograph taken from the same location during the transplanting season, Mar. 25, 1963.

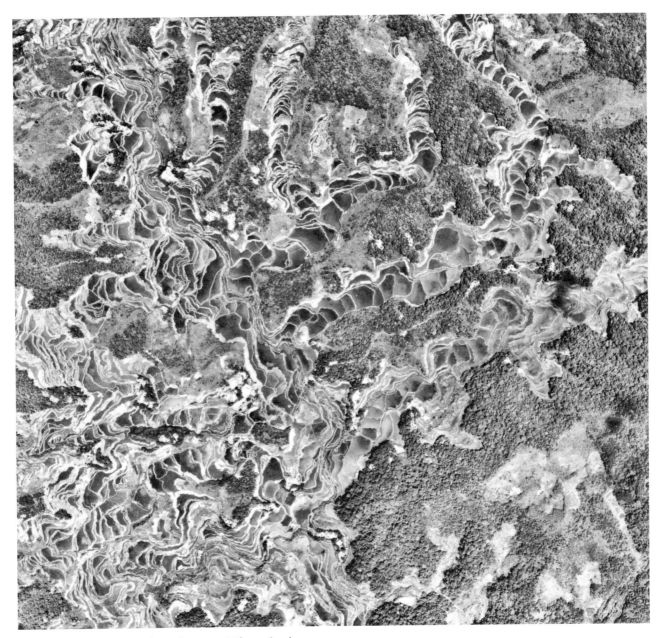

Fig. 57. Vertical aerial view of a central Ifugao landscape. Section of a 1:17,600-scale aerial photograph (reproduced without reduction from an electronically processed contact print) of a part of Kababuyan, Banaue, in the south-central sector of the mapped survey area, Apr. 23, 1963.

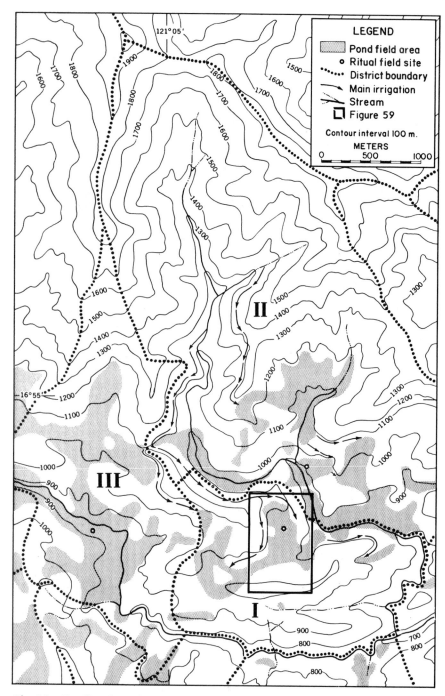

Fig. 58. Small-scale regional map of agricultural terrain in central Ifugao. District I is located within the focal area, as are most of two of the five adjacent districts (districts II and III), all of which lie within the northern part of the survey area.

Harold C. Conklin

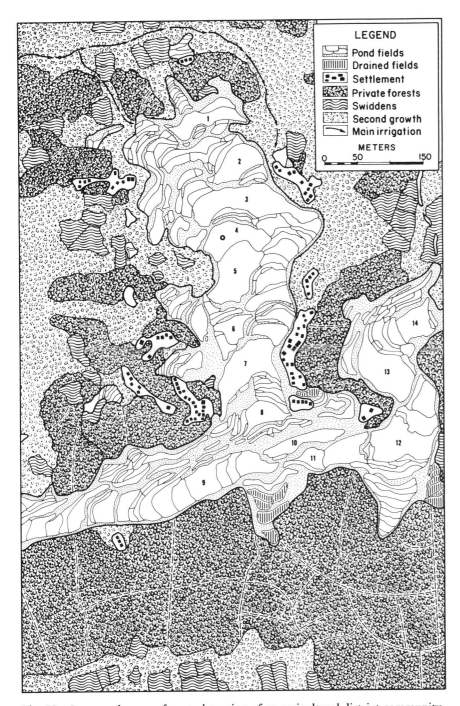

Fig. 59. Large-scale map of central portion of an agricultural district community. Settlement arrangement and agricultural terrain in part of district I (Bayninan), April 1963. Planimetric data were derived largely from aerial photogrammetric manuscript compiled at a scale of 1:2,500.

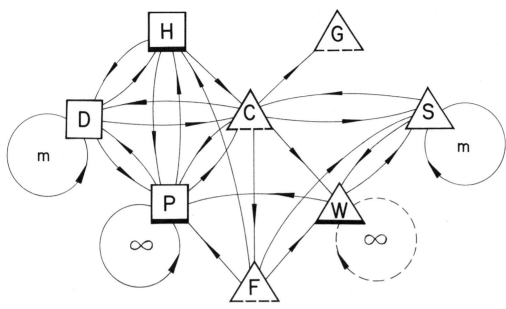

Fig. 60.   Graph of the eight land-form types in Ifugao.

respondingly adjacent nodes. Note, for example, the correlation between P and D on one side and W and S on the other in terms of recognized microclimatic and biotic variation paralleling the already indicated differences of slope and cultural evaluation. One can observe even more directly that such specific, hypothetical, one-step successions as:

$$G \to W, G \to D, P \to S, F \to G, F \to C$$

are explicitly excluded from this system.

From such observations, it is apparent that for a community of Ifugao farmers, an ideal long-term sequence begins in an initial, homogeneous, natural state of F and develops into an agriculturally dominated environment covered exclusively by P, W, and H. One of the easiest ways to assess the relative economic standing of an Ifugao agricultural district is to note the degree to which this target condition has been approached (cf. Figs. 53 and 57).

In addition to facilitating the analysis of ideal or potential patterns, however, the general digraph (Fig. 60) also serves as a base from which actual cases can be represented. In the recording of recurring subcycles (sequences passing through some but not all nodes), successions worked out for individual sites can be expressed as partial subgraphs. To illustrate, the history of a particular pond-field site first cleared in 1937:

$$F(n) \to S(4) \to W(6) \to P(2) \to D(2) \to C(6) \to S(5) \to W(3) \to P(-)$$
$$\text{[1937] [1941] [1947] [1949] [1951] [1957] [1962] [1965]}$$

can be represented in a graph (Fig. 61).

Such a series of short-term changes in the status of terrace land can be observed only at the periphery of an irrigated sector. At the "center" or the putatively oldest site of every agricultural district (*himpuntonāqan*), one finds a single, named, ritual plot or parcel (*puntonāqan*; Fig. 58), which is traditionally the first to be planted, transplanted, and harvested. Owners of land at and near such sites tend to keep walls and fields in excellent condition and in a perpetual P state. The validity of genealogically linked chains-of-title recounted to establish the relative age, size, and ownership of these core fields

Harold C. Conklin

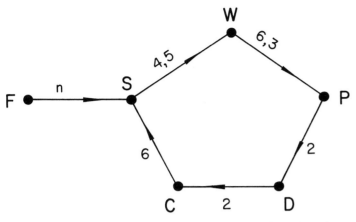

Fig. 61. Graph of the history of a pond-field site first cleared in 1937.

is easy to assume but difficult to check. In a few instances, photographs from the early 1900s have provided useful documentation of the remarkable continuity of pond-field margins and land use in these central areas (Fig. 56).

Aerial photographs can provide even better evidence, though the earliest available documentation of this type goes back only to 1945, when the purpose of such photography was primarily to locate General Yamashita's troops, and is of very uneven coverage and quality. Recent aerial photography of the area, flown for this project, meets the necessary standards of photogrammetric mapping. Coupled with detailed ground surveys, these photographs have been of immense help in relating Ifugao classifications and farming practices to locationally precise land units.

Mapping

In order to plot distances, areas, and gradients in an area of high relief, carefully compiled terrain maps are a necessity. Their previous unavailability for Ifugao severely limited the planimetric accuracy of even the best sketch maps (Beyer 1908; Lambrecht 1932:3–5) and village plans (Lambrecht 1929), and apparently discouraged any attempts to chart the irregular boundaries of the terraced pond-field areas. Fortunately, as a result of recent devel-

opments in high resolution aerial photography and machine mapping (Thompson 1966), it is now possible, with relatively few ground control points, to determine contour differences of less than two meters from 1:12,000 to 1:20,000 scale stereopairs, thus overcoming the formidable obstacles facing the unassisted ground surveyor and cartographer.

During the last five years, topographically reliable 1:50,000 sheets for most of northern Luzon have been published. Although the scale of these government maps is too small for detailed ethnographic use, they have greatly facilitated the regional interpretation of the new aerial photography covering the survey area and several thousand square kilometers of the surrounding cordilleran territory, especially to the north and west. Added to the products of the archival research, the new photography (Fig. 57) brought to more than 1,000 the number of vertical aerial prints used in this study.

In spite of many logistic, weather, and terrain difficulties, all photography and ground surveying necessary for the machine mapping phase of this project were completed in 1963. Four film-manuscript separations (topography, vegetation, drainage, and cultural detail) for map sections covering the survey area (at 1:5,000 scale, with four-meter contours) and the focal area (at 1:2,500 scale, with two-meter contours) were photogrammetrically plotted during 1963 and 1964. The required ground checking continued for a total of nine months at various periods between 1964 and 1966. Final drawings are now being made for publication. Through an examination of two sample derivative maps (Figs. 58, 59), I shall show the kinds of spatial detail covered, relate this information to the earlier analysis of Ifugao land use, and assess briefly the use of aerial photogrammetry for ethnographic research.

Regional Map. A regional map (Fig. 58) covering an area of about 18 square kilometers (7.0 square miles or almost 20 percent of the survey area) shows the distribution of inundated pond-field land in the focal area (I) and in the adjacent, similarly discrete, agricultural districts (especially the closely associated areas II and III). Arrows indicate major irrigation canals; hundreds of additional, separate, branching, or diversion channels provide the more than 10,000 individual plots within this three-district complex with varying degrees of controlled water supply. In all, pond fields cover about 15 percent of the total area of these districts. The surface and ground water necessary to maintain this type of permanent-field agriculture comes largely from the higher and steeper parts of the drainage basin, which are easily discerned on the map. The regional importance of this forested catchment area is reflected in a comparison of the approximate percentages of major land forms included (estimates based partly on more detailed base maps and photographs):

G	7.0%	(mostly ridges of intermediate elevation)
F	30.0%	(especially higher slopes and ridges; most of northern half of this map)
C	20.0%	(intermediate and lower slopes)
W	20.0%	(vicinity of inundated and more heavily populated areas)
S	6.0%	(mostly intermediate and lower slopes, especially those steeper than adjacent terraced sections)
H	0.5%	(adjacent to or near larger, broader pond fields)
D	0.5%	(scattered, in P area)
P	16.0%	(especially on more gently inclined slopes)
Total	100.0%	(entire surface area, including an embedded 1–2% of interstitial cliffs, rocky outcrops, stream beds, sandbars, and trails; cf. Figs. 57, 59.)

Many serious irrigation and land-use problems seem always to be set within a regional frame of reference. The ethnographic significance of this observation is underscored by a number of social and economic factors, such as the wide network of kin relationships among the inhabitants of clustered districts, the strictly cognatic and primogeniturally-weighted inheritance of irrigated land, and the principle of setting up conjugal residence as close as possible to the largest pond-field holding transmitted to a couple at marriage.

In 1963, the inhabitants of this three-district region numbered approximately 2,200. They were settled in more than 100 small hamlets, mostly between 900 and 1,100 meters above sea level, and were situated in or near the densest clusters of pond fields. Irrigated agricultural land for the three districts totaled approximately 285 hectares.

Subdistrict Map. A somewhat more detailed subdistrict map (Fig. 59) shows the way in which smaller segments of various land forms and residential clusters are articulated. It consists of an enlargement of the marked section on the regional map (Fig. 58) in the immediate vicinity of the Bayninan ritual plot (4, Fig. 59). Boundaries that are well established locally are delineated; some are clearly discernible even from the air (cf. Fig. 57). The density and extent of privately owned woodlots, the spatially intermediate character of second growth dominated by caneland, and the clustering of settlements in such a focal sector are also easily observed. Other differ-

Harold C. Conklin

ences between a core area and a district or district complex can be illustrated by contrasting the land-form percentages for the three districts I, II, and III with those for this central section of district I alone (Table 5). From the center of a district, G and F remain relatively remote, while W, P, and H are consistently clustered (cf. Fig. 57).

Because of the scale of reproduction and for greater clarity on the subdistrict map, many details have been excluded: contours, spot elevations, water courses (other than the main irrigation canals), trails, and separate level divisions within hamlets. A closer look at what has been included reveals that, aside from the houseyards (H), and in order of decreasing extent, four major land-surface types are represented: W, 22 hectares (about 54 acres); P, 20 hectares; C, 10–12 hectares; and S, 3–4 hectares. Five kinds of property units are delineated; W, 55 privately owned lots (120 for all of district I); P, more than 300 inundated plots (1,700+ for all of district I; within the territory covered by the map there are actually 417 plots, measurably delineated on larger scale maps, but many do not appear in this reproduction because of their small size—less than 15 square meters in area or less than two meters in width, comprising part or all of 87 privately owned parcels; S, 46 individually managed slope fields (90 for all of district I, this figure including 40 cleared initially in 1963); D, 13 individually managed dry terraces (80 for the whole district); and H, 11 of the 17 district I settlements (ranging in form from one to six hamlet terraces each). C areas, like the more distant F and G, are not divided sharply into discrete property units.

P areas receive the most attention in terms of time, labor, and capital, as well as in sociocultural evaluation. The numbers on the subdistrict map signify the principal pond fields of 14 (among 25) main parcels in this core area. Since 1962, these 14 plots and their associated subsidiary terraces have served as test fields for continuing agricultural and microecological study. The numeral progression also marks successive drops in elevation (the difference between fields 1 and 14 being more than 100 meters). These variations in parcel composition and

Table 5. Relative extent of major land forms within a region and at the center of a district.

| | Approximate percentage of surface area covered | |
Major land form type	Region comprised of districts I, II, III (Fig. 58)	Core area of district I (Fig. 59)
G	7.0	0.0
F	30.0	0.0
C	20.0	20.0
W	20.0	37.0
S	6.0	5.3
H	0.5	2.0
D	0.5	0.7
P	16.0	35.0

elevation are locally crucial in the routing of irrigation water and the building of drainage channels. Precise differences are easily obtained from the machine analysis of stereopairs of aerial photographs. These are listed along with data on parcel segmentation and ownership in Table 6. For example, while plots 1 and 9 are each planimetrically 400 meters removed from plot 14, the vertical difference between 1 and 14 is almost four times that between 9 and 14. The actual watercourse gradient through this area remains close to 10 percent.

Hydraulic, agronomic, and other cultural activities closely linked with these factors are numerous, as illustrated by a partial descriptive inventory taken from one field map of the ethnogeographically discrete sector lying between and including field 3 and the subsidiary plots below field 8. A former stream valley, this area averages about 150 meters in width and is bordered by steep concave slopes. It is relatively "flat," descending 40 meters through ten locally named pocket-like terraced subareas. Between the two main irrigation-drainage ditches running along the margins lie 105 pond-field plots, each at a slightly different level from its neighbor and with distinct bunds and embankments. Many of these wet fields have supporting or protective walls, terrace

Table 6. Ownership, composition, and elevation of principal plots of fourteen main pond-field parcels.

| Main pond field | Property holder | | Parcel composition | | | Surface elevation above P14 (in meters)[a] |
| | Lives in district I | Lives in district II | Subsidiary plots | | | |
			Above main plot	Below main plot	Total plots	
1	A[b]		2	5	8	104.8
2	B		6	4	11	86.2
3	C		0	13	14	78.3
4[c]	D		0	0	1	72.2
5		E	0	10	11	69.9
6	F		0	3	4	59.1
7	G		0	17	18	53.1
8	H		6	20	27	38.3
9	I		4	0	5	28.4
10	J		0	1	2	22.1
11	K		4	0	5	19.2
12	L		39	3	43	14.7
13	M		0	0	1	9.4
14	N		3	4	8	0.0
Totals	(12)	(1)	64	80	158	—

a. Photogrammetric heighting accuracy: ± 0.5 m.
b. Letters represent separate individuals.
c. Single-plot ritual field parcel.

Harold C. Conklin

steps, and sunken boundary markers of stone. Five plots —numbers 3, 4, 5, 7, and 8—are of considerable breadth. Each of these serves as the principal field of a separate holding. In all, there are 13 parcels, each marked with special ritual plants at particular points along the inner side of the principal field dike. Twelve plots contain seedbed sections. Owners work or manage their respective fields, except for seven mortgagees who farm temporarily hypothecated subsidiary plots or plot-sections. Irrigation and drainage control is maintained by a series of waterworks, which are mostly walled, lined, or reinforced with fitted stone: 13 irrigation inlets (including six culverts) and 13 drainage outlets connecting with the two main canals, 119 interterrace spillways, and 12 internal water sources (including five springs and one well). Finally, six artificially walled mudfish pits and eleven raised vegetable mounds have been constructed in some of the larger pond fields.

This type of culturally relevant information can be recorded and tallied with cartographic and ethnographic accuracy, but it cannot be derived from photointerpretation or photogrammetry alone. Many of these details were considered important enough by several Ifugao assistants (not owners of the parcels involved) to be added by them in December 1965 to a large-scale map of the area. Few of the distinctions could have been recorded directly from photographs by even the most skilled plotter.

For this type of ethnographic inquiry, it is important to recognize both the specific advantages as well as the very real limitations in the use of aerial photography and machine mapping, as well as in making direct ground observations and in obtaining information from local inhabitants. With data derived from the experiences of this project, I find it instructive to summarize such factors in tabular form (Table 7). Air photos give the field worker a visual overview of the landscape. They may serve as finding charts and as bases for profitable discussions with informants. Accurate maps are necessary for many types of measurement and for the assessment of relief and hydrography. Locationally, they provide an essential

plotting board. By themselves, however, these devices cannot provide information sufficient to determine the shape and occurrence of many kinds of ethnographically needed data. Personal observations and ground measurements are still required in cases where vegetation covers trails, water courses, dams, and marked property boundaries, and where the grain of terrestrial variation is too fine or too dense for photographic penetration. Moreover, the perceptions, categorizations, usages, and communicative interactions of one's informants frequently furnish the only source of information about the way in which complex and changing socioecological contexts and events are ordered.

In this brief report on recent ethnoecologically oriented research in the Philippines I have tried to indicate the general problems of recording, interpreting, and comparing man-environment relations in Ifugao. In analyzing the socially and culturally structured landscape, I have stressed the importance of detailed ethnographic mapping and the special opportunities, requirements, and limitations inherent in the use of aerial photography. Essential to this analysis was an explicit description of the systematic interrelations in time and space of locally distinguished and agriculturally significant land forms. I have also emphasized the advantages of combining multiple forms of data display and analysis and the use of varying types of field and archival documentation. A number of manuscripts on Ifugao and neighboring areas contain unique records worthy of further study and publication (Conklin 1967a). Similarly, unpublished photographs taken by individuals who traveled through the area after the 1880s may also provide invaluable and otherwise irretrievable information. As it is certain that many such early glass plates and prints remain buried in private collections and albums, I would appreciate hearing of their existence at any time.

This paper, in slightly different form, first appeared in *Transactions of the New York Academy of Sciences*, ser. II, vol. 30, no. 1 (1967):99–121. Text statements hold as of that date. Since then a number of directly related works have appeared, including

Table 7. Advantages and limitations of aerial photogrammetry in constructing ethnographically useful maps, with particular reference to Ifugao.

Pertinent data to be expressed cartographically	Determinable from information provided by			
	Air photos[a]	Machine plots[b]	Field observations[c]	Informants
Regional extent of irrigated fields	x[d]	y[e]		
Terrain contours		x		
Watershed drainage systems	y	x		
Wet-field plot boundaries	y	x	y	
Measurable areas, slopes, terrain elevations, and horizontal distances		x	y	
Boundaries between caneland and grassland or woodlots	y		x	y
External boundaries of swiddens	y		x	y
Extent of drained fields and pond field seedbeds	y	y	x	y
Delineation of houses and similar structures	y	y	x	y
Extent of individual or connected series of hamlet terraces		y	x	y
Form of terrace embankments			x	y
Network of irrigation channels leading to and within pond-field areas			x	y
Water sources (springs, etc.)			y	x
Boundaries of agricultural districts			y	x
Boundaries between private woodlots and other woodlots or public forests			y	x
Boundaries between adjacent swiddens			y	x
Stage of swidden cycle (e.g., 2nd year)			y	x
Economic value of land units (in terms of fertility, water rights, etc.)			y	x
Internal construction of pond fields			y	x
Ownership markers within pond-field parcels			y	x
Ritual pond fields				x
Composition of pond-field parcels				x
Pond-field parcel names, owners, pedigrees				x
Extent of locally named geographical units				x

a. Contact and enlarged prints of high resolution vertical aerial photography at a negative scale no smaller than 1:20,000. Low oblique aerial photographs, such as Fig. 53, are useful in survey work and as an adjunct to ground observations, but for mapping, they can be used only with difficulty.

b. Planimetric and topographic manuscript (preliminary maps), plotted photogrammetrically at a scale no smaller than 1:5,000 from vertical air photography and the results of third-order as well as fourth-order ground control.

c. Those that can be recorded on the ground by anyone who has learned the general land-form and land-use distinctions commonly made in Ifugao.

d. The x represents a primary or direct source of information.

e. The y represents a secondary, partial, or derived source of information.

Harold C. Conklin

an important source of Ifugao agricultural vocabulary (Newell 1968), a brief but perceptive account of Ifugao terracing practices (van Breeman et al. 1970), and a set of large-scale, ethnographically and photogrammetrically compiled land-use maps of north central Ifugao (Conklin 1972). Research reported on in this paper was supported in various ways by the National Science Foundation, the Yale University Concilium on International Studies, the Philippine National Museum, the International Rice Research Institute, and the Robert H. Lowie Museum of Anthropology, University of California at Berkeley. For help in preparing this report, I particularly want to thank Antonio S. Buangan, Alberto B. Bulatao, Hamako A. Butler, Jean M. Conklin, Pugguwon Lupaih, and Buwaya Tindungan.

Aerial Photography in Anthropology

Part Three
Aerial Photography in Anthropology

Thomas S. Schorr
A Bibliography, with Historical Sketch

Aerial photographs were put to use in anthropology shortly after the turn of the century, when J. E. Capper (1907) published views taken from a war balloon of the archaeological site at Stonehenge. Advances followed quickly on the heels of World War I, largely as an outgrowth of aeronautical achievements and intelligence operations (Rowe 1953:907).

As part of the continuing war effort, Great Britain, France, and Germany started the process of constructing and perfecting sizable military air forces, which involved the development of auxiliary technology, including optical devices for aerial navigation, target acquisition, fire control, and aerial photographic reconnaissance, along with the training of specialists to operate, maintain, and update these systems (Livingston 1964). Many British archaeologists as well as their counterparts in other nations found that their specialized knowledge and abilities enabled them to serve the interests of national emergency as intelligencers. Perhaps the best known example from the period just prior to the First World War involves the activities of Sir Leonard Woolley and his assistant, T. E. Lawrence, during the Sinai expedition of 1914, under the direction of Capt. S. F. Newcombe

(Garnett 1938:163–167; Knightley and Simpson 1971:38–40).

Archaeology Takes Off

When intelligence operations and cartography turned opportunely from laborious ground survey methods to the more efficient aerial photographic reconnaissance and photointerpretation as an alternate way of procuring vital information during the war, British archaeologists working in this area immediately became aware of a number of unique properties of information recorded by this method, which suit it ideally to site discovery and survey.

The images captured on aerial photographs best resemble unselective maps of all visible object phenomena as they relate in the time and space encompassed by the camera's field of view during the instant when the shutter was tripped. Very often, the photograph will reveal subtle features of long-obliterated structures in the terrain, soil formations, and vegetative cover, especially under the proper conditions of light and season, which are either invisible or easily overlooked in surface reconnaissance at close distances and at low angles of view. Some features, invisible to the eye at any angle, may be recorded for study by the use of special combinations of film and light filters. Moreover, the technique of taking overlapping photographs at calculated intervals along the course of a flight produces an exaggerated, three-dimensional model of the terrain when such pictures are viewed with a stereoscope, which reveals even the slightest undulation produced by subsurface remains and lends itself to precise measurement. As military intelligence demonstrated, prospecting in archaeology can also be accomplished by using existing photographs flown for other purposes.

Hence, the accuracy, rapidity, low cost, and overall convenience with which the new method could make entire regions accessible as never before to surveying and mapping, produced an enthusiastic acceptance of the method in the early decades of the twentieth century as an effective new tool in the archaeologist's kit (Crawford 1929, 1939, 1954; Daniel 1950; Poidebard 1929, 1934; Reeves 1936; Rey 1919; St. Joseph 1957, 1962; Scollar 1965; Steer 1947; Vaufrey 1946). A parallel course of development took place in Germany and France, and to a lesser extent in the Soviet Union. Photo intelligence during the two world wars revealed many new and spectacular sites of archaeological interest (Beazeley 1919, 1920; Rey 1921; Wiegand 1920), and archaeologists, having become skillful in the new technology and its methods, went on to perfect these means in peacetime and to stimulate others to apply them toward advancing the study of earth, nature, and man (Deuel 1969:19; Martin 1970, 1971; Riley 1945; St. Joseph 1966:15, 35; Scollar 1963, 1965; Tolstov, Andrianov, and Igonin 1962, 1971).

Leo Deuel wrote an engrossing and definitive "story of aerial archaeology," which portrays all of the effort, genius, frustration, and eventual success of the individuals who developed and proved this new method of discovery. Among the pioneers singled out by Deuel, O. G. S. Crawford receives recognition as the father of aerial archaeology (Deuel 1969:20, 24; Crawford 1923). Under his guidance and with techniques that he standardized, British archaeologists and their French colleagues took the lead in archaeological discovery from the air, applying the method with amazing results throughout the United Kingdom, France, Africa, Italy, the Near East, and Southeast Asia.

Inseparably connected with developments on the military side following World War I were the information requirements of expanding colonial empire administrations. It turned out that periodic aerial photographic reconnaissance, while satisfying the continuing need for strategic military information, could also yield a wide variety of essential demographic, social, cultural, and resource data with great efficiency and reliability over large territories. When compiled over time, these data were found to lend easily to statistical analysis of past changes and current trends. (Walker 1926, 1929; Bourne 1928, 1931; Crostwaite 1930; Cochrane-Patrick 1931a, 1931b; Robbins 1934). Archaeology benefited from the fallout of photographic data interpreted for other purposes, while social anthropology, being ancillary to the colonial administrations of the various countries involved, routinely utilized the method to further ethnographic aims (Griaule 1937: 471–475, 1946, 1948).

Although aerial photography in the Soviet Union also dates from World War I, it was not until the Khorezm expedition of 1940, under the direction of S. P. Tolstov, that it was adopted and used systematically in Soviet archaeology. Tolstov employed two aircraft to reconnoiter and obtain oblique air photographs of the enormous area to the east and south of the Aral Sea, through which course the lower portions of the Amu- and Syr-Darya (Igonin 1965). Work in the area intensified after 1946, by which time over 250 monumental remains from ancient Khorezm had been discovered by aerial photographic interpretation (Tolstov 1948; Tolstov, Andrianov, and Igonin 1962). A few years later, B. V. Andrianov organized a special task force to study the entire area of ancient Khorezm, locate new archaeological sites, interpret construction changes in irrigation networks that operated from the fifth century B.C. into the Middle Ages, compile detailed archaeological maps, and establish temporal and geographical relationships among the sites (Tolstov and Andrianov 1957; Tolstov, Andrianov, and Igonin 1962; Andrianov 1956, 1965, 1969; Igonin 1965, 1968). Since then, Soviet archaeologists have used aerial photography in other areas of Central Asia and Kazakhstan (Igonin 1965; Andrianov 1969) and have exerted a tremendous effort in systematizing air photo methods and techniques, particularly in the specialized archaeology of arid regions (Igonin 1971).

From the outset, American archaeologists lagged

Thomas S. Schorr

behind their Old World counterparts, largely because they were not involved in the military-colonial circumstances of exploring archaeologically significant regions with the new reconnaissance techniques. Yet Army Lieutenants H. R. Wells and A. C. McKinley were the first to take aerial photographs of a site, the Cahokia mounds, in the United States (Deuel 1969:221; Smithsonian Institution 1922:92–105); and in 1923, R. A. MacLean published the first American article on aerial archaeology in an apparent effort to stimulate more interest. Eventually, New World archaeologists were awakened at the end of the second decade when Charles A. Lindbergh accidentally discovered potential uses for the airplane in archaeological reconnaissance while working to establish new air routes in the Caribbean for Pan American Airways. Lindbergh and American archaeologists in general were evidently unaware of the aerial reconnaissance and photographic techniques that Crawford and others had by this time systematized and published (Deuel 1969: 190). In consultation with Alfred V. Kidder, Lindbergh made a number of successful trial runs using aerial photography over Pueblo Indian sites of Arizona and New Mexico (Kidder 1930, Weyer 1929). Together, they received the backing of the Carnegie Institution of Washington and, in the company of Mrs. Lindbergh, archaeologist Oliver H. Ricketson, and William I. Van Dusen of Pan American Airways, they attempted what turned out to be a largely unsystematic and unsuccessful aerial survey of the difficult Yucatan Peninsula for its traces of Maya remains. A University of Pennsylvania expedition during the following year "hardly improved on what was known from land surveys" (Deuel 1969:217, 212; Kidder 1929, 1930a, 1930b; Madeira 1931; Mason 1931; Ricketson and Kidder 1930). Yet the publicity from these ventures stimulated American archaeology into using the method, and shortly afterward, aerial archaeology went to Peru with the Shippee-Johnson expedition, where it has since been employed systematically for a longer period of time than in any other New World culture area (Johnson and Platt 1930; Shippee 1932a, 1932b; Ford and Willey 1949; Willey 1959; Schaedel 1951; Kosok 1965).

Over the years, aerial archaeology has advanced beyond site discovery and surface mapping to produce a number of specialized methods, techniques, and kinds of equipment for recording the progress of excavation and for mapping the spatial relationships among artifacts *in situ* (Guy 1932; Poidebard 1939; Bascom 1941; Miller 1957; Solecki 1952, 1957, 1958, 1960; Harp 1966; Petre 1966; St. Joseph 1966; Clark 1968; Whittlesey 1966, 1970; Conlon 1973). Through modifications and innovations, many methods originally developed in aerial photography have been extended into the study of underwater sites, opening up an entirely new sector of archaeological application (Bascom 1971; Bass 1966, 1968; Deuel 1969:288–292; Höhle 1971; Poidebard 1939; Throckmorton 1970). Finally, the development of the "direct historical approach" (Strong 1953), linking prehistory to history, and the growing concern with the study of long-range, regional continuities in cultural adaptive change have produced an indispensable reliance on the information associations that the aerial photographic method and its extensions can provide over large and widely separated areas of landscape (Harp 1967, 1970; Kosok 1965; Millon 1964, 1973; Sanders 1965; Spores 1969).

If discovery, reconnaissance, and photo mapping of archaeological sites are made infinitely easier from the air, interpretation of the meaning of the aerial images inevitably depends on the tedious procedures of the dirt archaeologist for verification. For at some stage during photointerpretation, regardless of purpose, the meaning of the images must be validated by reference to ground truth, what the images represent in reality. The problem for the archaeologist is made more complex, as the air view only records surface features, exteriors of past activity that may have become shrouded by time and the progressive transformations of the environment. Moreover, aerial reconnaissance has revealed enigmatic traces of prehistoric human social activity for which no close approximations are known to exist in the behavior of historic or contemporary peoples. The mysterious, delineated figurines discovered from the air near Nazca, Peru (Kosok and Reiche 1947, 1949; Reiche 1949; Kosok 1965), and the "ridged fields" that have been recently identified in aerial photographs from widespread regions of Central and South America (Denevan 1966, 1970; Parsons 1969; Parsons and Bowen 1966; Parsons and Denevan 1967; Smith, Denevan, and Hamilton 1968; Puleston and Puleston 1971; Siemens and Puleston 1972; Schorr 1973) can only have been produced and maintained by organized labor parties operating over time. Yet the purpose of these constructs and the manner in which they were used still defy adequate explanation.

Ethnography Tries Its Wings

Cultural geographers, in common with archaeologists, have long sought to abstract information on culture and social relations by analyzing the form of physical constructs and spatial arrangements produced by human populations over time. Sociocultural anthropologists as well have recognized the fact that the activities of social life produce characteristic patterns in the physical surroundings of human groups (Steward 1937, 1955; Hallowell 1955; Firth 1961:42; Keesing 1962:207; Hall 1968; Durbin 1968; Richardson 1969). In 1937, for example, Julian Steward noted that "the number and grouping of domiciles is, by analogy with historic societies, often suggestive of the kinship composition of the society." Later, speaking more figuratively, he referred to the "economic and ecological factors that shape society" and discussed "the degree and manner in which economic factors have combined with kinship, ceremonialism, inheritance, and other factors to produce observed social patterns" (1955:155). Felix Keesing posited the same consistent relationship in that housing bears "a close functional relation to the habits of social aggregation of the group" (1962:207). Recently archaeologists in the United States have even formed a new school based in these assumptions (Binford and Binford 1968; Bayard 1969; Ucko, Tringham and Dimbleby 1972). But aside from supplying classified inventories of the smaller objects of material culture, which for some reason were limited to the outer boundaries of the house construct, ethnographers, especially in the United States, have paid scant attention to analysis of the larger physical traits that define the shape of socioculturally specialized population groupings. For this reason, aerial reconnaissance and photointerpretation did not gain wide or early acceptance as an ethnographic tool, in spite of the method's long-standing geographical applications (MacFadden 1952; Davis 1954; Kedar 1958; Coppock and Johnson 1962; Deshler 1967), its increasing use in archaeology, and its highly successful entry into the sociological analysis of rural and urban phenomena (Alexander et al. 1966; Cissna 1963; Eyre et al. 1970; Gibbs 1961; Green 1955, 1956a, 1956b, 1957; Green and Monier 1953, 1959; Manji 1968; Monier 1958; Monier and Green 1953, 1957; Mumbower and Donoghue 1967; Pownall 1950; Richter 1969; Silberman 1959; Steiner 1967; Strandberg 1968a, 1968/69; Wittenstein 1952, 1954, 1955; Wobber 1969a, 1969b). Except for a few ethnographers working principally in France and England, the method went long unused.

John Rowe (1953:909) pointed out that the French have been the most systematic users of aerial photographic methods in ethnographic research. In part, this is a consequence of wartime and colonial requirements; but it is also owing to the strong alliance which has traditionally existed in that country between ethnology and cultural geography (Brunhes 1925; Chombart de Lauwe 1951, 1956; Deffontaines et al. 1949; Gourou 1936a, 1936b, 1955; Robequain 1929). The work of Marcel Griaule in French East Africa and Cameroon, dating from 1930, is the earliest instance of an explicit ethnographic application. His 1936 aerial photographic reconnaissance of the same region is probably the first of its kind undertaken solely for ethnographic purposes (Griaule 1937, 1946, 1948; Chombart de Lauwe 1951, 1956), although Ray Bourne had put the method to use in an economic development survey for the British Colonial Office a few years earlier in northern Rhodesia (Bourne 1923, 1931). Griaule's student, Paul-Henry Chombart de Lauwe also figures importantly—perhaps more than any other single individual—for his ethnographic applications of the method. Much of his work is dedicated to the study of patterns of structure and function that exist between the

Thomas S. Schorr

habitation complexes of different traditional cultures and their natural settings (Chombart de Lauwe 1965). The essays on family and habitation edited by Chombart de Lauwe (1959, 1960) contain a wealth of comparative cultural information derived from aerial photography and represent a monument to interdisciplinary collaboration in the analysis of problems related to the adaptation of dwellings to social requirements. The practical applications of this essentially ecological methodology extend to the planning and construction of experimental residential complexes that structure living space in a way that is conducive to the harmonious functioning of urban-industrial society. He also wrote a profusely illustrated little handbook (1951, 1956) of practical aerial photographic methods and techniques for use in geography, archaeology, and ethnology which has been translated and received wide distribution, although unfortunately, not in the English language.

In the Soviet Union, the contemporary problem of housing populations that were displaced by the Second World War is being handled within the framework of practical ethnography, involving the use of aerial photographic methods. New population centers have arisen as a result of postwar reconstruction, the eastward migration of large numbers of people, and the need to settle the sparsely populated lands of Central Asia. In these situations, aerial photographic interpretation provides an indispensable assist to the ethnographer in the comparative assessment of old and newly established settlement patterns, types of dwellings, and their relationships with the environment (Igonin 1967). Numerous French, English, and German ethnographers have also routinely used aerial photographs over the years in basic and applied ethnographic research (Dakeyne 1962; Gerresheim 1967; Gutkind 1952, 1956; Manshard 1965; Monkhouse 1959; Ominde 1962; Emrys Peters, personal communication; Porter 1956).

The first ethnographic application of the method in the New World occurred in 1948, when John Rowe acquired existing aerial photographs and, with the help of a light aircraft and a handheld camera, made some photos of his own over the region inhabited by the Guambiano Indians near the town of Silvia, Department of the Cauca, Colombia. The aerial photographs proved indispensable as map supplements for the cultural information they contained. Although Rowe did not pursue the method further, he indicated for American cultural anthropologists some of the advantages of using aerial photographs in ethnographic field work, particularly in the study of settlement patterns, land tenure, house types, cultivation cycles, irrigation and drainage, and the effects of seasonal variations. Moreover, Rowe recognized the method as an effective means for eliciting information from native informants (Rowe 1952:909–910, personal communication).

From 1960 on, aerial reconnaissance came into its own as an ethnographic field research tool among sociocultural anthropologists in the United States. At that time, three major field research projects began, each of which put aerial photographic reconnaissance to use. The Harvard Chiapas Project, headed by Evon Vogt, got underway in 1956 (Vogt 1969; Vogt and Romney 1971). To the north, the Teotihuacán Valley Project together with the Teotihuacán Mapping Project, combining archaeology with ethnography, began in 1960 (Millon 1964; Sanders 1965). In 1961, Harold Conklin initiated the field research phase of the Ifugao study (Conklin 1967). These projects included contract aerial reconnaissance, photogrammetry, cartography, and photointerpretation by commercially specialized firms, and provided opportunities for students of anthropology to receive training in the method and its techniques. A unique feature of these projects was their employment of native informants as photo interpreters (Collier and Vogt 1965; Conklin 1967; Price 1968). Other studies of shorter duration and on a slightly smaller scale also had their beginnings during the early years of the 1960s (Hackenberg 1967; Schorr 1965, 1968). The overall effect has been to stimulate an increasing recognition of the advantages that application of the method offers for ethnographic data gathering, especially in research that involves multidisciplinary investigation, a broader ecological view, time-depth surveys, and ethnoscientific classification.

New Developments

The popular notion that aerial reconnaissance entails the use of aircraft-mounted cameras and photosensitized films to record material patterns on the earth's surface gives only a partial idea of the range of data-gathering systems, techniques, and applications presently in service. Of late, the science of acquiring information about existing object phenomena at a distance, of which aerial photography represents only one specialty, is more accurately described by the phrase "remote sensing," for usually the sensing system does not enter into the domain or alter the state of the phenomenon being observed (American Society of Photogrammetry 1966, 1970; Colwell 1961a, 1963; Harp 1966; Gumerman and Lyons 1971:126; Lyons, Inglis, and Hitchcock 1972). Besides the visible light spectrum and adjacent portions of the infrared and ultraviolet which can be registered directly on film emulsions, the energy bands detected and recorded by modern remote sensing methods include emitted and reflected radiation generated by a variety of natural and manmade sources, such as the intermediate and far (thermal) infrared spectra (Adams et al. 1970; Colwell and Olson 1966; Estes 1966; Gumerman and Lyons 1971; Lopic 1968; Olson 1967; Schaber and Gumerman 1969; Wellar 1968); terrestrial gamma-ray spectra, magnetic anomalies, audio and radio frequency pulsing, continuous and pulsed laser emissions, microwave radiometry, and radar scanning (Simpson 1966; Crandall 1969; Viksne et al. 1970; Gumerman and Lyons 1971). Along with the continuing use of aircraft and balloons, the sensing from rockets, spacecraft, and satellites is now commonplace (Fischer 1968; Wobber 1969a, 1969b; Kolars and Apsbury 1967; Anderson 1971; Lyons, Inglis, and Hitchcock 1972). Image rectification, enhancement, pattern recognition, and interpretation for data readouts are becoming increasingly automated and computerized (Belcher 1970; Centner and Hietanen 1971; Jensen 1973; Schepis 1970; American Society of Photogrammetry 1969).

Training in photo interpretation has long been standard fare in the curricula of many university departments and schools, most commonly in the fields of earth sciences, ecology, sociology, agronomy, and forestry (Brock 1966; Johnson 1969; Kutdritskii, Popov, and Romanova 1966; Merchant 1963). Many anthropologists have also recognized applications and used these techniques profitably, although few departments of anthropology offer encouragement or training along these lines. In the future, graduate programs in anthropology can stand to benefit by introducing instruction in remote sensing as a routine part of field training, for these methods and techniques are not specializations in and of themselves but, as amply demonstrated, are tools having broad and overlapping applications in many areas of research (Brock 1970; Stone 1956).

The Bibliography

The bibliography that follows cannot be all-inclusive. Were it to include every work that discusses remote sensing information, methods, or techniques used by anthropologists, it would double in size and would consist mainly of brief reports or repetitious accounts of things archaeologists have spotted in an aerial view. It has therefore been structured so as to trace the historical development of aerial photography in anthropology, demonstrate results from the systematic anthropological application of aerial photographic reconnaissance, familiarize anthropologists with the kinds of data that can be derived from remote sensing, and teach techniques, resources, and methods of remote sensing, particularly aerial photography and photo interpretation, which are apt to be of use to the anthropologist. In addition, it includes all references cited in the various papers throughout this volume.

Abramson, Norman
1963. *Information Theory and Coding.* New York: McGraw-Hill.
Adamesteanu, D.
1967. "Viabilita Antica: Ancient Road Systems in the Plain of the Crati: A Contribution of Air Photography," in *The Search for Sybaris, 1960–1965,* Froelich Rainey, Carlo Maurilio Lerici, et al. Rome: Lerici Editori, pp. 265–269.

Adams, William, Larry K. Lepley, Clifton Warren, and
  Sen-Dow Chang
  1970. "Coastal and Urban Surveys with IR," *Photogrammetric Engineering* 36(2):173–180.
Agache, Roger
  1962. *Vues aériennes de la Somme et recherche du passé*. Amiens: Imprimerie Gogois.
  1963. "Détection des fosses combles sur terrains sans végétation grâce à l'humidité remanente des remblais. Le procédé des zingueurs," *Société de préhistoire française* 60(9–10):642–647.
  1964. "Aerial Reconnaissance in Picardy," *Antiquity* 33(150):113–119, plates 11–22.
  1964. *Archéologie aérienne de la Somme: Recherches nouvelles 1963–1964*. Amiens: Imprimerie Gogois.
  1965. "Découverte aérienne de la Picardie antique," *Archéologia* 6 (September–October):44–49.
——, Raymond Chevallier, and Giulio Schmeidt
  1966. *Études d'archéologie aérienne*. Paris: Service d'édition et de vente des publications de l'éducation nationale.
Alexander, R. H., et al.
  1966. "Remote Sensing of Urban Environments." *Proceedings of the Fourth Symposium on Remote Sensing of Environment*. Ann Arbor: The University of Michigan.
Allan, William
  1965. *The African Husbandman*. Edinburgh: Oliver and Boyd.
American Society of Photogrammetry
  1960. "Varied Applications of Photogrammetry," *Photogrammetric Engineering* 26(5).
  1963. "Uses of Photogrammetry," *Photogrammetric Engineering* 29(1).
  1966. *Selected Papers on Remote Sensing of Environment*. Ann Arbor: The University of Michigan.
  1969. "Activities and Work of Sustaining Members: IBM Corporation," *Photogrammetric Engineering* 35(12):1187.
  1970. "Remote Sensing and Photointerpretation," *Photogrammetric Engineering* 36(5).

Anderson, James R.
  1971. "Land-use Classification Schemes," *Photogrammetric Engineering* 37(4):379–387.
Andrianov, Boris V.
  1956. "Archeologotopograficheskie issledovania na zemliakh drevnego oroshenia Turtkul'skogo i Biruniiskogo raionov v 1955–1956 gg" (Research in the archeologotopography of irrigation in the Turtkul'ski and Biruniiski regions in 1955–1956), *Materialy Khorezmskoi Ekspeditsii*, vol. 1. Moscow: Akademia Nauk SSSR.
  1965. "Deshifrirovanie aerofotosnimkov pri izuchenii drevnikh orositel'nykh sistem" (Deciphering aerial surveys for the study of ancient irrigation systems), *Estestvennye nauki v arkheologii*, p. 261. Moscow: Akademia Nauk SSSR.
  1969. "Drevnie orositel'nye sistemy priaral'ia" (Ancient irrigation systems of the Aral Region). Akademia Nauk SSSR, Institut Etnografii im. N. N. Miklukho-Maklaĭa. Moscow: Izhatel'stvo "Nauka."
Anson, Abraham
  1963. "Photogrammetry as a Science and as a Tool," *Photogrammetric Engineering* 29(1):129–138.
Avera, Harmon Q.
  1963. "Photogrammetry and the Small Land Survey," *Photogrammetric Engineering* 29(1):96–99.
Avery, T. Eugene
  1968. *Interpretation of Aerial Photographs*. 2nd ed. Minneapolis: Burgess.
Bailloud, G., and Paul-Henry Chombard de Lauwe
  1952. "La photographie aérienne" in *La découverte du passé: Progrès récents et techniques nouvelles en préhistoire et en archéologie*, ed. Annette Laming. Paris: A. and J. Piccard, pp. 45–57.
Baker, W. A.
  1954. "Archaeology from the Air. A Rewarding Pursuit for the Private Pilot," *Flight and Aircraft Engineering*, Feb. 19, pp. 200–201.
Baker, Wilfred H.
  1960. *Elements of Photogrammetry*. New York: Ronald.

Bandi, Hans-Georg

1942. "Luftbild und Urgeschichte," *33ᵉ Annuaire*. Frauenfeld: Société suisse de préhistoire, pp. 145–153.

Baradez, Jean

1949. *Fossatum africae. Recherches aériennes sur l'organisation des confins sahariens à l'époque romaine*. Paris: Arts et métiers graphiques.

Barth, Fredrik

1967. "On the Study of Social Change," *American Anthropologist* 69(6):661–669.

Bartlett, John R.

1854. *Personal Narrative of Explorations and Incidents in Texas, New Mexico, California, Sonora, and Chihuahua*, vol. 2. New York: Appleton.

Barton, Roy Franklin

1919. "Ifugao Law," *University of California* (Berkeley) *Publications in American Archaeology and Ethnology* 15:1–186. Reprinted 1969, Berkeley and Los Angeles: University of California Press.

1922. "Ifugao Economics," *University of California* (Berkeley) *Publication of American Archaeology and Ethnology* 15:385–446.

Bascom, William R.

1941. "Possible Applications of Kite Photography to Archaeology and Ethnology," *Transactions of the Illinois Academy of Sciences* 34(2):62–63.

Bascom, Williard

1971. "Deep-Water Archaeology," *Science* 174:261–269.

Bass, George F.

1966. *Archaeology under Water*. New York: Praeger.

1968. *A Diversified Program for the Study of Shallow Water Searching and Mapping Techniques*. Philadelphia: University of Pennsylvania Museum.

Bayard, Donn T.

1969. "Science, Theory and Reality in the 'New Archaeology,' " *American Antiquity* 34:376–384.

Beazeley, G. A.

1919. "Air Photography in Archaeology," *The Geographical Journal* 53:330–335.

1920. "Surveys in Mesopotamia During the War," *The Geographical Journal* 55:109–127.

Belcher, Donald J.

1948. "Determination of Soil Conditions from Aerial Photographs," *Photogrammetric Engineering* 14(4):482–488.

1970. "Successful Computerization for Resources Mapping," *Journal of Remote Sensing* 1(1):7–10.

Bennett, R. R.

1931. "Cobá by Land and Air," *Art and Archaeology*, April, pp. 194–205.

Bennett, Wendell C.

1944. *Archaeological Regions of Colombia, a Ceramic Survey*. Yale University Publications in Anthropology 30. New Haven: Yale University Press.

Beresford, Maurice W.

1950. "Maps and Medieval Landscape," *Antiquity* 24:114–118.

——, and J. K. S. St. Joseph

1958. *Medieval England: An Aerial Survey*. Cambridge Air Survey 2. Cambridge, Eng.: Cambridge University Press.

Bertalanffy, Ludwig von

1968. *General System Theory*. New York: Brazillier.

Beyer, H. Otley

1908. "Preliminary Map of Ifugao Country." Scale 1:125,000. Office of Chief Engineer, Manila, Philippines.

Bigelow, George F.

1963. "Photographic Interpretation Keys—A Reappraisal," *Photogrammetric Engineering* 29(6):1042–1051.

Binford, Sally, and Lewis R. eds.

1968. *New Perspectives in Archaeology*. Chicago: Aldine.

Boserup, Esther

1965. *Conditions of Agricultural Growth*. Chicago: Aldine.

Bourne, Ray

1928. *Aerial Survey in Relation to Economic Development of New Countries, with Special Reference to an*

Investigation Carried Out in Northern Rhodesia.
Oxford Forestry Memoirs 9. Oxford: Clarendon Press.

1931. *Regional Survey and Its Relation to Stock Taking of the Agricultural and Forestry Resources of the British Empire.* Oxford Forestry Memoirs 13. Oxford: Clarendon Press.

Bowen, H. C.
1962. "Air Photographs and the Study of Ancient Fields in England," in *Proceedings of the International Symposium on Photointerpretation*, Delft, Netherlands.

Bradford, John S. P.
1947a. "Etruria from the Air," *Antiquity* 21:74–83.
1947b. "Buried Landscapes in Southern Italy," *Antiquity* 23:58–72.
1947c. "A Technique for the Study of Centuriation," *Antiquity* (Jan.): 197–204.
1952. "Progress in Air Archaeology," *Discovery* 13(6): 177–181.
1956. "Fieldwork on Aerial Discoveries in Attica and Rhodes," *The Antiquaries Journal*, January–April, pp. 57–69; July–October, pp. 172–180.
1957. *Ancient Landscapes: Studies in Field Archaeology.* London: G. Bell.
——, and P. R. Williams-Hunt
1946. "Siticulosa Apulia," *Antiquity* 20:191–200.

Branch, Melville C.
1971. *City Planning and Aerial Information.* Cambridge: Harvard University Press.

Bray, Warwick, and M. Edward Moseley
1971. "An Archaeological Sequence from the Vicinity of Buga, Colombia," *Ñawpa Pacha* 7-8:85–103, 5 plates. Berkeley: Institute of Andean Studies.

Breeman, Nico van, L. R. Oldeman, W. J. Plantinga, and W. G. Wielemaker
1970. "The Ifugao Rice Terraces," in *Aspects of Rice Growing in Asia and the Americas*, N. van Breeman et al. Wageningen: H. Veenen en Zonen, N. V., pp. 39–73.

Brock, Gerald C.
1970. *Image Evaluation for Aerial Photography.*
London and New York: Focal Press.

Brock, Robert H., Jr.
1966. "Courses Available in Photogrammetry," *Photogrammetric Engineering* 32(2):307–319.

Brookfield, Harold C.
1968. "New Directions in the Study of Agricultural Systems in Tropical Areas" in *Evolution and Environment*, ed. Ellen T. Drake. New Haven: Yale University Press, pp. 413–439.

Brunhes, J.
1925. *La géographie humaine*, vol. III: *La vision aérienne de la terre.* Paris: Alcan.

Buckley, Walter, ed.
1968. *Modern Systems Research for the Behavioral Scientist.* Chicago: Aldine.

Bullard, William R., Jr.
1960. "Maya Settlement Pattern in Northeastern Peten, Guatemala," *American Antiquity* 25(3):355–72.

Busacker, Robert G., and Thomas L. Saaty
1965. *Finite Graphs and Networks: An Introduction with Applications.* New York: McGraw-Hill.

Cameron, H. L.
1958. "History from the Air," *Photogrammetric Engineering* 24(3):366–375.

Cancian, Frank
1965a. *Economics and Prestige in a Maya Community: The Religious Cargo System in Zinacantan.* Palo Alto, Cal.: Stanford University Press.
1965b. "Efectos de los programas económicos del Gobierno Mexicano en las tierras altas mayas de Zinacantan," in *Estudios de cultura maya* 5:281–297.

Capper, J. E.
1907. "Photographs of Stonehenge, as Seen from a War Balloon," *Archaeologia* 60:571, plates 69–70.

Carls, Norman
1947. *How To Read Aerial Photographs for Census Work.* Washington, D.C.: Department of Commerce, Bureau of the Census.

Carpenter, Rhys
1963. "Discovery from the Air," in *Art and Archaeology*, ed. James S. Ackerman and Rhys Carpenter.

Englewood Cliffs, N.J.: Prentice-Hall, pp. 22–31.

Castellanos, Manuel
1968. Personal communication, Dec. 9. Manuel Castellanos was Director of the Oficina de Asuntos Indígenas in San Cristóbal las Casas, Chiapas, Mexico.

Centner, R. M., and E. D. Hietanen
1971. "Automatic Pattern Recognition," *Photogrammetric Engineering* 37(2):177–186.

Charlton, Thomas H.
1967. "Ethnohistory and Archaeology: Post-Conquest Sites." Paper presented at the 32nd Annual Meeting of the Society for American Archaeology, Ann Arbor, Michigan.

Chart, D. A.
1930. "Air Photography in Northern Ireland," *Antiquity* 4:453–459.

Chevallier, Raymond
1957. "Bibliographie des applications archéologiques de la photographie aérienne," *Bulletin d'archéologie marocaine* 2 (supplement).
1957. *Bibliographie des applications archéologiques de la photographie aérienne.* Milan, Rome: Lerici Foundation. Rev. ed., *Bulletin de l'archéologie marocaine* 2 (supplement).
1962. *L'archéologie aérienne en France.* Milan, Rome: Lerici Foundation.
1964. *L'avion à la découverte du passé.* Paris: Arthème Fayard.
1964. *L'étude des modes anciens d'utilization des teers (archéologie agraire) par la photographie aérienne et son intérêt pratique.* Paris.
1965a. "La révélation des paysages ensevelis," *Archéologia* 3 (March–April): 31–37.
1965b. *Photographie aérienne: Panorama intertechnique.* Paris: Gauthier-Villars.

Chisholm, Michael
1967. *Rural Settlement and Land Use.* New York: Science Editions.

Chombart de Lauwe, Paul-Henry
1948a. (ed.) *La découverte aérienne du monde.* Paris: Horizons de France.
1948b. "Vision aérienne du monde," in *La découverte aérienne du monde.* Paris: Horizons de France, pp. 19–56.
1948c. "L'évolution des rapports entre l'homme et le milieu," in *La découverte aérienne du monde.* Paris: Horizons de France, pp. 209–248.
1948d. "La vision aérienne, et les civilisations disparues," in *La découverte aérienne du monde.* Paris: Horizons de France, pp. 249–280.
1948e. "Exemple d'exploitation d'une vue aérienne," in *La découverte aérienne du monde.* Paris: Horizons de France, pp. 402–406.
1951a. *Photographies aériennes: L'étude de l'homme sur la terre.* Paris: A. Colin.
1951b. "Photographies aériennes, méthodes et procédés d'interprétation," in *La découverte du passé,* ed. Annette Laming. Paris: Librairie Armand Colin.
1952. *Paris et l'agglomération parisienne: L'étude de l'espace dans une grande cité,* vol. II: *Méthodes de recherche.* Paris: Presses Universitaires de France.
1956. *La fotografía aérea: Métodos, procedimientos, interpretación, el estudio del hombre sobre la tierra.* Trans. Luís Jordá. Barcelona: Ediciones Omega.
1959. "Le milieu et l'étude sociologique de cas individuels," *Informations Sociales* 2:41–54.
1960. "Sur l'évolution de l'habitation et le changement sociale dans la société industrielle," in *Famille et habitation,* ed. Paul-Henry Chombart de Lauwe et al., vol. II, *Un essai d'observation experimentale.* Paris: Centre National de la Recherche Scientifique, pp. 11–31.
1965. *Des hommes et des villes.* Paris: Editions Payot.
n.d. "Bibliographie de la découverte aérienne apliquée aux sciences humanines." Paris: L'École Pratique des Hautes Études.
———, et al.
1959. *Famille et habitation,* vol. I: *Sciences humaines et conceptions de l'habitation.* Paris: Centre National de la Recherche Scientifique.
1960. *Famille et habitation,* vol. II: *Un essai d'observation experimentale.* Paris: Centre National de la

Thomas S. Schorr

Recherche Scientifique.

Chorley, Richard J., and Peter Haggett
1968. *Socio-Economic Models in Geography.* London: University Paperbacks.

Cissna, Volney J., Jr.
1963. "Photogrammetry and Comprehensive City Planning for the Small Community," *Photogrammetric Engineering* 29(4):681–683.

Clarke, David L.
1968. *Analytical Archaeology.* London: Methuen.

Clarke, William C.
1966. "From Extensive to Intensive Shifting Cultivation: A Succession from New Guinea," *Ethnology* 5(4):347–359.

Cochrane-Patrick, C. K.
1931a. "Aerial Reconnaissance Mapping in Northern Rhodesia," *Geographical Review* 21:213–220.
1931b. "The Aerial Photograph as an Aid to Survey," *South African Survey Journal* 3:367–377.

Coe, Michael D.
1964. "The Chinampas of Mexico," *Scientific American* 211(1):90–98.
1966. *The Maya.* New York and Washington: Praeger.
1968. "San Lorenzo and the Olmec civilization," in *Dumbarton Oaks Conference on the Olmec*, ed. Elizabeth P. Benson. Washington: Dumbarton Oaks Research Library and Collection, Trustees for Harvard University, pp. 41–71.

——, and Kent V. Flannery
1964. "Microenvironments and Mesoamerican Prehistory," *Science* 143(3607):650–654.

Coleman, Charles G.
1960. "Recent Trends in Photographic Interpretation," *Photogrammetric Engineering* 26(5):755–763.

Collier, George A.
1968. "Land Inheritance and Land Use in a Modern Maya Community." Ph.D. dissertation, Harvard University.
1969. "Computer Processing of Genealogies and Analysis of Settlement Pattern," *Human Mosaic* 3(2):133–141.

——, and Victoria R. Bricker
1970. "Nicknames and Social Structure in Zinacantan," *American Anthropologist* 72(2):289–302.

——, and Evon Z. Vogt
1965. "Aerial Photographs and Computers in the Analysis of Zinacanteco Demography and Land Tenure." *Paper read at 64th Annual Meeting, American Anthropological Association, Denver.*

Collier, John, Jr.
1967. *Visual Anthropology: Photography as a Research Method.* New York: Holt, Rinehart, and Winston.

Colwell, Robert N., ed.
1960. *Manual of Photographic Interpretation.* Falls Church, Va.: American Society of Photogrammetry.
1961a. "Some Practical Applications of Multiband Spectral Reconnaissance," *American Scientist* 49(1):9–36.
1961b. *Developing the Aerial Photographic Specifications for Rasin-lay Surveys in California.* San Francisco: Wine Advisory Board.
1962. "Aerial Photographic Interpretation of Underground Objects, Materials, and Properties," *Proceedings of the Symposium on Detection of Underground Objects, Materials, and Properties,* Ft. Belvoir, Va., pp. 225–246.

——, et al.
1963. "Basic Matter and Energy Relationships Involved in Remote Reconnaissance," *Photogrammetric Engineering* 29(5):761–799.

——, and Don L. Olson
1966. "Thermal Infrared Imagery and Its Use in Vegetation Analysis by Remote Aerial Reconnaissance," in American Society of Photogrammetry, *Selected Papers on Remote Sensing of Environment*, Falls Church, Va.: American Society of Photogrammetry, pp. 77–91.

Conklin, Harold C.
1957. *Hanunóo Agriculture. A Report on an Integral System of Shifting Cultivation in the Philippines.* Forestry Development Paper, no. 12. New York: Food Agriculture Organization, United Nations.

1962. "Lexicographical Treatment of Folk Taxonomies," *International Journal of American Linguistics* 28(2), Part IV, *Problems in Lexicography*, ed. F. W. Householder and S. Saporta. Publication 21. Bloomington, Ind.: Indiana University Research Center in Anthropology, Folklore, and Linguistics, pp. 119–141.

1967a. "Ifugao Ethnobotany, 1905–1965: The 1911 Beyer-Merrill Report in Perspective," in *Studies in Philippine Anthropology: In Honor of H. Otley Beyer*, ed. M. D. Zamora. Quezon City, Philippines: Alemar-Phoenix, pp. 204–262. Reprinted in 1967 in *Economic Botany* 21(3):243–272. Baltimore.

1967b. "Some Aspects of Ethnographic Research in Ifugao," *Transactions of the New York Academy of Sciences*, 2nd ser. 30(1):99–121.

1972. *Land Use in North Central Ifugao: A Set of Eight Maps.* New York: American Geographic Society.

Conlon, V. M.

1973. *Camera Techniques in Archaeology.* New York: St. Martin's Press.

Coppock, J. T., and J. H. Johnson

1962. "Measurement in Human Geography," *Economic Geography* 38(2):130–137.

Couts, Cave J.

1961. *Hepah, California!* ed. Henry F. Dobyns. Tucson, Ariz.: Arizona Pioneer Historical Society.

Cowgill, Ursula M.

1961. "Soil Fertility and the Ancient Maya," *Transactions of the Connecticut Academy of Arts and Sciences*, New Haven, pp. 1–56.

Crandall, Clifford J.

1969. "Radar Mapping in Panama," *Photogrammetric Engineering* 35(7):641–646.

Crawford, Osbert Guy Stanhope

1923. "Air Survey and Archaeology," *The Geographical Journal* 61:342–366.

1924. "Archaeology from the Air," *Nature* 114:580–582.

1928. *Air Survey and Archaeology.* 2nd ed. Ordnance Survey Professional Papers, n.s. 7. London: H.M.S.O.

1929. "Air Photographs of the Middle East," *The Geographical Journal* 13:497–512.

1929. "Woodbury," *Antiquity* 3(12):452–455.

1929. *Air Photography for Archaeologists.* Ordnance Survey Professional Papers, 12. London: H.M.S.O.

1933. "Some Recent Air Discoveries," *Antiquity* 7:290–296.

1939. "Archaeological Air Photographs in England," *The Geographical Review* 29:671–672.

1953. *Archaeology in the Field.* New York: Humanities Press.

1953. *Said and Done: The Autobiography of an Archaeologist.* New York: Humanities Press.

1954. "A Century of Air-Photography," *Antiquity* 28:206–210.

1957. "Archaeology from the Air," in *A Book of Archaeology*, ed. Mary Wheeler. London: Cassell, pp. 83–89.

——, Erich Ewald, and Werner Buttler

1938. *Luftbild und Vorgeschichte.* Luftbild und Luftbildmessung, no. 16. Berlin: Lilienthal–Gesellschaft für Luftfahrtforschung, Hansa-Luftbild.

——, and Alexander Keiller

1928. *Wessex from the Air.* Oxford: Clarendon Press.

Crostwaite, H. L.

1930. "Aerial Survey of East and Central African Territories," *Journal African* 29:333–342.

Dakeyne, R. B.

1962. "The Pattern of Settlement in Central Nyanza, Kenya," *The Australian Geographer* 8(4):183–191.

Daniel, Glyn E.

1950. *A Hundred Years of Archaeology.* London: G. Duckworth.

Davis, Charles M.

1954. "Field Techniques," in *American Geography: Inventory and Prospects*, ed. Preston E. James and Clarence F. Jones. Syracuse: Syracuse University Press, pp. 507–516.

Deffontaines, Pierre

1948. *Géographie et religion.* Paris: Librairie Gallimard.

——, A. Leroi–Gourhan, and M. Jean-Brunhes-De-Lamarre

1949. *Revue de géographie humaine et d'ethnologie,*

4 vols. Paris: Librairie Gallimard.

Denevan, William M.

1966. *The Aboriginal Cultural Geography of the Llanos de Mojos of Bolivia.* Ibero-Americana no. 48. Los Angeles and Berkeley: University of California Press.

1970. "Aboriginal Drained-Field Cultivation in the Americas," *Science* 169:647–654.

Deshler, Walter W.

1967. "Culture Difference in East Africa as Read from the Air: The Case of Indigenous House Types." Department of Geography, University of Maryland, College Park, Md. (mimeo).

Deuel, Leo

1967. *Conquistadors Without Swords: Archaeologists in the Americas.* New York: St. Martin's Press.

1969. *Flights into Yesterday: The Story of Aerial Archaeology.* New York: St. Martin's Press.

Dill, H. W., Jr.

1959. "Use of the Comparison Method in Agricultural Airphoto Interpretation," *Photogrammetric Engineering* 25(1):44–49.

Drucker, Philip

1961. "The La Venta Olmec Support Area," *Kroeber Anthropological Society Papers* 25:59–72.

——, and Robert F. Heizer

1960. "A Study of the Milpa System of La Venta Island and Its Archaeological Implications," *Southwestern Journal of Anthropology* 16(1):36–45.

Durbin, Marshall

1968. " 'Comments' to Proxemics by Edward T. Hall," *Current Anthropology* 9(2–3):98–100.

Eccleston, Robert

1950. *Overland to California on the Southwestern Trail*, ed. G. P. Hammond and E. H. Howes. Berkeley: University of California Press.

Edel, Matthew

1966. "El ejido en Zinacantan," in *Los Zinacantecos: Un pueblo tzotzil de los altos de Chiapas*, ed. Evon Z. Vogt. Colección de antropología social. Mexico: Instituto Nacional Indigenista, pp. 163–182.

Engelbach, R.

1929. "The Aeroplane and Egyptian Archaeology," *Antiquity* 3:470–473.

Esher, Lord

1966. "Air Photographs and Contemporary Planning," in *The Uses of Air Photography*, ed. J. K. S. St. Joseph. New York: Day.

Estes, John E.

1966. "Some Applications of Aerial Infrared Imagery," *Annals of the Association of American Geographers* 56(4):673–682.

Eyre, L. Alan, Blossom Adolphus, and Monica Amiel

1970. "Census Analysis and Population Studies," *Photogrammetric Engineering* 36(5):460–466.

Firth, Raymond

1961. *Elements of Social Organization.* Boston: Beacon Press.

Fischer, William A.

1968. "Eros: Viewing the Earth from Space," *Geoscience News* 1(3):16–19.

Fisher, John J., and E. Zell Steever

1973. "35-mm Quardricamera," *Photogrammetric Engineering* 39(6):573–578.

Ford, James A.

1944. *Excavations in the Vicinity of Cali, Colombia.* Yale University Publications in Anthropology 31. New Haven: Yale University Press.

——, and Clarence H. Webb

1956. "Poverty Point: A Late Archaic Site in Louisiana," *Anthropological Papers of the American Museum of Natural History* 46(1).

——, and Gordon R. Willey

1949. "Surface Survey of the Virú Valley, Peru," *Anthropological Papers of the American Museum of Natural History* 43(1).

Frake, Charles O.

1962. "Cultural Ecology and Ethnography," *American Anthropologist* 64(1):53–59.

Frost, R. E.

1952. "Discussion of Photo Recognition: Analysis and Interpretation and Photo Keys," *Photogrammetric Engineering* 28(3):502–505.

Garnett, David, ed.
  1938. *The Letters of T. E. Lawrence.* London: Spring Books.

Geertz, Clifford
  1963. *Agricultural Involution: The Process of Ecological Change in Indonesia.* Berkeley: University of California Press.

Gerresheim, Klaus
  1968. *Luftbildauswertung in Ostafrika.* New York: Humanities Press.

Gibbs, Jack P.
  1961. *Urban Research Methods.* Princeton, N.J.: Van Nostrand.

Gillie, D.
  1956. "Location of Archaeological Sites by Air," *Explorers Journal* 34(2–4):15–18.

Gladwin, H. S., E. W. Haury, E. B. Sayles, and W. Gladwin
  1937. *Excavations at Snaketown, Material Culture.* Medallion Papers, no. 25. Gila Pueblo, Globe, Ariz.

Goodman, Marjorie Smith
  1959. "A Technique for the Identification of Farm Crops from Aerial Photographs," *Photogrammetric Engineering* 25(1):131–137.

Gossen, Gary H.
  1970. "Time and Space in Chamula Oral Tradition." Ph.D. dissertation, Harvard University.
  1974. *Chamulas in the World of the Sun: Time and Space in a Maya Oral Tradition.* Cambridge: Harvard University Press.

Gourou, Pierre
  1936a. *Esquisse d'une étude de l'habitation annamite dans l'Annam septentrional et central du Thanh Hoá au Binh-Dinh.* Paris: Les Éditions d'Art et d'Histoire.
  1936b. *Les paysans du delta tonquinois: Étude de géographie humaine.* Paris: Les Éditions d'Art et d'Histoire.
  1955. *Peasants of the Tonkin Delta: A Study of Human Geography,* 2 vols. trans. Richard R. Miller. New Haven: Human Relations Area Files Press.

Green, Norman E.
  1955. "Aerial Photography in the Analysis of Urban Structures, Ecological and Social." Ph.D. dissertation (microfilm), University of North Carolina, Chapel Hill.
  1956. "Scale Analysis of Urban Structures: A Study of Birmingham, Alabama," *American Sociological Review* 21(1):8–13.
  1956. "Aerial Photographic Analysis of Residential Neighborhoods: An Evaluation of Data Accuracy," *Social Forces* 35(2):142–147.
  1957. "Aerial Photographic Interpretation and the Social Structure of the City," *Photogrammetric Engineering* 23(1):89.

——, and Robert B. Monier
  1953. "Reliability and Validity of Air Reconnaissance as a Collection Method for Urban Demographic and Sociological Information." Technical Research Report, no. 11. Air University, Human Resources Research Institute, Maxwell Air Force Base, Ala.

——, and Robert B. Monier
  1959. "Aerial Photographic Interpretation and the Human Ecology of the City," *Photogrammetric Engineering* 25(5):770–773.

Griaule, Marcel
  1937. "L'emploi de la photographie aérienne dans la recherche scientifique," *L'antropologie* 40:469–475.
  1946. *Emploi de l'aviation dans la recherche ethnographique.* Paris: National Congress of French Aviation.
  1948. "L'ethnographie," in *La découverte aérienne du monde,* ed. Paul-Henry Chombart de Lauwe. Paris: Horizons de France, pp. 177–208.

Gumerman, George J., and Thomas R. Lyons
  1971. "Archaeological Methodology and Remote Sensing," *Science* 172:126–132.

Gutkind, E. A.
  1952. *Our World from the Air: An International Survey of Man and His Environment.* London: Chatto and Windus.
  1956. "Our World from the Air: Conflict and Adaptation," in *Man's Role in Changing the Face of the Earth,* ed. William L. Thomas, Jr. Chicago: University of Chicago Press, pp. 1–44.

Guy, P. L. O.

Thomas S. Schorr

1932. "Balloon Photography and Archaeological Excavation," *Antiquity* 6:148–155.

Hackenberg, Robert A.

1964. "Changing Patterns of Pima Indian Land Use," in *Indian and Spanish-American Adjustments to Arid and Semiarid Environments*, ed. C. L. Knowlton. Committee on Desert and Arid Zone Research, no. 7. Washington, D.C.: American Association for the Advancement of Science, pp. 6–15.

1967. "Parameters of an Ethnic Group: A Method for Studying the Total Tribe," *American Anthropologist* 69(5):478–492.

Haggett, Peter

1965. *Locational Analysis in Human Geography.* London: Arnold.

Hall, Edward T.

1968. "Proxemics," *Current Anthropology* 9(2–3):83–108.

Hallowell, A. Irving

1955. "Cultural Factors in Spatial Organization," in *Culture and Experience*, ed. A. Irving Hallowell. Philadelphia: University of Philadelphia Press, pp. 184–202.

Halseth, Odd S.

1932. "Prehistoric Irrigation in Arizona," *The Masterkey* 5:165–175.

Hammond, Rolt

1967. *Air Survey in Economic Development.* London: Muller.

Harp, Elmer, Jr.

1966. "Anthropology and Remote Sensing," *Proceedings of the Fourth Symposium on Remote Sensing of Environment.* Ann Arbor: The University of Michigan.

1967. "Experimental Air Photo Interpretation in Archaeology," *Photogrammetric Engineering* 33(6):676.

1968. "Anthropological Interpretation from Color," in *Manual of Color Aerial Photography*, ed. J. T. Smith. Falls Church, Va.: American Society of Photogrammetry.

1968. "Optimum Scales and Emulsions in Air Photo Archaeology." Paper read at the 8th International Congress of Anthropological and Ethnological Sciences, Tokyo.

Hastings, James R., and Raymond Turner

1965. *The Changing Mile: An Ecological Study of Vegetation Change with Time in the Lower Mile of an Arid Region.* Tucson: The University of Arizona Press.

Haury, Emil W.

1967. "The Hohokam, First Masters of the American Desert," *National Geographic* 131(5):670–701.

Hayden, Julian D.

1945. "Salt Erosion," *American Antiquity* 10(3):373–378.

1957. "Excavations, 1940, University Ruin," *Southwestern Monuments Association, Technical Papers*, no. 5.

Heath, G. R.

1957. "Correlations Between Man's Activity and His Environment Which May be Analyzed in Photo Interpretation," *Photogrammetric Engineering* 13(1):108–114.

Heizer, Robert F.

1959. *The Archaeologist at Work.* New York: Harper.

Heleva, M. U. V.

1958. *Integration of Field and Photogrammetric Methods in Large-Scale Mapping.* Quebec: Annuaire de la Corporation des Arpenteurs-Géometres de la Province de Quebec.

Henshall, Janet D.

1968. "Models of Agricultural Activity," in *Socio-Economic Models in Geography*, ed. R. J. Chorley and Peter Haggett. London: University Paperbacks, pp. 425–458.

Hinton, Page

1967. "A Comparative Analysis of the Selected Maya Settlement Patterns." Freshman seminar paper on the Maya, Harvard Chiapas Project.

Höhle, Joachim

1971. "Reconstruction of the Underwater Object," *Photogrammetric Engineering* 37(9):948–954.

Hoover, J. W.

1929. "The Indian Country of Arizona," *Geographical Review* 19:38–60.

Howe, G. M.

1951. "A Note on the Application of Air Photography to the Agricultural Geography of North-West Cardiganshire," *Geography* 36:15–20.

Igonin, Nicolai I.

1965. "Primenie aerofotosiemki pri izuchenii arkheologicheskikh pamiatnikov" (Application of aerial survey to the study of archeological monuments). *Akademia Nauk SSSR, Institut Arkheologii*, pp. 257–262. Moscow: Izhatel'stvo "Nauka."

1967. "Ispol'zovanie materialov aerofotosiemki v etnograficheskikh issledovaniakh" (The application of air photo surveys to ethnographic research), *Sovietskaiă Etnografiă* 5:143–153.

1968. "Issledovanie arkheologicheskikh pamiatnikov po materialam krupnomasshtabonoi aerofotosiemki" (Study of archeological monuments through large-scale air photo surveys), *Istoriă, Arkheologiă i Etnografiă Srednei Azii* 257–268. Akademia Nauk SSSR, Institut Etnografii im. N. N. Miklukho-Maklaiă. Moscow: Izhatel'stvo "Nauka."

1971. *Krupnomasshtabnoe kartografirovanie arkheologicheskikh pamiatnikov aridnoi zony na osnove materialov aerofotosiemki* (The preparation of large-scale maps of arid-zone archaeological monuments on the basis of air photo surveys). Moscow: Moskovskii Institut Inzhenerov Geodezii, Aerofotosiemki i Kartografii.

Jakobson, Roman

1957. *Shifters, Verbal Categories, and the Russian Verb.* Russian Language Project, Department of Slavic Languages and Literatures, Harvard University, Cambridge, Mass.

Jensen, Niels P.

1968. *Optical and Photographic Reconnaissance Systems.* New York: John Wiley.

1973. "High-Speed Image Analysis Techniques," *Photogrammetric Engineering* 39(12):1321–1328.

Johnson, G. R., and R. R. Platt

1930. "Peru from the Air," *American Geographical Society*, special publication no. 12.

Johnson, Philip L.

1969. ed. *Remote Sensing in Ecology.* Athens: University of Georgia Press.

1971. "Remote Sensing As a Tool for Study and Management of Ecosystems," in *Fundamentals of Ecology.* Ed. Eugene P. Odum. Philadelphia: W. B. Saunders, pp. 468–483.

Johnson, Robert

1967. "The Tile Ratio: An Index of Cultural Change in Chiapas." Freshman seminar paper on the Maya, vol. 3, Harvard Chiapas Project, Harvard University.

Judd, Neil M.

1929. "Arizona Sacrifices Her Prehistoric Canals," *Explorations and Fieldwork of the Smithsonian Institution*, pp. 177–182.

1931. "Arizona's Prehistoric Canals from the Air," *Explorations and Fieldwork of the Smithsonian Institution* 3111:157–166.

Karan, Pradyumna Prasad

1960. "Land Use Reconnaissance in Nepal by Aero-Field Techniques and Photography," *Proceedings of the American Philosophical Society* 104(2):172–187.

Kedar, Yehuda

1958. "The Uses of Aerial Photographs in Research in Physiogeographic Conditions and Anthropogeographic Data in Various Historic Periods," *Photogrammetric Engineering* 24(4):584–587.

Keesing, Felix M.

1962a. *Cultural Anthropology.* New York: Holt, Rinehart, and Winston.

1962b. *The Ethnohistory of Northern Luzon.* Palo Alto: Stanford University Press.

Kennedy, Daniel, et al.

1963. "Panel: Use of Aerial Photographs for Cadastral Surveys," *Photogrammetric Engineering* 29(5):850–871.

Kidder, Alfred V.

1929. "Air Exploration of the Maya Country," *Bulletin*

of the Pan American Union, December, pp. 1200–1205.

1930. "Colonel and Mrs. Lindbergh Aid Archaeologists," *The Masterkey*, January, pp. 5–17.

1930. "Five Days over the Maya Country," *The Scientific Monthly*, March, pp. 193–205.

King, J. E.
1962. "Advantages of Photogrammetry in Cadastral Surveying," *Survey and Mapping* 22(1):97.

Knightley, Phillip, and Colin Simpson
1971. *The Secret Lives of Lawrence of Arabia*. New York: Bantam Books.

Kohn, C. F.
1951. "Aerial Photographs in Geological Analysis of Rural Settlements," *Photogrammetric Engineering* 17:759–771.

Kolars, John, and George Apsbury
1967. "Settlement Patterns in the Nile Delta and the Salton Sea Area," *Earth Resource Surveys from Spacecraft*. Washington D.C.: National Aeronautics and Space Administration.

Kosok, Paul
1965. *Life, Land and Water in Ancient Peru*. New York: Long Island University Press.

——, and Maria Reiche
1947. "The Mysterious Markings of Nazca," *Natural History* 56(5):200–207, 237–238.

1949. "Ancient Drawings on the Desert of Peru," *Archaeology*, December, pp. 206–215.

Kroeck, Richard M.
1966. *A Manual for Users of Aerial Photography of the Highlands of Chiapas, Mexico*. Vidya Report no. 233, prepared for the Department of Social Relations, Harvard University. Palo Alto: Itek Corporation.

Kruckman, Laurence
1972. "The Techniques and Application of Aerial Photography to Anthropology: A Bibliography," *Exchange Bibliography* 339. Monticello, Ill.: Council of Planning Librarians.

Kutdritskii, D. M., I. V. Popov, and E. A. Romanova
1966. *Hydrographic Interpretation of Aerial Photo-*

graphs. Jerusalem: Israel Program for Scientific Translation.

Labat, Pierre
1959. "La maison et la famille dans diverses civilisations," in *Famille et habitation*, vol. I: *Sciences humaines et conceptions de l'habitation*. Paris: Centre National de la Recherche Scientifique, pp. 29–45.

Lambrecht, Francis
1929. "Ifugao Villages and Houses," *Publication of the Catholic Anthropological Conference* 1(3):117–141.

1932–1951. "The Mayawyaw Ritual," *Publication of the Catholic Anthropological Conference* 4:1–754.

Laming, Annette, ed.
1952. *La découverte du passé: Progrès récents et techniques nouvelles en préhistoire et en archéologie*. Paris: Piccard.

Leach, Edmund R.
1961. *Pul Eliya, a Village in Ceylon: A Study of Land Tenure and Kinship*. New York: Cambridge University Press.

Light, Richard, and Mary Upjohn
1938. "Contrasts in African Farming. Aerial Views from the Cape to Cairo," *Geographical Review* 28(4): 529–555.

Lindbergh, Charles A.
1929. "The Discovery of Ruined Maya Cities," *Science* 70(1817):12–13.

Linton, David
1961. "Aerial Aid to Archaeology," *Natural History* 70:16–27.

Livingston, Robert G.
1964. "A History of Military Mapping Camera Development," *Photogrammetric Engineering* 30(1):97–110.

Lopic, Jack Van
1968. "Infrared Mapping: Basic Technology and Geoscience Applications," *Geoscience News* 1(3):4–7, 24–31, 36.

Lyons, E. H.
1964. "Recent Developments in 70 mm. Stereo-Photography from Helicopters," *Photogrammetric*

Engineering 30(5):750–756.

Lyons, Thomas R., Michael Inglis, and Robert K. Hitchcock
1972. "The Application of Space Imagery to Anthropology," *Proceedings of the Third Annual Conference on Remote Sensing in Arid Lands.* Tucson: University of Arizona, pp. 243–264.

MacFadden, Clifford H.
1949. "Some Preliminary Notes on the Use of the Light Airplane and 35 mm. Camera in Geographic Field Research," *Annals of the Association of American Geographers* 39(3):188–200.
1952. "The Use of Aerial Photographs in Geographic Research," *Photogrammetric Engineering* 18:732.

MacLean, R. A.
1923. "The Aeroplane and Archaeology," *American Journal of Archaeology*, 2nd ser. 27:68–69.

Madeira, Percy C., Jr.
1931. "An Aerial Expedition to Central America," *Museum Journal* 22(2):95–153. Philadelphia: University of Pennsylvania.

Maitland, P.
1927. "The 'Works of the Old Men' in Arabia," *Antiquity* 1:197–203.

Malinowski, Bronislaw
1935. *Coral Gardens and Their Magic*, vol. 2. London: Allen and Unwin.

Manji, Ashraf S.
1968. *Uses of Conventional Aerial Photography in Urban Areas: Review and Bibliography.* Evanston, Ill.: Remote Sensing Laboratory, Department of Geography, Northwestern University.

Manshard, W.
1965. "Kigezi (Südwest-Uganda): Die agrargeographische Struktur eines ostafrikanischen Bergeslandes," *Die Erdkunde* 19(3):192–210.

Marlar, Thomas L., and Jack N. Rinker
1967. *A Small, Four Camera System for Multi-Emulsion Studies in Aerial Photography.* Hanover, N.H.: Photographic Interpretation Division, U.S. Army Cold Regions Research and Engineering Laboratory.

Martin, Anne-Marie
1970. "Geschichte und Möglichkeiten der Luftbild-Archäologie," in *Landeskundliche Luftbildauswertung im mittel europäischen Raum*, vol. 10. Bonn-Bad Godesberg: Institut für Landeskunde.
1971. "Archaeological Sites: Soils and Climate," *Photogrammetric Engineering* 37(4):353–357.

Mason, J. A.
1931. "The Air Survey in Central America," *University Museum Bulletin* 2(3):73–75, 78–79, plates I–III. Philadelphia: University of Pennsylvania.

Matheny, Ray T.
1962. "Value of Aerial Photography in Surveying Archaeological Sites in Coastal Jungle Regions," *American Antiquity* 28:226–230.

Meggers, Betty J.
1954. "Environmental Limitation on the Development of Culture," *American Anthropologist* 56(5):801–824.
——, and Clifford Evans
1956. "Archaeological Investigations at the Mouth of the Amazon," *Smithsonian Institution, Bureau of American Ethnology, Bulletin* 167:6–11.

Meighen, C. W., D. M. Pendergast, B. K. Swartz, Jr., and M. D. Wissler
1958a. "Ecological Interpretation in Archaeology, Part I," *American Antiquity* 24(1):1–23.
1958b. "Ecological Interpretation in Archaeology, Part II," *American Antiquity* 24(2):131–150.

Merchant, Dean C.
1963. "A Survey of Courses Offered in Photogrammetry," *Photogrammetric Engineering* 29(6):960–965.

Miller, Edward
1958. "Review of Medieval England: An Aerial Survey," *Antiquity* 32:281.

Miller, William C.
1957. "Uses of Aerial Photographs in Archaeological Field Work," *American Antiquity* 23:46–62.

Millon, René
1964. "The Teotihuacan Mapping Project," *American Antiquity* 29(3):345–352.

1973. ed. *Urbanization at Teotihuacán, Mexico,* vol. 1. Austin: University of Texas Press.

Molano, Juan O. P.
1801. "Letter to the Provincial (Francisco Piñero)," datelined Bayombong, Aug. 5. Santo Domingo, Quezon City, Philippines: Archivo de la Provincia del Santísimo Rosario, Sección "Cagayán."

Monier, Robert B.
1958. "Verification of Aerial Photographic Analysis of Urban Residential Structures: A Study of Rochester, New York." Lackland Air Force Base, Texas: Air Force Personnel and Training Research Center.
———, and Norman E. Green
1953. "Preliminary Findings on the Development of Criteria for the Identification of Urban Structures from Aerial Photographs," *Annals of the Association of American Geographers* (special volume), Spring.
1957. "Aerial Photographic Interpretation and the Human Geography of the City," *The Professional Geographer* 9(5):2–7.

Monkhouse, F. J.
1959. *Landscape from the Air.* Cambridge, Eng.: Cambridge University Press.

Mouterde, René, and Antoine Poidebard
1945. *Le Limes de Chalcis: Organisation de la steppe en haute Syrie romaine,* 2 vols. Paris: Librairie orientaliste Paul Geuthner.

Müller, W.
1960. "Aerofotografische Faktoren bei der erforschung antiker Städteanlagen." *Halle-Wittenberg Gesellschafts und Sprachwissenschaftliche Reihe* 9:403–410.

Müllerried, Federico K. G.
1957. *Geología de Chiapas.* México, D. F.: Gobierno del Estado de Chiapas.

Mumbower, Leonard E., and James A. Donoghue
1967. "Urban Poverty Study: Aerial Photographs Facilitate the Analysis of a Variety of Socio-economic Aspects of a City," *Photogrammetric Engineering* 33(6):610–618.

Munson, Patrick J.
1967. "A Hopewellian Enclosure Earthwork in the Illinois River Valley," *American Antiquity* 32(3):391–393.

National Academy of Sciences, National Research Council
1966. *Spacecraft in Geographic Research.* Washington, D.C.: U.S. Government Printing Office.

National Aeronautics and Space Administration
1970. *Aerial Archaeology in the Space Age,* HHN–107. Scalera, N.M.: NASA Historical Division, Office of Policy.

National Park Service
1965. *Archaeological Photointerpretation.* Palo Alto: Itek Corporation.

Naval Reconnaissance and Technical Support Center
1967. *Image Interpretation Handbook.* TM 30–245, NAVAER 10–35–685, AFM 200–35. Washington, D.C.: U.S. Government Printing Office.

Newell, Leonard E.
1968. *A Batad Ifugao Vocabulary.* New Haven: Human Relations Area Files.

Norcross, Theodore W.
1963. "Values and Uses of Photogrammetry," *Photogrammetric Engineering* 29(1):146–148.

Nunnally, Nelson R., and Richard E. Witmer
1970. "Remote Sensing for Land Use Studies," *Photogrammetric Engineering* 36(5):449–453.

O'Neill, H. T.
1953. "Keys for Interpreting Vegetation from Air Photographs," *Photogrammetric Engineering* 19(3): 422–424.

Odum, Eugene P.
1969. "The Strategy of Ecosystemic Development," *Science* 164:262–270.

Olson, Charles E., Jr.
1960. "Elements of Photographic Interpretation Common to Several Sensors," *Photogrammetric Engineering* 26(4):651–656.
1967. "Accuracy of Land-Use Interpretation from Infrared Imagery in the 4.5 to 5.5 Micron Band," *Annals of the Association of American Geographers* 57(2):382–388.

Ominde, S. H.
1962. "Land and Population in the Western Districts of Nyanza Province, Kenya." Ph.D. diss., University of London.

Osterhoudt, Frank
1965. "Land Titles in Northeast Brazil. The Use of Aerial Photography," *Land Economics* 41(4):387-392.

Parry, C. C.
1857. "Report on United States and Mexican Boundary Survey by William H. Emory," Sen. Ex. Doc. No. 108, 34th Congress, 1st. session, Vol. 1, Cong. Doc. Series No. 832, pp. vi, 1, 24, 95-96.

Parsons, James J.
1969. "Ridged Fields in the Rio Guayas Valley, Ecuador," *American Antiquity* 34(1):76-80.

——, and William A. Bowen
1966. "Ancient Ridged Fields of the San Jorge River Floodplain, Colombia," *Geographical Review* 56(3): 317-343.

——, and William M. Denevan
1967. "Pre-Columbian Ridged Fields," *Scientific American* 217(1):92-100.

Petre, A.
1966. "Noi metode technice de prospectiuni archeologice," *Studii se Cercetari de Istorie Veche* 17(1): 197-209.

Poidebard, Antoine
1929. "Les révélations archéologiques de la photographie aérienne: Une nouvelle méthode de recherches d'observations en région de steppe," *Illustration*, Mar. 25.
1934. *La trace de Rome dans le désert de Syrie: Le limes de Trajan à la conquête arabe, recherches aériennes (1925-1932)*, 2 vols. Paris: Librairie orientaliste Paul Geuthner.
1934. "La trace de Rome dans le désert de Syrie . . . recherches aérienne (1925-1932)," *Antiquity* 8:373-380.
1938. "La recherche des civilisations anciennes," *Comptes rendus du Premier Congrès de Géographie Aérienne*, pp. 258-262.
1939. *Un grand port disparu, Tyr: Recherches aériennes et sousmarines, 1934-36.* Paris: Geuthner.

Porter, P. W.
1956. "Population Distribution and Land Use in Liberia." Ph.D. diss., London School of Economics and Political Science.

Pownall, L. S.
1950. "Aerial Photographic Interpretation of Urban Land Use in Madison, Wisconsin," *Photogrammetric Engineering* 16(3):414-426.

Pozas, Ricardo
1959. *Chamula: Un pueblo indio de los altos de Chiapas.* Memórias del Instituto Nacional Indigenista, 8. México, D.F.: Instituto Nacional Indigenista.

Price, Richard
1968. "Land Use in a Maya Community," *International Archives of Ethnography* 51:1-19.

——, and Sally Price
1970. "Aspects of Social Organization in a Maya Hamlet," *Estudios de cultura maya* 8:297-318.

Puleston, Dennis E., and Olga Stavrakis Puleston
1971. "An Ecological Approach to the Origins of Maya Civilization," *Archaeology* 24(4):330-337.

Pyddoke, Edward
1961. *Stratification for the Archaeologist.* London: Phoenix House.

Redfield, Robert
1952. "The Primitive World View," *Proceedings of the American Philosophical Society* 96(1):30-36.

Reeves, Dache M.
1936. "Aerial Photography and Archaeology," *American Antiquity* 2(2):102-107.

Reiche, Maria
1949. *Mystery on the Desert: A Study of the Ancient Figures and Strange Delineated Surfaces Seen from the Air near Nazca, Peru.* Lima: Editora Médica Peruana, S. A.

Rey, P. León O.
1919. "La photographie aérienne au service de l'archéologie," *La Nature* 2360(117).
1921. *Observations sur les premiers habitats de la Macédoine, recueillies par le Service Archéologique*

Thomas S. Schorr

de l'Armée d'Orient, 1916–1919 (région de Salonique). Paris: E. de Boccard.

Richardson, Miles
1969. "The Spanish American (Colombian) Settlement Pattern as a Socio-Cultural Stage and Cues for Behavior." Paper presented at the 68th Annual Convention of the American Anthropological Association, New Orleans.

Richter, Dennis M.
1969. "Sequential Urban Change," *Photogrammetric Engineering* 35(8):764–770.

Ricketson, Oliver G., Jr., and A. V. Kidder
1930. "An Archaeological Reconnaissance by Air in Central America," *Geographical Review* 20:177–206.

Riley, D. N.
1945. "Aerial Reconnaissance of the Fen Basin," *Antiquity* 19:145–153.
1946. "The Technique of Air Archaeology," *The Archaeological Journal* 101:1–16.

Rinker, Jack N., and Robert E. Frost
1968. *Environmental Analysis and Remote Sensing.* Hanover, N.H.: U.S. Army Terrestrial Science Center.

Robbins, C. R.
1934. "Northern Rhodesia: An Experiment in the Classification of Land with the Use of Aerial Photography," *The Journal of Ecology* 22(1):88–105.

Robequain, Charles
1929. *Le Thanh hod: Étude géographique d'une province annamite.* Publications de l'École Française d'Extrême-Orient, 23–24. Paris: Van Oest.

Roberts, F. H. H., Jr.
1954. "River Basin Surveys," *Report of the Bureau of American Ethnology*, 60(2), Appendix 5. Washington, D.C.: Smithsonian Institution.

Romney, A. Kimball
n.d. *The Processing of Genealogical Data.* Palo Alto: Stanford University Press, in press.

——, and Roy Goodwin D'Andrade
1964. "Cognitive Aspects of English Kin Terms," in *Transcultural Studies in Cognition*, ed. Romney and D'Andrade. *American Anthropologist* 66(3):part 2: 146–170.

Rowe, John Howland
1953. "Technical Aids in Anthropology: A Historical Survey," in *Anthropology Today*, ed. A. L. Kroeber. Chicago: University of Chicago Press, pp. 895–940.

St. Joseph, J. K. S.
1945. "Air Photography and Archaeology," *Geographical Journal* 105:47–61.
1951a. "Air Reconnaissance of North Britain," *Journal of Roman Studies* 41:52–65.
1951b. "A Survey of Pioneering in Air Photography," in *Aspects of Archaeology in Britain and Beyond*, ed. W. F. Grimes. London: Edwards, pp. 303–315.
1955. "Air Reconnaissance in Britain, 1951–55," *Journal of Roman Studies* 45:82–91.
1958. "Air Reconnaissance in Britain, 1955–57," *Journal of Roman Studies* 48:86–101.
1961. "Air Reconnaissance in Britain, 1958–1960," *Journal of Roman Studies* 51:119–135.
1962a. "Aerial Reconnaissance in Wales," *Antiquity* 35(140):263–275.
1962b. "Air Photography and Archaeology in Britain, Recent Results," *Proceedings of the International Symposium on Photointerpretation held at Delft, Netherlands.* Delft: International Society of Photogrammetry.
1962c. "Air Reconnaissance in Northern France," *Antiquity* 35:279–286.
1966. "The Scope of Air Photography," in *The Uses of Air Photography*, ed. J. K. S. St. Joseph. New York: Day, pp. 14–35.

Sanders, William T.
1965. "The Cultural Ecology of the Teotihuacan Valley." Mimeo. University Park: Pennsylvania State University.

——, and Barbara J. Price
1968. *Mesoamerica: The Evolution of a Civilization.* New York: Random House.

Sauter, M. R.
1947. "L'exploration archéologique aérienne en Suisse," *L'anthropologie* 51(3–4):362–363.

Schaber, Gerald G., and George J. Gumerman
1969. "Infrared Scanning Images: An Archaeological

Application," *Science* 164(3875):712–713.

Schaedel, R. P.

1951. "Lost Cities of Peru," *Scientific American* 185(2):18–23.

Schepis, Eugene L.

1970. "Datamap: A Practical Remote Sensing Application," *Journal of Remote Sensing* 1(1):15–17.

Schmidt, Erich F.

1940. *Flights over Ancient Cities of Iran.* Oriental Institute of the University of Chicago. Chicago: University of Chicago Press.

Schorr, Thomas S.

1965. "Cultural Ecological Aspects of Settlement Patterns and Land Use in the Cauca Valley, Colombia." Ann Arbor: University Microfilms.

1968. "Cauca Valley Settlements," *XXXVII Congreso Internacional de Americanistas, Argentina 1966, Actas y Memórias* 1:449–466. Buenos Aires: Librart S. R. L.

1973. "The Structure, Purpose and Social Organization of Pre-Columbian 'Ridged Field' Systems." Paper read at the 72nd Annual Meeting, American Anthropological Association, New Orleans.

Schuyler, Robert L.

1970. "Archaeology in Outer Space," *Space World* 75:13.

Scientific American

1965. "Cities," *Scientific American* 213(3), special issue.

Scollar, Irwin

1963. "Einige Ergebnisse der archäologischen Luftbildforschung im Rheinland während des Jahres 1962," *Bonner Jahrbücher* 163:305–310.

1963. "Review of the International Colloquium on Air Archaeology," *Antiquity* 37(148):269.

1965. *Archäologie aus der Luft: Arbeitsergebnisse der Flugjahre 1960 und 1961 im Rheinland.* Düsseldorf: Rheinland-Verlag.

Scott, William Henry, trans.

1965. "A Description of the Customs of the Peoples of Kiangan, Bunhian and Mayoyao, 1857," by Fray

Ruperto Alarcón, *Journal of Folklore Institute* 2(1):78–100.

Secretaría de Industria y Comercio

1963. *VIII censo general de población, 8 de junio, 1960.* México, D.F.: Dirección General de Estadística, Estado de Chiapas.

Service d'Édition et de Vente des Publications de l'Education Nationale

1964. *Colloque International d'Archéologie Aérienne.* Paris: Bibliothèque Générale de l'École Pratique des Hautes Études, Section VI.

Seymour, T. D.

1957. "The Interpretation of Unidentified Information —A Basic Concept," *Photogrammetric Engineering* 23(1):115–121.

Shepard, James R.

1964. "A Concept of Change Detection," *Photogrammetric Engineering* 30(4):648–651.

Shippee, Robert

1932a. "Great Wall of Peru and Other Aerial Photographic Studies by the Shippee-Johnson Peruvian Expedition," *Geographical Review* 22(1):1–29.

1932b. "Lost Valleys of Peru: Results of the Shippee-Johnson Peruvian Expedition," *Geographical Review* 22(4):562–581.

1933. "Air Adventure in Peru," *National Geographic Magazine*, January, pp. 80–120.

Siemens, Alfred H., and Dennis E. Puleston

1972. "Ridged Fields and Associated Features in Southern Campeche: New Perspectives on the Lowland Maya," *American Antiquity* 37(2):228–239.

Silberman, Leo

1959. "Sociogrammetry," *Photogrammetric Engineering* 25(3):419–423.

Simpson, Robert B.

1966. "Radar: Geographic Tool," *Annals of the Association of American Geographers* 56(1):80–96.

Skinner, G. William

1964. "Marketing and Social Structure in Rural China, Part I," *Journal of Asian Studies* 24(1):363–399.

1965. "Marketing and Social Structure in Rural

China, Part II," *Journal of Asian Studies* 24(2): 195–228.

Smith, C. T., William M. Denevan, and P. Hamilton
1968. "Ancient Ridged Fields in the Region of Lake Titicaca," *Geographical Journal* 134:353–367.

Smith, H. T. U.
1954. "Aerial Photographs in Quaternary Research," *Quaternaria* 50:81–96.

Smith, J. T., ed.
1968. *Manual of Color Aerial Photography.* Falls Church, Va.: American Society of Photogrammetry.

Smithsonian Institution
1922. *Explorations and Field-Work of the Smithsonian Institution in 1921.* Publication 2669. Washington, D.C.: Smithsonian Institution.

Solecki, Ralph S.
1952. "Photographing the Past," *Missouri River Basin Papers Report*, September.
1957. "Practical Aerial Photography for Archaeologists," *American Antiquity* 22:337–351.
1958. "Consideration in the Interpretation of Aerial Views in Archaeology," *Photogrammetric Engineering* 24:798–802.
1960. "Photo Interpretation in Archaeology," in *Manual of Photographic Interpretation*, ed. R. N. Colwell. Falls Church, Va.: American Society of Photogrammetry, pp. 717–733.

Southworth, Clay H.
1919. *Supplementary Exhibits*, vol. 1: *History of Irrigation Along the Gila River*, Appendix A.

Spencer, J. E., and G. A. Hale
1961. "The Origin, Nature, and Distribution of Agricultural Terracing," *Pacific Viewpoint* 2(1):1–40.

Spores, Ronald
1969. "Settlement, Farming Technology, and Environment in the Nochixtlan Valley," *Science* 166(3905):537–569.

Steer, Kenneth
1947. "Archaeology and the National Air-Photograph Survey," *Antiquity* 21(81):50–53.

Steiner, Dieter
1969. "Zur Technik und Method der Landnutzungsinterpretation von Luftbildern," *Berichte zur Deutschen Landeskunde* 29(1):99–130.
1967. *Index to the Use of Aerial Photographs for Rural Land Use Studies.* Bad Godesberg: Bundesanstalt für Landeskunde und Raumforschung.

Steward, Julian H.
1937. "Ecological Aspects of Southwestern Society," *Anthropos* 32:87–104.
1955. *Theory of Culture Change.* Urbana: University of Illinois Press.
1968. "Causal Factors and Processes in the Evolution of Pre-farming Societies," in *Man the Hunter*, ed. R. B. Lee and Irven DeVore. Chicago: Aldine Press, pp. 321–334.
———, et al.
1955. "Irrigation Civilizations: A Comparative Study." Social Science Monographs, 1. Washington, D.C.: Pan American Union.

Stone, Kirk H.
1956. "Air Photo Interpretation Procedures," *Photogrammetric Engineering* 22(1):123–132.
1959. "World Air Photo Coverage," *The Professional Geographer* 11(3):2–5.
1961. "World Air Photo Coverage," *Photogrammetric Engineering* 27(2):214–227.

Strandberg, Carl H.
1962. "Ancient Indian Fishtraps: The Potomac River," *Photogrammetric Engineering* 28:475–478.
1967a. *Aerial Discovery Manual.* New York: Wiley.
1967b. "Photoarchaeology: Reconnaissance Tests Using Color, as Well as Other Films, Indicate That Exploration Studies May Be Reduced from Months to Hours," *Photogrammetric Engineering* 33(10): 1152–1157.
1968a. "Aerial Photography, Part I," *Photographic Applications in Science, Technology and Medicine*, Fall, pp. 25–30.
1968/1969. "Aerial Photography, Part II," *Photographic Applications in Science, Technology and Medicine*, Winter, pp. 41–47.

1969. "Aerial Photography, Part III," *Photographic Applications in Science, Technology and Medicine*, Spring, pp. 23–29, 40–41.

Strong, William Duncan
1953. "Historical Approach in Anthropology," in *Anthropology Today*, ed. Alfred L. Kroeber. Chicago: University of Chicago Press, pp. 386–397.

Thompson, J. Eric S.
1934. *Sky Bearers, Colors and Directions in Maya and Mexican Religion*. Publication 436. Washington, D.C.: Carnegie Institution of Washington.

Thompson, Morris M., ed.
1966. *Manual of Photogrammetry*, 3rd ed., 2 vols. Falls Church, Va.: American Society of Photogrammetry.

Throckmorton, Peter
1970. *Shipwrecks and Archaeology: The Unharvested Sea.* Boston: Little, Brown.

Tolstov, S. P.
1948. *Drevnii Khorezm* (Ancient Khorezm). Moscow: Akademia Nauk SSSR.
——, and B. V. Andrianov
1957. "Novye materialy po istorii irrigatsii Khorezm" (New material on the history of irrigation in Khorezm), *Kratkie Soobshcheniya Instituta Etnografii* 26. Moscow: Akademia Nauk SSSR.
——, Boris V. Andrianov, and Nicolai I. Igonin
1962. "Ispol'zovanie aerometodov v arkheologichekikh issledovaniakh" (Use of aerial methods in archeological research), *Sovetskaia Arkheologiia* 1:1–15.

Tomlinson, R. F., and W. G. E. Brown
1962. "The Use of Vegetation Analysis in the Photo Interpretation of Surface Material," *Photogrammetric Engineering* 28(4):584–591.

Ucko, Peter J., Ruth Tringham, and G. W. Dimbleby, eds.
1972. *Man, Settlement and Urbanism*, Cambridge: Schenkman.

U.S. Army Map Service
1954. *Map Intelligence*, 2nd ed. Army Map Service Training Aid, no. 6. Washington, D.C.: U.S. Army Corps of Engineers.

U.S. Naval Photographic Interpretation Center
1950. "Pacific Landforms and Vegetation," OPNAV 16–UP107, PIC Report 7, NAVAER 10–35–560. Washington, D.C.: Department of the Navy.

Vaufrey, R.
1946. "La photographie aérienne et la préhistoire," *L'anthropologie* 50(1–2):291–293.

Vera, Luis
1964. *Técnicas de inventario de la tierra agrícola. La experiencia del proyecto aerofotogramétrico OEA/Chile.* Washington, D.C.: Pan American Union.

Viksne, Andris, Thomas C. Liston, and Cecil D. Sapp
1970. "SLR Reconnaissance of Panama," *Photogrammetric Engineering* 36(3):253–259.

Villa Rojas, Alfonso
1945. *The Maya of East Central Quintana Roo*. Publication 559. Washington, D.C.: Carnegie Institute.
1968. "Los conceptos de espacio y tiempo entre los grupos mayances contemporáneos," Appendix to *Tiempo y realidad en el pensamiento maya*, Miguel León-Portilla. Serie de culturas mesoamericanas 2. Instituto de Investigaciones Históricas. México, D.F.: Universidad Nacional Autónoma de México.

Vogt, Evon Z.
1956. "An Appraisal of Prehistoric Settlement Patterns in the New World," in *Prehistoric Settlement Patterns in the New World*, ed. Gordon R. Willey. Viking Fund Publications in Anthropology, no. 23. New York: Wenner–Gren Foundation for Anthropological Research. pp. 173–182.
1961. "Some Aspects of Zinacantan Settlement Patterns and Ceremonial Organization," *Estudios de cultura maya* 1:131–145.
1964. "The Genetic Model and Maya Cultural Development," in *Desarrollo cultural de los Mayas*, ed. Evon Z. Vogt and Alberto Ruz Lhuillier. México, D.F.: Universidad Nacional Autónoma de México, pp. 9–48.
1966. (ed.) *Los Zinacantecos: Un pueblo tzotzil de los altos de Chiapas.* Colección de Antropología Social, vol. 7. México: Instituto Nacional Indigenista.
1967. "Field Notes From the Summer of 1967."

Thomas S. Schorr

Harvard Chiapas Project, Harvard University.

1969a. "Chiapas Highlands," in *Handbook of Middle American Indians*, ed. Robert Wauchope, vol. 7: *Ethnology*. Austin: University of Texas Press, pp. 133–151.

1969b. *Zinacantan: A Maya Community in the Highlands of Chiapas*. Cambridge: Harvard University Press.

1970. *The Zinacantecos of Mexico: A Modern Maya Way of Life*. New York: Holt, Rinehart, and Winston.

n.d. *Tortillas for the Gods: A Symbolic Analysis of Zinacanteco Ritual*. Forthcoming.

——, and A. Kimball Romney

1971. "The Use of Aerial Photographic Techniques in Maya Ethnography," *VII Congrès International des Sciences Anthropologiques et Ethnologiques* II: 156–171. Moscow, Aug. 3–10, 1964.

Wagner, Philip L.

1960. *The Human Use of the Earth*. Glencoe: Free Press.

Walker, G. L.

1926. "Prospecting for Copper by Airplanes," *Engineering and Mining Journal* 22:576–578.

1929. "Surveying from the Air in Central Africa," *Engineering and Mining Journal* 25:49–52.

Warneck, Peter E.

1963. "Photogrammetry and Property Survey," *Photogrammetric Engineering* 29(4):594–595.

Wedel, Waldo R.

1953. "Prehistory and the Missouri Development Program Summary Report on the Missouri River Basin Archaeological Survey in 1948," *Bureau of American Ethnology Bulletin* 154:1–59.

Wellar, Harry S.

1968. "On Applications of Aerial Infrared Imagery," *Annals of the Association of American Geographers* 58(2):411–413.

Weyer, Edward M., Jr.

1929. "Exploring Cliff Dwellings with the Lindberghs," in *World's Week*, December, pp. 52–57.

Whittlesey, Julian Hill

1966. "Bipod Camera Support: An Aluminum A-Frame Simplifies Recording for Archaeology," *Photogrammetric Engineering* 32(6):1005–1010.

1970. "Tethered Balloon for Archaeological Photos," *Photogrammetric Engineering* 36(2):181–186.

Wiegand, Theodor

1920. *Sinai*. Berlin: W. de Gruvter.

Willey, Gordon R.

1953. *Prehistoric Settlement Patterns in the Virú Valley, Peru*. Bulletin of the Bureau of American Ethnology, no. 155. Washington, D.C.: Smithsonian Institution.

1956. "Problems Concerning Prehistoric Settlement Patterns in the Maya Lowlands," in *Prehistoric Settlement Patterns in the New World*, ed. Gordon R. Willey. Viking Publications in Anthropology, no. 23. New York: Wenner-Gren Foundation for Anthropological Research, pp. 173–182.

1959. "Aerial Photographic Maps as Survey Aids in Virú Valley," in *The Archaeologist at Work*, ed. Robert F. Heizer. New York: Harper, pp. 203–207.

Williams-Freeman, F. P.

1928. "Views of Wessex from the Air by O. G. S. Crawford and Alexander Keiller," *Antiquity* 2:508–510.

Williams-Hunt, P. D. R.

1948. "Archaeology and Topographical Interpretation of Air Photographs," *Antiquity* 22(86):103–105.

1949. "Anthropology from the Air," *Man*, May, pp. 49–51.

1950. "Irregular Earthworks in Eastern Siam: An Air Survey," *Antiquity* 24(93):30–36.

Willingham, J. W.

1959. "Obtaining Vertical Aerial Photographic Coverage with a 35mm Camera," *Journal of Forestry* 57(2):108–110.

Witenstein, Matthew M.

1952. "The Application of Photo Interpretation to Urban Area Analysis," *Photogrammetric Engineering* 18(3):490–492.

1954. "Photosociometrics: The Applications of Aerial

Photography to Urban Administration and Planning Problems," *Photogrammetric Engineering* 20(3): 419–427.

1955. "Uses and Limitation of Aerial Photography in Urban Analysis and Planning," *Photogrammetric Engineering* 21(4):566–572.

Wittfogel, Karl

1955. "Developmental Aspects of Hydraulic Societies," in *Irrigation Civilizations: A Comparative Study*, Julian H. Steward et al. Washington, D.C.: Pan American Union, pp. 43–52.

Wobber, Frank J.

1969a. "Aerial and Orbital Images in Urban Environment Studies, Part I," *Photogrammetric Applications in Science, Technology and Medicine*, July, pp. 21–29.

Wong, K. W.

1969. "Research in Universities in U.S. and Canada in 1968," *Photogrammetric Engineering* 35(12):1263–1267.

Woodbury, Richard B., and J. Q. Ressler

1962. "Effects of Environmental and Cultural Limitations upon Hohokam Agriculture, Southern Arizona," in *Civilizations in Desert Lands*, ed. R. B. Woodbury. Anthropological Papers, no. 62. Salt Lake City: University of Utah, pp. 41–56.

Wrigley, E. A.

1968. "Demographic Models and Geography," in *Socio-Economic Models in Geography*, ed. R. J. Chorley and Peter Haggett. London: University Paperbacks, pp. 189–215.

Wurman, Richard Saul, and Scott W. Killinger

1967. "Visual Information Systems," *Architecture Canada*, March, pp. 37–44. Reprinted in 1968 in *Ekistics* 26(153):224–288.

The diversity of source materials assembled here could hardly have been evaluated effectively were it not for the generous assistance of B. V. Andrianov, N. I. Igonin, Froelich Rainey, Martha R. Bell, David V. Hughey, Catherine Marshall, Thomas R. Lyons, and Edward B. Sisson, as well as the other authors of this volume.

Thomas S. Schorr

Index